Electronic Networks

Crossing Boundaries/Creating Communities

Edited by Tharon Howard and Chris Benson
with Rocky Gooch and Dixie Goswami

Boynton/Cook Publishers
HEINEMANN
Portsmouth, NH

Boynton/Cook Publishers, Inc.
A subsidiary of Reed Elsevier Inc.
361 Hanover Street
Portsmouth, NH 03801-3912
http://www.boyntoncook.com

Offices and agents throughout the world

Library of Congress Cataloging-in-Publication Data
Electronic networks : crossing boundaries/creating communities /
    edited by Tharon Howard . . . [et al.].
        p.   cm.
    Includes bibliographical references.
    ISBN 0-86709-454-0
    1. English language—Composition and exercises—Study and
teaching—United States—Computer-assisted instruction.
2. Education—United States—Data processing. 3. World Wide Web
(Information retrieval system) 4. Group work in ecducation—United
States. 5. Community education—United States. I. Howard, Tharon W.
LB1576.7.E54   1999
371.33'4—dc21   98-47059
                                                                              CIP

Editor: Peter R. Stillman and Ray Coutu   .
Production: Melissa L. Inglis
Cover design: Joni Doherty
Manufacturing: Louise Richardson

Printed in the United States of America on acid-free paper
03 02 01 00 99   DA   1 2 3 4 5 6 7 8 9

*To countless students who inspired
and informed us and this book.*

Contents

Preface

Dixie Goswami and Tharon Howard

Although this is a traditional book published in a medium that makes it difficult for authors to have "a conversation" with each other and their readers, our purpose here is to encourage conversation among teachers interested in using networking technologies in their classrooms. We didn't want this to be yet another book that hyped the Internet or raved about the ways electronic discussion groups exemplify poststructuralist theories of discourse. Instead, we wanted a book in which teachers could reflect critically on what happened when they moved their classes into electronic spaces.

This book acknowledges that while some schools using computer technologies are achieving impressive results, technology adopted in a vacuum is no panacea. Parents, teachers, and policy makers are concerned about spending billions on technology at a time when large numbers of children and young people aren't mastering basic reading and writing skills, much less learning to navigate new information highways. One way to read this book is to look for conditions and activities that ensure the success with computers that these authors describe. Taken as a whole, this book is an argument for building a human infrastructure at the same pace we are installing computers and wiring, for developing effective ways to assess whether students are truly benefiting from technology, and for addressing issues of resistance and equitable use. The book argues, too, that teachers and young people who are active members of small-scale networks that support collaborative inquiry have opportunities to establish contact and cooperative relationships with others, which in some places is viewed with alarm.

A driving force behind this book is the concept of the "teacher as researcher." The discourse among teachers sharing their insights into classroom practices is often overlooked, undervalued, or even devalued, dismissed as "merely anecdotal" by many traditional empirical researchers. Consequently, even when the methodology of the teacher-researcher is informed by accepted ethnographic practices such as triangulation, clearly defined participant-observer roles, or other established qualitative measures, it is often difficult for teacher-researchers to give voice to their work in traditional print media. Teacher-researchers have, thus, found spaces for their conversations in the electronic communities that have developed on computer networks. Computer networking provides teacher-researchers (and their student collaborators) with an important source of data not previously available: transcripts of electronic exchanges available for analysis and interpretation. Studying the discourse informs and changes the online communication and at the same time generates new questions about language and learning and new approaches to research design for systematic, intentional studies. Substantial samples of classroom discourse, transcribed and available for analysis, are not available to most teachers: easy and relatively inexpensive access to electronic discourse places language at the center of classroom-based inquiries; moreover, computer conferencing facilitates collaborative work that promotes analysis and reflection.

On conferencing systems such as BreadNet, used by several hundred students, faculty, and alumni of the Bread Loaf School of English of Middlebury College, or Internet discussion groups such as ACW-L, PURTOPOI, NCTE-TALK, and MediaMOO (see Chapter 1 for a list of other groups), teachers interested in using network technologies in their classrooms share their ideas and experiences with other teachers. For many years now, these electronic communities have functioned as what Diana Crane called "invisible colleges" or collectives, whose members collaboratively create and share knowledge with one another. In cases like BreadNet, these electronic communities have collectively developed a body of experience in teaching with networks that is well over a decade old.

The obvious problem with these electronic communities is that they are largely unknown to the very people who may need them most—teachers or school administrators who are beginning to consider ways of incorporating network technologies into their pedagogies. If you don't know the "secret handshake" for getting on the Net, then you can't benefit from membership in electronic communities. Or if once online you can't locate these communities, then you can't participate in the conversations and profit from the experience of those who have learned how to avoid some of the land mines that litter the terrain of cyberspace. There is thus a need for texts that cross the boundaries between traditional media and networks, texts that share the insights of experienced teacher-researchers in a medium that is more accessible to those who want those insights. We hope that this book is such a text.

Structurally, the book is divided into three parts. Part 1 provides an introduction to networked classrooms. It begins with Susan Hilligoss's excellent introduction to the wide variety of classroom

projects that can be used in networked environments. Hilligoss not
only helps us see the range of possibilities for networked projects, she
also introduces many of the fundamental issues that teachers must
consider, and the Web sites, books, journals, email lists, and other
resources that teachers need.

John Barber's chapter provides an engaging history of computers,
tracing their evolution from early mechanical devices in the 1830s to
today's Internet-accessible desktop PC.

Donna Ashmus provides an introduction to how the World Wide
Web functions and how it can be used in the classroom. Like
Hilligoss, Ashmus lists a number of Web sites teachers will want to
investigate.

Part 1 concludes with Tharon Howard and Jane Perkins's look at
the future of composition in networked environments and the ways
new digital media will force us to rethink and reshape the "writing"
process. Howard and Perkins provide basic technical introductions
to digital audio editing, digital video capture, graphic image manipulation, and other aspects of multimedia authoring. Then they provide
detailed descriptions of the hypermedia authoring processes they use
with their students.

Where Part 1 introduces the range of possibilities for networked
classroom projects, Part 2 describes the actual implementation of projects. In this section, teacher-researchers reflect critically on various
networked writing projects—both successful and unsuccessful—and
they draw conclusions and offer practical advice on teaching in networked environments. Part 2 begins with Elisa Sparks's energetic
account of how she used the World Wide Web and listserv conferences to turn her science fiction literature course into an active learning community. Sparks's chapter contains much practical advice for
teachers, beginning with a list of the reasons she moved from a traditional classroom format to the Web. She then discusses the resources
needed to complete class assignments and what teachers need to learn
in order to conduct successful "webbed" projects. She also covers
how teachers can integrate technology into a syllabus without bump-
ing out significant content.

Anna Citrino and Brian Gentry discuss the consequences networked projects can have, focusing primarily on their impact on the
communities in which students live. This chapter describes an
online narrative-writing project that connected Native Alaskan students, Kuwaiti students, and rural western American students, and it
describes some of the effects—both positive and negative—such
cross-cultural linkages can have for students, parents, and the surrounding community.

Tom McKenna and Rob Baroz examine a publication project that took place between classes in Alaska and Vermont. McKenna claims the project was a failure—though some readers may disagree with this assessment, given what his students learned about audiences and the consequences of writing. McKenna traces a trail of events and closely examines the students' texts in order to find the pedagogical, cross-cultural, and rhetorical causes of the problems students encountered. Both McKenna and Baroz raise important questions about using expressivist writing pedagogy in networked classrooms, and McKenna's close readings of student exchanges offer important insights into the ways students construct their readers during networked projects and the consequences of doing so.

Like the previous two chapters, Kurt Caswell and Doug Wood's chapter shows what motivated teachers can accomplish with very limited technology. All three of these chapters describe projects where the only resources a teacher had were a single computer and a modem. Caswell and Wood's chapter describes a cross-cultural exchange between Caswell's Japanese English-language students and Wood's South Carolina middle school students. The authors discuss the technological, age, and cultural barriers that had to be addressed in the project, and they offer compelling excerpts from students, which argue for the pedagogical importance of this kind of networked classroom activity.

Part 2 concludes with Claire Bateman and Chris Benson's description of an online poetry exchange between five rural South Carolina classrooms. Like McKenna, Bateman and Benson raise important questions about the sometimes threatening consequences that networked projects can have for our students when we ask them to use writing for communicative purposes with authentic audiences. Yet, the authors also show how teachers can use this rhetorical situation to change student writing from merely another academic exercise into meaningful, active learning experiences.

Part 3 moves away from the project-based focus to explore the institutional changes brought about by the introduction of networking technologies in the classroom. The chapters in this section move beyond the adaptations that individual teachers must consider for their assignments, responses to students, syllabi, etc., and examine how institutional infrastructures and organizational cultures need to be adapted to fully support new technologies. The section begins with Lucy Maddox's description of a network of teachers of Native American students who use computer conferencing to raise important cultural questions, design appropriate curriculum, and confer about educational issues specific to Native American students. Maddox concludes by explaining the cross-age, cross-institutional, and cross-cultural benefits she observed in a networked writing exchange between graduate students in a Native American literature class at Georgetown University and middle school students at Laguna Middle School on the Laguna Reservation.

Next is Rocky Gooch's discussion of questions frequently asked by teachers who use the computer conferencing system BreadNet. From his perspective as the person responsible for training teachers to use the network, Gooch describes the emerging characteristics of professional development programs that provide teachers/users with positive experiences in linking them across diverse schools.

Philip Sittnick's chapter describes how Laguna Middle School was forced to adapt to the impacts of technology over time. Because the school is operated by the Lagunas, a Native American tribe in New Mexico, Sittnick is able to use the differences between Laguna and mainstream cultures to call attention to the tacit socioeconomic and cultural forces at work during these periods of technological adaptation. Sittnick recounts how his school and the surrounding community successfully dealt with such changes both in terms of infrastructure and personnel and curricular revision.

Wayne Butler's chapter is also a story of culture clashes brought about as a result of network technologies; however, Butler's focus is on the differences between the workplace culture of high school teachers and that of university teachers. The chapter describes a cross-age, cross-institution collaborative project in which college students serve as mentors for high school students. Butler enumerates the many impediments that had to be collaboratively resolved because of the fundamental differences in institutional cultures, and like Caswell and Wood's chapter involving cross-age tutoring, the discussion serves as a successful model for teachers who might wish to engage in this increasingly popular method of networking classes.

The final chapter in this section also calls attention to the differences between K–12 and college workplace cultures; however, Rickly's emphasis is on the differences in reward and promotion systems. A critical discussion for any teacher or administrator thinking about working with technology, Rickly's chapter argues that the technological expertise teachers must develop in order to successfully integrate networked projects into their classrooms must be rewarded and valued in the same fashion as any other professional activity teachers perform. Rickly describes strategies for bringing about institutional changes in review, promotion, and/or tenure procedures, and she provides practical systems that administrators and teachers may use as they evaluate the instructional technologies and projects we develop.

As this overview of the book's tripartite structure shows, the editors and contributors have tried to put together a collection that will encourage other teachers to cross their own institutional and technological boundaries. It doesn't take much more than a single PC and a modem to bring about radical change in the classroom. We have tried to give the kind of practical advice that will enable others to join the "invisible colleges" already on the Net or, better yet, begin to build new electronic communities there. Obviously, we hope that this book encourages teachers to incorporate networking technologies into their classes and that it stimulates ideas for new networked projects appropriate for those courses. However, we also hope that the discussions of the problems, challenges, and dangers found in almost every chapter of this book will serve as a cautionary tale. As Elisa Sparks points out, incorporating networking technologies into the classroom takes stamina and hard work. This is a common observation in our experience. In networked classes, the resources are expensive, the faculty learning curve is high, the financial incentives are often poor, the logistics of collaboration are frustrating, and the risk of failure is large—yet, for the teachers who contributed to this book, the benefit to our students and the professional support we obtain within those electronic communities make the risk of border crossing worth taking.

Acknowledgments

The editors owe a great debt to the writers who contributed to this collection. Their perceptions of how communications technology has shaped their practice and the fascinating stories they had to offer provided encouragement and direction in shaping the book. We gratefully acknowledge the contributions of the students whose writing is reproduced in this collection.

We thank James Maddox, director of the Bread Loaf School of English, whose belief in the power of content-based networks for encouraging change in geographically isolated schools and communities played a key role in our undertaking. We are beholden to many members of the faculty of the Bread Loaf School of English, Professor Lucy Maddox of Georgetown University, and Professor Jacqueline Jones Royster of The Ohio State University, in particular. Caroline Eisner, director of the Bread Loaf School of English Computer Center, provided invaluable help to teachers studying online discourse.

The DeWitt Wallace–Reader's Digest Fund has supported the Bread Loaf Rural Teacher Network generously for six years, enabling several hundred rural teachers to integrate technology with ongoing professional development and their best teaching practices: that support is reflected throughout this book.

We thank Lisa Luedeke and Ray Coutu of the editorial staff at Heinemann Publishing for their encouragement and patience in bringing this book to press. Peter Stillman, formerly of Heinemann and now executive editor at Calendar Islands Publishers, was instrumental in developing the ideas presented in this book. Without his encouragement and guidance and his belief in teachers as writers, this project never could have succeeded.

We offer our sincere gratitude to Robert Becker, Director of the Strom Thurmond Institute of Government and Public Affairs at Clemson University, for encouraging and supporting this work. Carolyn Benson and Martha Morris of the Thurmond Institute provided essential administrative support and expert proofreading.

We are grateful to the 1993–1996 Instructional Technology Committee members of the National Council of Teachers of English for their support and encouragement of teachers who create electronic communities of learners.

1

Getting Started in a Networked Writing Classroom
Projects and Resources

Susan Hilligoss
Clemson University

What if you were assigned to teach in a computer classroom? How would that environment affect your teaching? Where would you get help to learn the technology? If you are reading this book, you are probably already contemplating using instructional technology to teach writing. You may already have used word processing and electronic mail for your work. You may have surfed the World Wide Web for information. Perhaps you are already asking students to incorporate these resources in their writing. Now, you are preparing to conduct a class using networked computers. Besides technical skills, you want to learn how computers can enhance good writing pedagogy. After a brief introduction to key issues in teaching writing in a networked classroom, this chapter will describe the types of projects that networked classrooms make possible and explain a number of electronic and print resources that you can go to for help.

What Is a Networked Writing Classroom?

Networked writing classrooms contain personal computers that are physically linked to each other by cables and may also offer access to the worldwide array of interconnected computers called the Internet. They are conceived as *classrooms* and offer opportunities for learning to write far beyond individuals' use of word processing to create printed texts. According to Tharon Howard (1992), unlike a so-called

1

computer lab, a networked computer classroom "is designed to allow for group interaction and communitarian activity" (50). It may also have facilities to allow demonstrations by students and teachers.

What Makes Networked Writing Classrooms Different?

Writing teachers and researchers have observed that networked computers change the way that writers write, readers read, and learners interact with each other and the teacher. Many of these changes support "an *active, interactive* theory of learning" (Moran 1992, quoting Richard Lloyd-Jones and Andrea Lunsford, 12) in ways that traditional classrooms do not.

Changed Relationships to Readers, Texts, and Authority

Networked computers provide writers with much more than the ability to compose, revise, and print documents via word processing. Teachers and scholars note that in a networked classroom, your audience is right there, writing back to you. Gail Hawisher (1992) has observed that electronic conferencing, a major function of networked computers, became widely available to writing teachers just as social constructivist views of language gained acceptance. She summarizes the conclusions of research studies that looked at why electronic conferencing is useful in composition classes: Electronic conferences are text-based, provide "real and expanded" audiences for writers, help build community, and encourage personal engagement. Networked writing also offers fewer contextual cues to the writer's status. In at least some cases, these reduced contextual cues encourage otherwise reticent communicators to participate and decrease "leader-centered communication" (84–90). Thus, computer-mediated communication has the potential to increase democratic participation in groups. For writers, by far the most important features of well-organized networked activities are the opportunity to write for actual readers who need the information, to solve problems collaboratively with readers and fellow writers, and to reflect on one's work (Bowen 1994, 119). Networked communication has demonstrated the potential to empower students to take charge of their learning.

The new technology can also bring new problems: Electronic communication may encourage "flaming," that is, emotionally charged attacks on another writer or writers (Howard 1997, 176). It can increase writers' fear of rejection, also called "communication anxiety" (Hawisher 1992, 92); some writers may decrease participation to the point of being "silenced." Using email, for example, requires some knowledge of netiquette, or the conventions of format, ethics, and courtesy that have grown up around this new medium. Computers, especially since the advent of the World Wide Web and CD-ROM technology, can also contribute to sensory overload. Teachers may have difficulty adapting their approaches to a networked classroom, especially if they are used to instructor-centered communication (Klem and Moran 1992). Finally, networks can replicate old problems. Old hands at using computers for teaching and learning agree: Computers don't turn bad pedagogy into good. Drill and practice on a computer is still drill and practice. Ineffective approaches to learning are only magnified in a networked classroom. The key to success is to be constantly open to your own learning and to plan reasonable, pedagogically sound activities that fit the students, the resources, and the setting.

Changed Texts

Communicating electronically has also brought changes to texts. Electronic mail and real-time "chat" rooms are often quite informal, more like conversation than writing. Readers read the screen differently from the way they read texts on paper (Haas 1989). In addition, electronic texts on the World Wide Web and in multimedia presentations have a significant new feature, called hypertext. Hypertext is nonlinear text; through links that the writer provides, readers may choose to order the segments in different ways. In general, electronic text seems more fluid and less stable than print. In a networked classroom, teachers and learners are confronted with new ways of both reading and writing.

What Kind of Project Can You Do in a Networked Classroom?

Networked classrooms provide teachers and students with a large number of writing-based projects that stress active learning in a community of writers and readers. These activities can be divided into two main categories: those that emphasize conferencing, including electronic mail (email) and "real-time" conferencing; and those that emphasize publishing, including digital, desktop, and multimedia authoring. The following descriptions focus on projects that have actual audiences and carry the potential to build a community of writers and readers. For that reason, projects that employ computing but do not necessarily involve an audience, such as researching topics on the World Wide Web (an extraordinarily valuable resource), are excluded from this discussion.

Electronic Mail and Email-Based Conferencing

Electronic mail is a staple in networked writing classrooms and the contemporary workplace. Regardless of the type of activities that you plan, email will probably figure in some way. Email-based conferencing systems go a step further, allowing messages to be posted to an entire group. Each member can retrieve the messages at her or his convenience. So email-based systems are called *asynchronous*, literally, "not at the same time" (Howard 1997, 172). They may be referred to as listservs, listprocs, majordomos, electronic discussion lists, or sometimes (erroneously) electronic bulletin boards. The Internet's Usenet groups are also asynchronous. For writing classrooms, asynchronous conferencing is a readily available and powerful tool.

Email Pen Pals   Because it is so immediate, email allows pen pals many more potential exchanges than regular mail does. As with paper pals, email pen pals may be more motivated to write and read because they are writing for a partner of similar age and to exchange real information (Schwartz 1990, 21). Email pen pal projects can be adapted for many purposes and are common ways to get started with networked computing. For example, you may want to encourage expressive writing as students get to know someone in another class or at a distance, and then encourage collaboration on one or more transactional assignments. Students can compare their daily lives and move into different circumstances of education, geography, social conditions, and economics (Bowen 1994). Pen pal projects are also useful for students learning to write English as a second or foreign language. While simple in approach, pen pal projects may be unwieldy to administer (Susser 1993).

Email File-Sharing or Writer's Exchanges   As students develop drafts, email allows them to send versions of their work to other writers and the teacher, who can reply in writing. In the networked environment, in which comments typed and there is no special privileged place (the margins of a conventional written text) for teachers' comments, teachers and student writers may concentrate more on coaching and practicing (Bowen 1994; Susser 1993). Writers can also collaborate more easily by sharing files.

Cross-Age Peer Tutoring and Mentoring   The main advantage of using networked computers for cross-age peer-tutoring projects is that both tutor and tutee have ample writing opportunities. Networks also allow tutoring relationships to occur across school boundaries and may make such projects more feasible than face-to-face and print-based projects. A number of projects have paired teachers in training with elementary, secondary, or college students (Mason et al. 1994;

Coogan 1995). Mentoring may also involve an outside expert, such as a professional poet in "electronic residency" (see Chapter 9) who responds to students' writing (Susser 1993).

Email Listservs or Discussion Groups   An email listserv "list" distributes messages to all members of that list. Once a writer posts an email message to the class list address, it is sent to everyone else in the class. The messages remain on the system so that students can read and respond at their convenience. One basic and important use of email lists is to post class materials. As students log on to the system each day, they can be greeted by a "Class News" bulletin, directing them to a variety of assignments, resource materials, and comments on previous work (Carbone et al. 1993).

A more powerful use of listservs is to hold a discussion group over several weeks or an entire term. For example, students in a class can write an email journal of responses to the assigned reading in the course. Students read assignments and write email responses to the list. Each response is sent to everyone else as a new email message, which other students can then read and respond to. Such a project encourages students to write to each other as well as to the teacher, answer each other's questions, state a point of view, support or challenge others' claims as well as their own, and pose new questions. Here is a sample email message from a graduate class listserv. The seminar topic was electronic literacies:

    Date: Thu, 29 May 1997 17:15:23 -0400
    Reply-To: ELECTRONIC_LITERACIES <9705ENGL__801001-
    L@CLEMSON.EDU>
    From: Heather
    To: 9705ENGL__801001-L@CLEMSON.EDU
    Subject: Re: Comment on Selfe article

    Vicki

    Just a comment from me on the informality/formality of my respons-
    es. So far I've been really good about trying to check my spelling
    and keep my punctuation fairly regular—however, I normally just
    send very messy messages via email and have just cleaned up my act
    a little for this particular audience. I don't know what Selfe, et al
    would say about that . . . I do know I am conscious of audience
    even in this medium, however, and I send more polished messages
    to professors than to my friends and to my mother than to my sib-
    lings . . . and to people I don't know than to people I do . . . Heather

Writers can be assigned to initiate questions on new readings, and this kind of empowerment is important for the list's success. The teacher's handling of the list responses also contributes to the success or failure of a listserv. For example, it is unreasonable to expect that online conversations will automatically lead to exciting face-to-face discussions — the points may have been sufficiently made online (Elred 1991).

Listservs also create a unique record for reflection. Days after the initial postings, having gathered more information or reflected on the assignment, students can return to their messages and post new responses. Because the messages stay on the system until deleted, they can be collected in a journal or archive. Writers can then examine the archive for topics and rhetorical strategies. Advanced classes have undertaken "microethnographies" that include these archives in their study (Blair 1996).

"Real-Time" Conferencing

What if you wanted everyone to prepare an assignment and, during class, have an online written "discussion" that mirrors an in-class oral discussion? To do that, you would employ another form of electronic-conferencing system, called "real-time" conferencing. One analogy for real-time conferencing is a conference telephone call in which everyone gets the chance to talk. Sometimes these conferences are referred to as "chats." To participate, writers must all be online at the same time. Thus, this type of conferencing is called *synchronous*.

The computer screen is usually divided into an individual participant's writing area and an area that shows the messages from all participants, that is, the online conference itself. Because the conference is synchronous, writers' messages appear on everyone else's computer screen almost instantaneously. Earlier messages scroll off the screen to make room for new ones. Athough the transcript of a chat can be printed or saved for future reference, the messages are usually not stored, unlike email-based conferencing. The lack of storage reflects the nature of conversation or chat.

Real-time conferencing has several forms, including ENFI (Electronic Networks for Interaction), INTERCHANGE, MUDs (Multi-User Dimensions), and, on the Internet, Internet Relay Chat (IRC). These vary considerably in the features that they offer groups of writers. Some, like MUDs and IRCs, are not educational in purpose and may tie up network resources, so that users at a site may be prohibited from connecting to them (Howard 1997, 179). One of the most common real-time systems for classroom use is the MOO (Multi-User Dimension, Object-Oriented).

MOOs   In a MOO, a group can "meet" in a virtual space or "room." A MOO enables users not only to communicate directly with each other by typing in their messages, but also use writing to take

Figure 1-1

The chat function of FirstClass Intranet Software
lets users "speak" via computer.

Private Chat

Participants:　Chris Benson
　　　　　　　Nona Edelson

☐ Scroll Lock　☑ Sounds

[Invite...]　[Send]

Chris Benson has joined the chat.
Nona Edelson has joined the chat.
Nona Edelson: Good morning, Chris
Chris Benson: Hello Nona; how are you this morning?
Nona Edelson: Fine and you?
Chris Benson: Good. Thanks for inviting me to your journalism class next week. I was
wondering if there particular topics you'd like me to address with your students.
Nona Edelson: Actually, there are several. My students are curious about what careers
are available to them with a journalism background, besides, of course, reporting
Chris Benson: I can certainly tell them about the boom in desktop publishing
opportunities.
Chris Benson: Are they interested in a workshop on technical stuff like page layout?
Nona Edelson: That would be pertinent, since we have two full computer labs this year
and students are now involved with some more sophisticated computer functions
Chris Benson: Okay, I'll spend about 15 minutes discussing career opportunities in
publishing and then the rest of the time we'll work on page layout.
Nona Edelson: Right now, we are doing the cut and paste method of layout and I find I wind
up doing most of it. I think if the students were trained to layout the paper on computer, it
would alleviate me of some work
Chris Benson: I can show them some useful shortcuts and techniques with desktop
publishing. I'll see you next Wednesday at 1:15. See you then.

many virtual actions, actions that others online can see on their screens. Through simplified programming commands, participants may write out gestures and facial expressions like waving and smiling to accompany their remarks. They may write out characteristics for their entrances and exits into the space, or develop characteristics for their online personae. They may create, locate, and examine objects in the room. They may explore and even create other spaces that are virtually connected in the MOO. How do writing classes use MOOs? Many projects that involve small writing groups can successfully utilize a MOO. You may ask a group of writers to enter the MOO space every day, having put their assignment on a virtual "desk." During their time online, they can brainstorm in writing with each other and create a draft, which they leave in the room to return to in the next conference, or for you or another group to read. MOOs have an immediacy, informality, and often intimacy that mirror face-to-face groups. However, unlike face-to-face writing groups, MOO groups must use writing for all social interactions, an advantage in a writing class. Writers have many opportunities to observe how their writing is interpreted by others. MOOs encourage active learning and initiative because they are also "constructed social spaces" that allow participants the power to imagine and create new aspects of the space itself, all through the medium of writing. The participants may make the space into a virtual campus, café, or company. Another advantage of real-time conferencing is that participants do not need to be in the same physical location. Thus, MOOs are especially useful for groups communicating across distances. Classes across town or across the world can be paired and communicate via the MOO.

OWLs (Online Writing Labs)   Writing centers have taken advantage of both conferencing and digital publishing. Students and tutors can confer in a MOO space and maintain contact via email exchanges. Tutors can thereby assist students at different locations. Lab hours and services, as well as reference materials and assignments, can be posted online via Gopher or the Web. Because online writing labs are well established at universities and even secondary schools, a body of published reflection and scholarship about their use is developing (*Computers and Composition* 1995).

Digital Publishing

Carrying a document or project to a final, polished form for presentation to a number of readers is a staple of writing classes. The new technology provides opportunities to enhance portfolios, class anthologies, newsletters, instructional manuals, and other genres as well as produce entirely new forms of individual and collaborative work. Publishing focuses more on the document than on the immediacy of readers, so it is important that class publishing activities also use the conferencing features of the networked classroom as students negotiate each stage to the finished product. Digital publishing takes advantage of the ability to distribute text information on floppy disks, CD-ROMs, and electronic networks—listservs and the Internet. Compared with print (which is treated under desktop publishing), digital publishing offers features like color and sophisticated typography, page layout, and graphics at relatively little expense per item distributed. Digital publishing on school networks and the Internet also offers the opportunity to reach hundreds, even thousands, of readers.

Electronic Portfolios   One form of digital publishing, which may also be combined with various conferencing techniques, is the creation of electronic portfolios on floppy disks or even CD-ROMs. These may be individual portfolios over the term or the result of group projects on a particular topic. They may include not only writing but also drawings, charts, photos, and, with a CD-ROM recorder, even short audio and video clips in which the student comments on or reads a piece of writing (see Chapter 4).

Newsletters, Anthologies, Guides, Reports   The popular activity of creating a class (or group) newsletter, anthology, magazine, report, or guide to a specific topic is well adapted to digital publishing, whether on floppies, CD-ROMs, Gopher, the Web, or simply a listserv. These projects can include both individual and collaborative authoring, using any of the conferencing techniques described. Some of these methods of publishing are strictly text-based, such as listservs and Gopher. Others, including floppies, CD-ROMs, and the Web, both support and encourage graphical information. For some projects, especially guides to particular topics, this ability to publish images such as photographs without expensive printers is especially valuable.

Publishing on a Gopher Site   Gopher is a popular text-only electronic publishing system accessible to users of the Internet (Howard 1997, 176). Many schools and colleges maintain Gopher sites with information about many subjects, from descriptions of courses to online reference works to class projects. Users work through highly organized menus to access the information. Although Gopher supports only text, publishing a class project to thousands of potential readers can be a satisfying experience for writers.

Publishing on a Web Site   Even more satisfying than publishing on a Gopher site is producing a page or pages that appear on the World Wide Web. Since the early 1990s explosion of the Web owing to the availability of graphical "browsers" such as Mosaic, Netscape Navigator, and Microsoft Internet Explorer, many classes have produced Web projects. These range from a study of Galileo by middle school students to a collaborative arts anthology by secondary students at a county-funded summer arts camp to hypertextual research papers by graduate students. Web pages support graphics, sound, animation, and short video clips as well as text. They also offer new genres and new means of organization, through hypertext links. One writerly exploration of this feature is hypertextual fiction or poetry. As with Gopher, you must have permission to publish from a particular site and adhere to the site guidelines. Web publishing may also require some knowledge of HyperText Markup Language, called HTML, a "tagging" system for documents that is somewhat like a computer programming language.

Desktop Publishing

Desktop publishing, or "word publishing" as Patricia Sullivan (1992) calls it, is the personal computer version of traditional print publishing. It takes advantage of graphical user interfaces (GUIs) and what you see is what you get (WYSIWYG) technology in computers and printing. Thus, with a graphical word processing or inexpensive page-layout program, plus an ink-jet or laser printer, students can explore the interactions of typography, page layout, and graphics to obtain professional-looking documents. With an inexpensive digital camera to take photographs, or using images obtained from sources such as published CD-ROMs or the Web (make sure that the images are "royalty free" to avoid copyright infringement), writers can illustrate their work as well. Producing a portfolio, anthology, newsletter, or manual using desktop publishing remains an important function of classroom computing. Students have the satisfaction of participating in a time-honored technical process and in effect hand-creating a physical product that has the authority traditionally granted print. This type of ownership, from conception to physical printed pages, is a legacy of the personal computer revolution and immensely valuable (Sullivan 1992). However, these same features are also desktop publishing's drawback. It is an older technology that focuses on individual authorship and invests much in a fixed text.

Multimedia Authoring

Multimedia refers to computer integration of text, sound, animation, and video. Multimedia is resource-intensive; that is, it requires powerful computers and a great deal of storage space. The Web's multimedia capabilities have been discussed earlier. Because of the availability of multimedia authoring software for education and the development of inexpensive CD-ROM recorders, teachers and students have more and more opportunities to create "stand alone" multimedia on CD-ROMs. Multimedia virtually demands a collaborative approach. The process can be complex, the talents required are many, and every stage requires collaboration and the negotiation of meanings. That is, it is probably a good idea to incorporate writing through email or conferencing. Although English classes have been involved in multimedia at least since the late 1980s (Dryden 1994), there is not a large body of research or published material on writing classrooms that integrate multimedia. The projects that multimedia supports are many.

Guides   For any subject, students can produce full-featured guides or narratives that require ample writing. For example, in a literature class they may put together a multimedia literary history of an important figure or year. Their written explanations can be illustrated with photographs, historical drawings, and music clips. Technical writing students can produce manuals with online documentation and animated sequences of processes. Discovering a logical and usable structure for the guide allows students to explore options in organization. Hypertext links can offer users several paths through the material, and student multimedia authors must anticipate how users might want to travel. Multimedia resumes can be constructed in the same way.

Personal and Creative Writing   Writers can construct multimedia presentations of their expressive and creative writing, using color, drawings, and photographs to accompany the text, and laying down a sound track or adding a video or voice-over of themselves reading. They can experiment with hypertext linking by segmenting the text and offering the reader different paths through it. They can put together an illustrated commonplace book of favorite quotations plus their interpretations and comments, with or without musical and visual accompaniment.

What Electronic Resources Exist for Writing Teachers?

Some of the best information about teaching writing in computer classrooms comes from electronic resources. They can provide information that is more current than print resources. Furthermore, certain resources, like listservs, put you in touch with others who have similar concerns and who may have considerable expertise.

Listservs

Electronic discussion groups cover almost any topic imaginable. Listserv groups tend to focus on professional issues, although they vary considerably in formality and tone. Subscribing to a discussion group, or "list," allows you to read what others in the field consider important issues, to contribute to ongoing discussions, and to ask questions. Some lists are very active; subscribers may receive a hundred or more messages a week, so it is a good idea to limit subscriptions to one or two lists at first.

How to Subscribe to a Listserv   To subscribe to a list, first you must find the email address of the discussion group (not the individual who moderates it). Usually this address includes the term *listserv* or *listproc*. Then send an email message, leaving the subject line of the message blank. In the body of the message, type a single-line message. If you do not have information about the format for the message, try using this one: SUBSCRIBE LISTNAME YourFirstName YourLastName

The following example demonstrates how to subscribe to "Penpal," a list that puts teachers in touch with other teachers for electronic projects:

TO: listserv@unccvm.uncc.edu
SUBJECT:_____
SUBSCRIBE penpal-L Susan Hilligoss

Useful Listservs   These few examples are to help you get started. The Alliance for Computers and Writing Web site (discussed below) describes other listservs related to writing, composition, and computers.

- ACW-L: Alliance for Computers and Writing, not limited to members. Subscription address: listproc@unicorn.acs.ttu.edu
- humanist: Computers and humanities. Subscription address: listproc@lists.Princeton.edu
- penpal-L: Connects teachers to each other for projects. Subscription address: listserv@unccvm.uncc.edu
- rural: Rural schools and telecommunications. Subscription address: listproc@itc.org
- RHETNT-L: Online rhetoric and writing. Subscription address: listserv@mizzou1.missouri.edu
- WCENTER: Writing centers. Subscription address: listproc@unicorn.acs.ttu.edu
- TCC-L: Teachers in Community Colleges. Subscription address: LISTSERV@UHCCVM.UHCC.HAWAII.EDU
- CREWRT-L: Creative Writing. Subscription address: listserv@mizzou1.missouri.edu

Web Servers

If you have a connection to the Internet, the World Wide Web offers countless resources related to education, computing, and writing. Each Web site has an electronic address, called a Uniform Resource Locator (URL) that begins with *http://*. (The acronym URL is not part of the address). You may search the Web for specific information using one of two methods, a subject guide or a search engine, or you may go to a known site by typing its URL into the location or address area of your browser. Once you have reached a site, links connect you to other information and sites. You can connect to the

Web from text-only communications software, but a graphical browser such as Mosaic, Netscape, or Internet Explorer allows you access to greater information through images and even sound and video.

Search Engines   Search engines match keywords to a database. (The "engine" is a software program.) You type in a keyword or keywords that specify your topic as much as possible and the engine presents the links that match. Different search engines produce very different results, based on the database's size and frequency of update, as well as the software's design and speed. They also differ in ease of use for new searchers and the handling of complex searches ("Kansas City Public Library: Introduction to Search Engines" 1997). Some tools also allow searches of Usenet news groups and classified ads in addition to the Web. Popular search engines include:

- AltaVista: http://www.altavista.digital.com/
- HotBot: http://www.hotbot.com/index.html
- Infoseek: http://www.infoseek.com/
- Lycos: http://www.lycos.com/
- Magellan: http://searcher.mckinley.com/
- Open Text: http://www.opentext.com/
- WebCrawler: http://webcrawler.com/
- Yahoo: http://www.yahoo.com/

Subject Guides   Subject guides classify sites just as the classified section of the telephone directory classifies businesses. They present information in an outline format and are helpful for general topics. For example, connecting to Yahoo allows you to choose the topic "Education" and under it, "K–12" and then "Distance Learning." The categories of a subject guide also help you learn keywords for a search engine search.

Specific Sites   For questions about computers and writing, one of the best places to start is the Alliance for Computers and Writing (ACW) Web site (http://english.ttu.edu/acw/). These pages have links to hundreds of other sites related to computers and writing. As you consider the following list, be aware that, as with everything else on the Web, a site may give links to a much wider range of topics than its own coverage suggests. Also be aware that URLs frequently change, as sites are switched to other servers (or occasionally are removed from the Web).

Computers and Writing in General

- Alliance for Computers and Writing (ACW) Web site: http://english.ttu.edu/acw/
- *Computers and Composition* (journal): http://www.cwrl.utexas.edu/~ccjrnl/toc.html
- National Writing Centers Association: http://www2.colgate.edu/diw/NWCA.html
- Bread Loaf School of English Writing Resources for Teachers: http://breadweb.middlebury.edu/resources/comp.html

MOOs

- Composition in Cyberspace (funded by the Annenberg/CPB Project): http://www.du.org/cybercomp.html
- MOO Central: http://www.pitt.edu/~jrgst7/MOOcentral.html

OWLs

- Webb School of Knoxville Online Writing Lab: http://gateway.webb.pvt.k12.tn.us/owl/webbowl.html
- Purdue Online Writing Lab, Purdue University: http://owl.english.purdue.edu/
- Networked Writing Environment, University of Florida: http://www.ucet.ufl.edu:80/writing/nwe.html
- Online Writery, University of Missouri: http://www.missouri.edu/~writery/

Literature and Humanities

- The Voice of the Shuttle, Alan Liu: http://humanitas.ucsb.edu/
- The Electronic Text Center at the University of Virginia: http://etext.lib.virginia.edu/uvaonline.html

Classrooms and Computing
(Includes Projects and Classroom Funding)

- Classroom Connect: http://ns.wentworth.com/classroom/
- The Schoolhouse Networking Operations Center: http://sunsite.unc.edu/cisco/
- Illinois State Board of Education: http://www.isbe.state.il.us/homepage.html
- International Telecomputing Consortium (rural teachers): http://www.itc.org/
- Web66: A K12 World Wide Web Project: http://web66.coled.umn.edu/

- "Bill of Rights and Responsibilities of Electronic Learners": http://www.aahe.org/

What Print Resources Exist for Writing Teachers?

Today, there is a wealth of information about computer-mediated communication, much of it authored by teachers experienced in using networked classrooms. Although the field is interdisciplinary, this section emphasizes resources by writing teachers themselves. Incidentally, many of the resources listed below have a site on the World Wide Web that gives contact information. Some addresses (URLs) are given below.

Research and Scholarship

Journals   Since 1983 the journal *Computers and Composition* has provided cutting-edge research and commentary in the field. Published three times a year, with back issues and current abstracts available on the Web (http://www.cwrl.utexas.edu/~ccjrnl/toc.html), the journal has published special issues on electronic portfolios and online writing centers (OWLs). Many established journals in English, rhetoric, and composition now also regularly contain articles on computers and writing. Browsing these can familiarize you with issues.

Newsletters   Rural teachers embraced information technology early. The *Bread Loaf Rural Teacher Network Magazine* features classroom projects and stories of teachers and learners across North America. A copy may be requested from the Bread Loaf School of English, Middlebury College, Middlebury, VT. As this book goes to press, an online version of the magazine will soon be available through the Web site of Middlebury College at www.middlebury.edu/.

Online Journals   The following journals exist only online. They combine research and commentary with forays into the shape and texture of discourse in the new media.

- *Kairos: A Journal for Teachers of Writing in Webbed Environments*: http://english.ttu.edu/kairos/index.html
- *Computer-Mediated Communication Magazine* (*CMC Magazine*): http://www.december.com/cmc/mag/masthead.html
- *RhetNet, A Cyberjournal for Rhetoric and Writing:* http://www.missouri.edu/~rhetnet/
- *CWRL: The Electronic Journal for Computer Writing, Rhetoric and Literature:* http://www.en.utexas.edu/~cwrl/

Essay Collections   Scholarly collections offer convenient reviews of issues. Of particular interest to teachers beginning to use instructional technology is *Re-Imagining Computers and Composition: Teaching and Research in the Virtual Age*, edited by Gail E. Hawisher and Paul LeBlanc (1992), which includes a list of terms and definitions related to computing by Richard Selfe as well as Charles Moran's comparison of traditional writing classrooms with networked classrooms. Another recent collection is *Literacy and Computers: The Complications of Teaching and Learning with Technology*, edited by Cynthia L. Selfe and Susan Hilligoss, which has sections on networked communication and hypertext (1994). Others include *Computers and Community: Teaching Composition in the Twenty-First Century*, edited by Carolyn Handa (1990) and *Evolving Perspectives on Computers and Composition Studies: Questions for the 1990s*, edited by Hawisher and Selfe (1992).

Books   A useful orientation to the scholarship is the history by Gail E. Hawisher, et al. called *Computers and the Teaching of Writing in American Higher Education, 1979–1994: A History* (1996). It summarizes a quarter-century of involvement and research, and contains an extensive bibliography. Personal in tone and accessible to a wider range of readers than its title might imply, *Computers and the Teaching of Writing* gives many insights into the parallel development of composition studies and instructional technology. It is part of the book series *New Directions in Computers and Composition Studies* published by Ablex.

Two major studies of digital texts, Richard A. Lanham's *The Electronic Word: Democracy, Technology, and the Arts* (1993) and Jay David Bolter's *Writing Space: The Computer, Hypertext, and the History of Writing* (1991), characterize the nature of electronic discourse in comparison with traditional forms in the Western literate tradition. Both Tharon Howard and Stephen Doheny-Farina examine the meaning of *community* in relation to electronic networks. In *A Rhetoric of Electronic Communities* (1997), Howard surveys theoretical constructions of community from linguistics, philosophy, and rhetoric, including feminist perspectives, and then develops a conception that can be applied to electronic networks. He applies this idea to his study of people's writing on PURTOPOI, a discussion list that he created and administered in the early 1990s. In *The Wired Neighborhood* (1996), Doheny-Farina applies communitarian principles to electronic networks, focusing on localized communities and K–12 schools. In a semester-long study detailed in *Link/Age:*

Composing in the Online Classroom (1997), Joan Tornow examines a writing class using an ethnographic approach, narrative, and many examples of her students' writing. *Link/Age* is a readable example of teacher research in a networked classroom.

Textbooks

Many of the current "computers and writing" textbooks focus on assisting students in using the Internet for exploration as well as traditional research. Increasingly, these texts are by teachers of writing who have ample experience in networked classrooms. The following are aimed at college writers, but most can be adapted for secondary students.

Handbooks and Rhetorics   Eric Crump and Nick Carbone's *English Online: A Student's Guide to the Internet and World Wide Web* (1997; to be retitled *Writing Online*) has an exceptionally clear presentation of the Internet and a strong research section that recognizes the problem of electronic plagiarism and dishonesty. William Condon and Wayne Butler's *Writing the Information Superhighway* (1997) integrates a rhetoric with a guide to online writing, from composing with a word processor to collaborating online to critiquing and authoring Web pages. *Online! A Reference Guide to Using Internet Sources* (1997) by Andrew Harnack and Eugene Kleppinger is typical of the convenient small-format handbooks. Among the more specialized texts are Dawn Rodrigues's *The Research Paper and the World Wide Web* (1997) and Carol Lea Clark's *Working the Web: A Student Guide* (1997). The latter takes readers through basic HTML and graphic formats to create Web pages, in addition to search strategies for research papers. All of these include ample Web resources for specific subjects; a note of caution, however: the addresses (URLs) quickly become outdated.

Readers   Thematic anthologies allow a class to study the issues of technology as students write using computers. Anthologies also offer teachers themselves a convenient way to learn about those issues. Victor Vitanza's *Cyber/Reader* (1996) accents the dislocations and novelty of cyberspace, including contrasts with the printed word and libraries, while Gail E. Hawisher and Cynthia L. Selfe's *Literacy, Technology, and Society: Confronting the Issues* (1997) emphasizes the social, ethical, and political implications of computers and research concerning those effects. Both anthologies contain classic articles and fiction; both are for college students, first-year and advanced.

What Are Some Other Sources?

Conferences and Workshops

At their annual meetings, the National Council of Teachers of English and the Conference on College Composition and Communication frequently run preconvention or postconvention workshops on using computers to teach writing. There are also convention-sponsored demonstrations staffed by experienced writing instructors. The Computers and Writing Conference is an annual national event that includes online participation from teachers who cannot attend the physical convention. In-service workshops are sponsored by many school districts, colleges, and universities. The best-known for writing pedagogy is the annual summer institute Computers in Writing-Intensive Classrooms, held at Michigan Technological University. The two-week workshop uses a fully equipped, state-of-the-art computer facility designed especially for English teachers.

Organizations

The following organizations are helpful to writing teachers.

Alliance for Computers and Writing   ACW, founded in 1993, exists to help writing teachers at all levels use "computer technologies and networks to improve their classroom writing instruction." The alliance's more than six hundred members are teachers and researchers from elementary and secondary schools, community colleges, and four-year colleges and universities, including a number outside the United States. The association is "based on the idea of people working together to overcome the difficulties and realize the amazing opportunities of computers and the Internet revolution" (Frequently Asked Questions About ACW-L 1997). In addition to an email discussion list, the alliance maintains nineteen regional associations of teachers who meet and discuss issues of instructional technology. The alliance also has taken over most of the functions of the now defunct Megabyte University, a pioneering electronic discussion list for computers and writing.

National Council of Teachers of English   NCTE has an Instructional Technology Committee that considers issues important to its membership. NCTE also sponsors many interest groups called "assemblies," some of which are active in computers and writing, such as the National Writing Centers Association and the Assembly on Computers and English.

Educom   One of the oldest associations devoted to technology in education, Educom is a nonprofit consortium of higher education institutions dedicated to furthering and facilitating the use of information technology for "active and learner-centered" collaborative learning that is also cost-effective ("Educom" 1997). It is concerned with policy-making issues.

Works Cited

Blair, K. L. 1996. "Microethnographies of Electronic Discourse Communities: Establishing Exigency for E-Mail in the Professional Writing Classroom." *Computers and Composition* 13 (1): 85–91.

Bolter, J. D. 1991. *Writing Space: The Computer, Hypertext, and the History of Writing.* Hillsdale, NJ: Lawrence Erlbaum.

Bowen, B. A. 1994. "Telecommunications Networks: Expanding the Contexts of Literacy." In *Literacy and Computers: The Complications of Teaching and Learning with Technology*, eds. C. L. Selfe and S. Hilligoss. New York: MLA.

Carbone, N., Moran, C., Van Denakker, S., Federenko, E., Daisley, M., McComas, D., and Ostermiller, D. 1993. "Writing Ourselves Online." *Computers and Composition* 10 (3): 29–48.

Clark, C. L. 1997. *Working the Web: A Student Guide.* New York: Harcourt-Brace.

Computers and Composition. 1995. 12 (2). Special issue on online writing labs.

Condon, W., and W. Butler. 1997. *Writing the Information Superhighway.* Boston: Allyn and Bacon.

Coogan, D. 1995. "E-Mail Tutoring, a New Way to Do New Work." *Computers and Composition* 12 (2): 171–81. (URL: http://www.cwrl. utexas.edu/~ccjrnl/Archives/v12/12_2_html/feature.html)

Crump, E., and N. Carbone. 1997. *English Online: A Student's Guide to the Internet and World Wide Web.* Boston and New York: Houghton Mifflin.

Doheny-Farina, S. 1996. *The Wired Neighborhood.* New Haven, CT: Yale University Press.

Dryden, L. M. 1994. "Literature, Student-Centered Classrooms, and Hypermedia Environments." In *Literacy and Computers,* ed. C.L. Selfe and S. Hilligoss, 282–304. New York: Modern Language Association.

"Educom." 1997. Http://www.educom.edu/. Cited 15 July 1997.

Elred, J. M. 1991. "Pedagogy in the Computer-Networked Classroom." *Computers and Composition* 8 (2): 47–61.

"Frequently Asked Questions About ACW-L." 1997. Version 3.1. January. http://www.daedalus.com/acwfaq.html. Cited 29 June 1997.

Haas, C. 1989. "Seeing In on the Screen Isn't Really Seeing It." In *Critical Perspectives in Composition Instruction,* eds. G. Hawisher and C. Selfe. New York: Teachers College Press.

Handa, C. A., ed. 1990. *Computers and Community: Teaching Composition in the Twenty-First Century.* Portsmouth, NH: Boynton/Cook.

Harnack, A., and E. Kleppinger. 1997. *Online! A Reference Guide to Using Internet Sources*. New York: St. Martin's Press.

Hawisher, G. E. 1992. "Electronic Meetings of the Minds: Research, Electronic Conferences, and Composition Studies." In *Re-Imagining Computers and Composition: Teaching and Research in the Virtual Age*, eds. G. E. Hawisher and P. LeBlanc. Portsmouth, NH: Boynton/Cook.

Hawisher, G. E., and P. LeBlanc, eds. 1992. *Re-Imagining Computers and Composition: Teaching and Research in the Virtual Age*. Portsmouth, NH: Boynton/Cook.

Hawisher, G. E., and C. L. Selfe, eds. 1992. *Evolving Perspectives on Computers and Composition Studies: Questions for the 1990s*. Urbana, IL: National Council of Teachers of English.

———. 1997. *Literacy, Technology, and Society: Confronting the Issues*. Upper Saddle River, NJ: Prentice Hall.

Hawisher, G. E., P. LeBlanc, C. Moran, and C. L. Selfe. 1996. *Computers and the Teaching of Writing in American Higher Education, 1979–1994: A History*. Norwood, NJ: Ablex.

Howard, T. W. 1992. "WANS, Connectivity, and Computer Literacy: An Introduction and Glossary." *Computers and Composition* 9 (3): 41–58.

———. 1997. *A Rhetoric of Electronic Communities*. Greenwich, CT: Ablex.

"Kansas City Public Library: Introduction to Search Engines." 1997. Reviewed by M. Pedram. Revised 30 January 1997 (http://www.kcpl.lib.mo.us/search/srchengines.htm).

Klem, E., and C. Moran. 1992. "Teachers in a Strange Land: Learning to Teach in a Networked Writing Classroom." *Computers and Composition* 9 (3): 5–22.

Lanham, R. A. 1993. *The Electronic Word: Democracy, Technology, and the Arts*. Chicago: University of Chicago Press.

Mason, L. D., A. Hill Duin, and E. Lammers. 1994. "Linking Learners: Structuring a Mentoring via Telecommunications Course." *Computers and Composition* 11 (2): 123–35.

Moran, C. 1992. "Computers and Writing: A Look to the Future." In *Re-Imagining Computers and Composition: Teaching and Research in the Virtual Age*, eds. G. E. Hawisher and P. LeBlanc. Portsmouth, NH: Boynton/Cook.

Rodrigues, D. 1997. *The Research Paper and the World Wide Web*. Upper Saddle River, NJ: Prentice Hall.

Schwartz, H. 1990. "Ethical Considerations of Educational Computer Use." In *Computers and Writing: Theory, Research, Practice*, eds. D. Holdstein and C. L. Selfe. New York: MLA.

Selfe, C. L., and S. Hilligoss, eds. 1994. *Literacy and Computers: The Complications of Teaching and Learning with Technology*: New York: Modern Language Association.

Sullivan, P. 1992. "Taking Control of the Page: Electronic Writing and Word Publishing." In *Evolving Perspectives on Computers and Composition Studies: Questions for the 1990s,* eds. G. E. Hawisher and C. L. Selfe. Urbana, IL: National Council of Teachers of English.

Susser, B. 1993. "Networks and Project Work: Alternative Pedagogies for Writing with Computers." *Computers and Composition* 10 (3): 63–89.

Tornow, J. 1997. *Link/Age: Composing in the Online Classroom.* Logan, UT: Utah State University Press.

Vitanza, V. J. 1996. *Cyber/Reader.* Boston: Allyn and Bacon.

2

A Brief, Selective, and Idiosyncratic History of Computers

John F. Barber

The plot of the popular 1997 science fiction film *Independence Day* shows the nations of Earth racing to ward off an alien invasion. Their secret weapon is computer technology, which allows instantaneous sharing of information and collaboration, as well as the introduction of a computer virus which eventually weakens the aliens' defenses and hastens their defeat. The computer saves humankind.

Yet, for some educators and administrators, computers *are* the aliens, intent on taking over and controlling everything we are and all that we do. They stand like deer in the headlights on the so-called information superhighway, lamenting the degree to which computer technology—from the coffeemaker in the faculty lounge to classroom pedagogy and curricula—is bearing down on their everyday lives.

Others embrace the light. They agree with Arthur C. Clarke (1986), who sees computer networks as the basis for sharing information in the future. Speaking specifically of education, Clarke predicts,

> The technologies that are changing society—communications satellites, fiber-optic cable, interactive TV, computers—will also change the way in which education is delivered. One result will be tremendous diversity in the educational system. Master teachers may address thousands of students scattered on several continents simultaneously, for instance. The technology that will make such courses available, teleconferencing, will soon be commonplace. (76–77)

Computers—we vilify, avoid, and lament, or deify, embrace, and celebrate them. In either case, given their prominence, it is easy to feel that computers and technology related to them have always been, and will continue to be, with us. While the latter is probably true, what we think and know of computers is relatively a twentieth-century phenomenon. During the past few decades computer technology was developed, marketed, and politicized by what President Dwight D. Eisenhower first called the military-industrial complex. It is only recently that we have begun to explore and extrapolate the community-building and egalitarian potentials of networked computers. As a result, we find ourselves at a crossroads: On the one hand, computer networks can increase the hegemony of big business and government control over individuals. On the other hand, they can encourage and empower individuals and collaborative communities. In short, the rapid commercialization and concern for control of computer networks like the Internet and the World Wide Web conflict with notions of grassroots participatory democracy.

Howard Rheingold (1993) says computer-mediated communication (CMC) has the potential to change our lives on three different, but strongly influential, levels.

1. Our perceptions, thoughts, and personalities are changed by the way we use a new medium and the way it uses us.

2. The nature of person-to-person interaction in CMC challenges us to consider whether it is possible for us to build some kind of community together.

3. The political implications of CMC are two-fold—either the Panoptican proposed by Jeremy Bentham (a combination of architecture and optics that makes it possible for a single prison guard to see every inmate and yet no prisoner can see anyone else; the net result is that all prisoners conform their behavior because they believe they are under constant surveillance)—or open discussion or debate in the public sphere of civil society. (13–15)

The battle lines in this debate are increasingly being drawn in the area of our vested interest: education, teaching, and learning. Our roles in this debate, as teachers and educators, become clear: We must help keep our students and ourselves from becoming victims. One way to do this is to take a cue from historians, who have long argued that unless we understand the past, we will not be prepared to deal with the future.

This may be difficult, however. For most of our students, computers and computer technology have always been an integral part of their lives. Probably their earliest toys contained computer chips that produced sounds or images. Many had access to computers before attending school. Many may even have had experience with computer networks like the World Wide Web. For our students, a time before computers is inconceivable.

But there was such a time, and where my colleagues in this volume discuss the present theory and future implications of computers in the classroom, I'd like to talk more generally about what computers are, how they came into being, how they have developed from large machines for calculating projectile trajectories to laptop cultural artifacts of connectivity and communication. I would also like to review some of the speculations regarding what computers might become, and how we might use them.

As my title suggests, this chapter traces briefly, selectively, and in an idiosyncratic way, the history of computers, emphasizing the use of electronic networks to cross boundaries and build collaborative communities in the writing classroom. This history is by no means exhaustive, nor is it meant to be inclusive. Surely I have missed some important developments, but my goal is to provide an engaging historic overview, rich with anecdote and up-to-date enough so as to inform our present use of computer technology.

Pre-Twentieth-Century Computing

In *The Age of Intelligent Machines* (1990), Raymond Kurzweil defines a computer as "a machine capable of automatically performing (that is without human intervention) sequences of calculations, and of choosing between alternate sequences of calculations based on the results of earlier calculations" (169). Yet, "intelligent" machines for performing mathematical calculations were built in Europe prior to the twentieth century. For example, French philosopher Blaise Pascal built a calculating machine for his father, the local tax collector, in 1642. Pascal called his machine the Pascaline. A machine for performing multiplication by repeating additions was built thirty-nine years later, in 1671, in Germany, by Gottfried Wilhelm von Leibniz, although there is no record of what Leibniz called his machine.

In England, in 1822, the British government agreed to fund the construction of the difference engine, a mechanical adding machine proposed by Charles Babbage. The British government was interested in using Babbage's machine, which could only perform addition (all other mathematical calculations had to be reduced to a series of additions) to perform astronomical and navigational calculations. Babbage was not able to produce a working model of his difference engine because no craftsman could produce the necessary precision parts, and in 1833 the government withdrew support.

However, the following year, Babbage started developing a more powerful calculating machine, one that could add, subtract, multiply, and divide directly, without the aid of the other three operations. He called this new machine the analytical engine and designed it to be controlled by cards punctured by strategically placed holes, similar to the cards used to control the figured weaving produced by Jacquard looms, named after their French inventor, Joseph-Marie Jacquard. In 1800 Jacquard redesigned an automated silk weaving loom built sixty years earlier but never used because silk weavers in Lyon, France, felt the loom threatened their jobs. One change in Jacquard's design was the addition of punched metal cards. The holes in the cards acted as instructions for particular patterns woven by the loom.

Babbage adapted Jacquard's punched cards for his analytical engine. The holes in the cards acted as instructions, telling Babbage's machine how to accomplish calculations. Different cards had instructions for different calculations. Taken together, a stack of these cards has come to be called a program which, according to Steven Levy (1984), is "a series of instructions which yield some expected result, just as the instructions in a recipe, when precisely followed, lead to a cake" (5).

Lacking funds and the ability to manufacture precision parts, Babbage was unable to build a full-scale model of his analytical engine just as he had been unable to produce his difference engine.[1] Despite this failure, Babbage did, as Jeremy Bernstein (1963) points out, develop components for his mechanical "engines," which are standard in today's electronic computers. What Babbage called the "store" is now called the computer's "memory." His "mill" we know today as the central processing unit or CPU. Babbage's "shuttle," a device for moving numbers back and forth between the store and the mill, is today's computer "bus." What Babbage envisioned as ways to get numbers in and out of his machines are known today as computer "input-output devices."

Following Babbage's use of punched cards, Herman Hollerith, of Manhattan, New York, developed a punched-card-controlled calculating machine that was able to tabulate the 1890 U.S. Census in just two years, a big improvement in efficiency over previous years. By contrast, the 1880 census had required the efforts of hundreds of people over a time period of nearly eight years to compile. Hollerith based his punched-card technology on the same Jacquard loom used by Charles Babbage, and upon the player piano, developed by John McTammany in 1876. McTammany got the idea for a self-playing piano controlled by rolls of perforated paper while repairing a music box. McTammany patented his invention in 1881, but died a pauper from defending his patent rights against violators.

Hollerith cards, about the size of dollar bills, were soon used in a variety of office machines. In 1896 Hollerith founded the Tabulating Machine Company, which merged with several other concerns to become the Computing Tabulating Recording Company (CTR) in 1911. In 1924 CTR changed its name to International Business Machines (IBM).

Twentieth-Century Computing

During the twentieth-century, ideas and technology related to computers advanced rapidly with each decade. Calculating machines combining mechanics and electronics were built, the basic technologies for present-day electronic computers were developed, and theories of information as packets of electrical signals that could be easily transmitted and manipulated by computers were adopted. During the twentieth-century, the so-called computer age has come into being, and computer technology has become a part of the fabric of our culture, beginning in 1906 when Lee De Forest developed a vacuum tube that became the basis for a revolution in electronic devices.

In 1910, the same year Halley's Comet provided a spectacular night-sky show, the Great Brass Brain, an eleven-foot-long, seven-foot-high calculator for predicting ocean tides, was built for the U.S. Coast Guard. Dials, thirty-seven in total, one for each variable in the prediction model, were set by hand. The machine operated by hand cranking. It was retired in 1966.

People quickly focused on the perceived dehumanizing effects of mechanical calculating machines. In 1921 Czech dramatist Karel Čapek coined the term *robot* from a Czech word meaning "forced labor" to describe the mechanical people in his science fiction drama *R. U. R.* (Rossum's Universal Robots), which premiered at the National Theater in Prague, Czechoslovakia, on 26 January 1921. The term *robot* was introduced to Americans when the Theater Guild produced Čapek's play on 9 October 1922. Soon after that, the term was known around the world (Gannett 1959).

Elmer Rice produced a play in 1923 called *The Adding Machine*, which satirized burgeoning numbers of office counting and writing machines. The play's protagonist, Mr. Zero, was portrayed as a "slave to a contraption of steel and iron" (Roszak 1986, 5).

The 1930s

In 1930, the same year the ninth planet, Pluto, was discovered, Vannevar Bush, a professor at the Massachusetts Institute of Technology, built an electromechanical calculating machine he called a "differential analyzer." His machine, the first analog computer, contained two thousand vacuum tubes, 150 electric motors, nearly two hundred miles of wiring, and thousands of electrical relay switches. An analog computer is designed to model, predict, or measure a certain event by imitating, through programmed instructions, that event. Without extensive reprogramming, an analog computer cannot accomplish more than one task (Jennings 1990, 33). Bush's machine was programmed (given operating directions) by plugging wires into circuit boards connected to the electrical relays. Bush's calculating machine, a progenitor of present-day credit-card-size electronic calculators, weighed one hundred tons.

Four years later, Konrad Zuse, of Germany, began work on digital computers, building several during World War II. Zuse's calculating machines were, however, never recognized or utilized by the German military. According to Anthony Ralston and Edwin Reilly (1983), instead of mimicking only one model or prediction, like an analog computer, a digital computer "uses numerical data, in the form of on-off electrical pulses (bits), to represent many situations. Instead of measuring, a digital computer counts. The output of a digital computer is separate, discrete, and discontinuous" (1577–1578).

Without knowing he was on a parallel path with Zuse, Alan Turing, an English mathematician, published a paper in 1937 entitled "On Computable Numbers, with an Application to the Entscheidungsproblem [decision-making problem]" in which he described a calculating machine, similar to those designed and built by Zuse, that used binary digits to solve mathematical problems. Turing's paper was the foundation for the binary memory system used in all modern computer systems.

During World War II, Turing worked with top-secret calculating machines to break the German signal codes. One machine, an eight-foot-tall bronze column called the Bronze Goddess, was used to break a German code called Enigma. Another machine, called Colossus, was used to break a more difficult German code, nicknamed Fish. Of Colossus, Karla Jennings (1990) writes that it

> had about 1,500 vacuum tubes and used punched paper tape for programming. Members of the Women's Royal Naval Service (WRENS) stood at toggle switches as a cryptoanalyst shouted programming instructions above the roar of clicking relays. . . . Most of the pioneer computer projects used women operators to grind through equations or help program the machine, just as women did the laborious data processing on Hollerith machines. (36)

In 1938 Claude Shannon's master's thesis, "A Symbolic Analysis of Relays and Switching Circuits" (Shannon and Weaver 1949),

applied Boolean logic (binary arithmetic) to electric switching circuits, and with the work of Zuse and Turing, helped pave the way for
electronic digital computers.

The 1940s

From this point until well after the end of World War II, the development and utilization of computer technology was an exclusive military province. In 1941 John Atanasoff, professor of physics at Iowa
State University, and his graduate student Clifford Berry built an electronic computer, the ABC (Atanasoff-Berry Computer), a machine
about the size of a large desk, that could solve linear equations. Their
computer was not programmable. Lack of funding and the start of
American involvement in World War II prevented the ABC from
becoming fully operational.

The same year, Helmut Hoelzer, an electrical engineer on Werner
von Braun's German rocketry staff, built an electronic analog computer. After World War II, both von Braun and Hoelzer went to work
building rockets for the United States' NASA space program.

In 1943 John Eckert and John Mauchly, of the University of
Pennsylvania, began developing ENIAC (Electronic Numerical
Integrator and Computer) for the U.S. Army. Intended to produce bal-
listic tables, ENIAC became operational in 1945, too late for the war
effort, and was thus used to solve scientific computations until 1955.
According to James Trager (1992), ENIAC was the first fully electronic, general purpose programmable digital computer. ENIAC was one
hundred feet long, ten feet tall, and three feet wide—a space equivalent
to a two-car garage. It used eighteen thousand radio tubes, which could
be turned on and off faster than mechanical relay switches. ENIAC
could complete forty-five hundred calculations a second despite the
fact that it used lots of electricity and broke down frequently. Mauchly
got many ideas for this computer after visiting John Atanasoff at the
University of Iowa in 1941. When IBM turned down their request for
research funding, Eckert and Mauchly started their own computer company called UNIVAC (UNIVersal Automatic Computer) in 1947.
Eckert and Mauchly built and sold their first UNIVAC computer to the
United States Census Bureau in 1951 (Trager 1992, 900).

The following year, IBM was more generous with funding,
awarding $5 million to Howard Aiken, a Harvard University
Engineering School mathematics professor, who built a programmable computer called the Harvard Mark I Automatic Sequence
Controlled Calculator, which used punched tape for programming,
and vacuum tubes and relays to calculate problems. Of the Mark 1,
Trager writes,

The Mark I was 51 feet long and 8 feet tall, had 760,000 parts (including thousands of mechanical relay switches), 500 miles of wiring, required 4 seconds to perform a simple multiplication problem, 11 seconds for division, and broke down frequently. When Eckert and Mauchly's ENIAC finally became operational in 1945, it was 2,000 times faster than Aiken's Mark I computer, which quickly became obsolete. (889)

As an offshoot of their work on ENIAC, John Eckert and John Mauchly began work in 1945 for the U.S. Army on the EDVAC (Electronic Discrete Variable Automatic Computer). EDVAC used four thousand tubes and ten thousand crystal diodes. It was to be a computer that used a permanently stored program, thus eliminating the necessity to program it by using punched cards or paper or magnetic tape. Based on their work, John von Neumann wrote and published a paper entitled "First Draft of a Report on the EDVAC," in which he explained concepts for a computer with a permanently stored program. The first computers with stored memory were often called "Neumann computers." John Kemeny (1972) writes about hearing von Neumann lecture at Los Alamos in 1946 and propose designing a fully electronic computer using a binary number system and incorporating internal memory and stored programs. Because this computer could carry out any calculation, it would be called a "universal computer" (3–7). Inspired by the stored-program concept presented by von Neumann in 1945, M. V. Wilkes designed EDSAC (Electronic Delay Storage Automatic Calculator) at Cambridge University in 1946. EDSAC became operational in 1949.

Addressing a different audience than von Neumann, Edmund Berkeley published a popular computer book, *Giant Brains, or Machines That Think*, about these new and amazing "mechanical brains" (he never used the word "computer") in 1949. As glorious as they seemed, these first computers were not without problems. Radio tubes and mechanical switches constantly broke down and programs often malfunctioned. These problems were called "bugs," and Naval Captain Grace Murray Hopper, who worked on the Mark I computer at Harvard in 1945, tells a colorful story about the origin of the term:

> We were building Mark I—and Mark I stopped. We finally located the failing relay and, inside the relay, beaten to death by the relay contact, was a moth about three inches long. So the operator got a pair of tweezers and carefully fished the bug out of the relay and put it in the log book. He put scotch tape over it and wrote, "First actual bug found." And the bug is still in the log book under the scotch tape and it is in the Museum of the Naval Surface Weapons Center at Dahlgren, Virginia. (quoted in Jennings 1990, 64)

The source of many "bugs" was addressed in 1948 when William Schockley, Walter Brattain, and John Bardeen introduced the transistor to replace the glass vacuum tube. AT&T and Bell Labs licensed the technology to the Sony Corporation in 1950. Sony improved production and cut costs, launching a revolution in microelectronics.

The same year, 1950, Alan Turing's now classic paper, "Computing Machinery and Intelligence," answered the question "Can a computer think?" with a simple "imitation test," now called the Turing Test. Turing determined that if written responses are collected from a computer and a human, both hidden from view or sequestered in another room, and another human can't tell which response the computer generated, then "fair play" obliges one to accept the fact that a computer can think. Turing reasoned that we have no way of knowing if a person is thinking except by his or her responses, and it is unfair to impose a different set of response criteria on a computer (Jennings 1990, 47–48). Turing's article was published in *Mind*, a philosophical journal, and was instrumental in the later development of artificial intelligence as a subset of computing science, where the philosophical debate surrounding his contentions continues.

While Turing was concerned with whether computers could think, Eckert and Mauchly were concerned with bankruptcy. They sold their UNIVAC computer and company to Remington Rand, which later became Sperry Rand, as it is known today. The following year, 1951, Remington Rand introduced the UNIVAC computer on a commercial basis. Its first customers included the U.S. Bureau of Census, which used the UNIVAC computer to tabulate the 1950 census. This was the beginning of the commercial computer age and marks the first use of a computer for business (Capron and Perron 1993, 551–52).

The 1950s

Computers soon were used for other purposes as well. In 1952 CBS television used a UNIVAC computer to predict, correctly, the election of Dwight Eisenhower. The UNIVAC predicted 438 electoral votes for Eisenhower, who finished with 442. Karla Jennings (1990) writes that this was the television debut of the computer age.

> Analyzing three percent of the returns, [the UNIVAC computer] predicted Eisenhower winning by a landslide. But polls showed a close race, and Eisenhower was a Republican, while the Democratic South hadn't even been counted yet! So, officials from Remington Rand, UNIVAC's manufacturer, tampered with the data to make UNIVAC broadcast a close race. But when more returns showed Eisenhower burying [Adlai] Stevenson, the president of Remington Rand appeared on [television] to explain to viewers that they'd

fudged the data because they couldn't believe their own computer. (27–28)

Computers now had business, and income, potential. In 1953 IBM introduced its first computer, called the IBM 701, to compete with Remington Rand. The following year Chinese American computer engineer An Wang founded Wang Laboratories in Lowell, Massachusetts, to make small business calculators. This marked the first application of small computers for business uses. Wang also did some pioneer work on magnetic memory, which later became the basis for all modern computing technology. IBM passed UNIVAC in computer sales in 1955 with seventy-six installations and with orders for 193 machines; this compared to UNIVAC's forty-six installations and orders for sixty-five. With little difference between the two computers, IBM built its lead on salesmanship and service (Trager 1992, 950). By 1959, two thousand computers were delivered to U.S. business offices, universities, laboratories, and other buyers, and the debate began as to whether computers created or destroyed jobs.

Concurrent with the development of early computers were five publications establishing the theory, language, and metaphors that continue to drive much of the thinking surrounding present-day computer technology and its use. The first was *Cybernetics; or Control and Communication in the Animal and the Machine* (1948), written by Norbert Wiener, a mathematician at the Massachusetts Institute of Technology. The second, also written by Wiener, was a popularized version of his earlier work, called *The Human Use of Human Beings: Cybernetics and Society* (1959). In both, Wiener introduced the term *cybernation*, which he defined as the new, automated technology surrounding the developing calculating machines. He also introduced and defined *feedback*, a key term for his concept of cybernation, as the ability of a computing machine to use the results of its own performance as self-regulating information and to adjust itself as part of an ongoing process. Wiener claimed that through perfecting feedback and the rapid manipulation of data by machines, the developing science of *cybernetics*—a term he coined from the Greek word for pilot, *kubernetes*, to embrace theories of control, feedback, and information transfer—would gain a deeper understanding of human life as being, essentially, the processing of information.

Wiener used the term *cybernetics* as a metaphor for the human mind, claiming as precedent James Watt's use of the word *governor* for the mechanical regulator on Watt's steam engine. Wiener's metaphor describes the mind as a sort of automatic pilot, which can be controlled through feedback loops of self information. From this notion comes the beginnings of cognitive science. For an historical overview of cybernetics and cognitive science, see Daniel Bell (1982).

The third and fourth publications appeared simultaneously in July 1949. Claude Shannon, a mathematician employed by the Bell Telephone Laboratories in New Jersey, published a two-part paper (the second, and concluding, part was published in October 1949) concerning a theory dealing with the statistical considerations of the accurate transmission of information. Warren Weaver, the Rockefeller Foundation's director of natural sciences, published an article in *Scientific American* (1949) outlining Shannon's work in lay terms. Both Shannon's two-part paper and a slightly more technical version of Weaver's article were published as *A Mathematical Theory of Communication* in 1949.

The fundamental problem of communication, as Shannon saw it, was to successfully transmit and receive messages. The message's meanings were not important. "These semantic aspects of communication," Shannon (1949) wrote, "are irrelevant to the engineering problem" (379). The problem was getting the message, not the feeling, and not necessarily the meaning, from one point to another efficiently and effectively. This set the stage for messages to be seen as discrete packets of information—devoid of human thoughts, feelings, and ideas—that could be encoded and decoded by mathematical algorithms and sent electronically from place to place. It was decades before the telephone company tried, at least semantically, to put feeling and emotion back into telephone messages with marketing campaigns urging us to "reach out and touch someone."

The implication of Shannon's work is an information theory in which "information" is not connected to the semantic contents of messages but is instead a quantitative measure of communicative exchange, especially when it takes place through some mechanical channel that requires messages to be encoded and decoded into electronic impulses.

Finally, Vannevar Bush, director of the Office of Scientific Research and Development during World War II, coordinated the application of six thousand research scientists' activities to America's wartime efforts and encouraged making the technology developed during the war available to the general public. One of the ideas Bush discussed was the first proposal for a system of associative indexing to be used in the mechanical storage and retrieval of information. Bush called his microfiche-based system Memex (memory extender) and specified fast access to information, the ability to annotate information, the ability to link information, and the ability to store a trail of links as characteristics of a system to approximate the way the human mind works by association. Said Bush (1945),

> With one item in its grasp, it snaps instantly to the next that is suggested by the association of thoughts, in accordance with some intri-

cate web of trails carried by the cells of the brain. . . . Man cannot hope fully to duplicate this mental process artificially, but he certainly ought to be able to learn from it. . . . Selection by association, rather than by indexing, may yet be mechanized. (106)

Bush recognized the connected nature of information stored in human memory and felt his Memex storage and retrieval system would support the human intellectual process by establishing trails through mechanically stored information.

The 1960s

The early development and application of computer technology and communication theory was directed toward large business and scientific laboratory customers. No thought was given, by large computer companies, to building computers for small businesses, let alone individual users. Outlining the situation, Howard Rheingold (1991) says that in 1950 "there were no more than a dozen computers in the United States" (74). Since then computers have changed, according to Bruce Sterling (1992), from fearsome high-tech totems to everyday pillars of human community (14). Entrepreneurial companies sprang up in garages and warehouses and began building small computers designed for individual users, "the people." The term *computer age* was first used in 1962 (Lubar 1993, 319), and this was the beginning of the "micro" or "personal" computer, small enough to fit on a desktop, powerful enough to provide some service to an individual.

One early service was psychiatric therapy. In 1963 Joseph Weizenbaum, an MIT computer scientist, released a computer conversational program called ELIZA that modeled nondirective ("Rogerian") psychiatric therapy. ELIZA became an instant success with the artificial intelligence community, and with those sufficiently persuaded of the program's humanity to reveal intimate details of their private lives. For these users, ELIZA clearly passed the Turing Test. But for the skeptical, according to Osborne Hardison, Jr. (1989), the success of ELIZA raised questions about the Turing Test itself.

> Who has to be persuaded in order for the Turing Test to be passed? Who decides who has to be persuaded? Should there be a "supreme court" of judges who must be persuaded before it can be said that the Turing Test has been "passed"? If so, who appoints the judges? (328)

Weizenbaum came to regret writing the ELIZA program, seeing that people wanted to believe in machine intelligence and personification, to the detriment of those same human attributes. Weizenbaum argues that there is a difference between humans and computers and that there are certain tasks that computers "*ought* not be made to do, independent of whether computers *can* be made to do them" (1976, *x*).

Another attempt at directing the growing abilities of computer technology toward providing personal services came in 1963 when Douglas Englebart published a paper entitled "A Conceptual Framework for the Augmentation of Man's Intellect." Throughout his career, Englebart worked to define the functions computers needed in order to augment human abilities. These functions included links between texts, electronic mail, document libraries, personal storage spaces for computer users, computer screens with multiple windows, and facilitation of work done on a computer by more than one user. Englebart invented the mouse (a computer input device that allows a user to select items on the computer screen and implement instructions), an outliner and idea processor, and online help systems integrated with computer software (Berk and Devlin 1991, 13–14).

From here, the pendulum swung back and forth between the profit motivations of big business and the collaborative, community-building concerns of grassroots users. In 1964 IBM became the computer industry leader, with its introduction of the System 360 computer. This computer was named "the 360" because it was supposed to provide 360 degrees, or complete, coverage of all business computational needs. IBM also coined the term *word processing* as a way to market a new product, a typewriter that recorded words on a magnetic tape. IBM estimated the market was five thousand machines.

Douglas Englebart and Theodor Nelson designed computer systems in the 1960s that implemented Vannevar Bush's notion of connected text. Nelson called Bush's notion of trails between stored information "links" and coined the term *hypertext* to denote a nonsequential, branching method of reading, writing, and storing and retrieving information connected by these links, spawning a new genre of computer technology and applications (Berk and Devlin 1991, 14; Nelson 1992, 48–49).

In 1967, trying to cut its costs, IBM stopped providing software for its computer equipment, relying instead on third parties to provide it. This launched the computer software industry, and in 1975 Microsoft, which later became the world's largest seller of computer software, was founded by Bill Gates (age nineteen) and Paul Allen (age twenty-two). Gates dropped out of Harvard to devote his attention to writing software, and became a billionaire before age thirty.

Finally, at the end of the decade, in 1969, ARPANET (Advanced Research Projects Agency Network), a joint project between the Defense Department, military and defense contractors, and universities doing defense research, was established to allow researchers at locations far removed from each other to share computer hardware and programs. ARPANET was, arguably, the first computer network designed for the interactive sharing of information and certainly the first to incorporate the concept of packet switching, or breaking messages into small parts, each of which is routed over the network to a destination where they are reassembled again.

The notion of packet switching began in 1949 with Claude Shannon's work at the Bell Telephone Laboratories in New Jersey. Shannon had proposed breaking communications into discrete packets of information that could be encoded and decoded by mathematical algorithms and sent electronically from place to place. His work was continued in the 1950s when the RAND Corporation studied the effects of a nuclear war on communication systems. The idea was to develop a decentralized communications system that would seek out undamaged routes for the reliable transmission of information. The most effective way to accomplish this, according to the RAND studies, was through packet switching.

The proposal was to separate all messages into small pieces of data, or packets, each with addressing information attached that indicated where it originated, where it was heading, and how many packets constituted the complete message. Routers throughout the network would read this information and pass the packets along to the next reliable node of the network. As nodes failed, the routers would determine alternative routes for the packets. If the receiving node did not receive all the packets it expected, it would ask the transmitting node to resend the packets.

According to Hafner and Lyon (1996), this packet switching scheme, along with a decentralized network consisting of a series of nodes around the country, became the basis for ARPANET. Although built for sharing research activities, the network was quickly used for personal communications by its original handful of users. One of the first large, public, network-based discussion lists developed around the theme of science fiction in the late 1970s (Rheingold 1993, 77). As more and more people began using the computer network for personal or political purposes, and as more and more computers were added, ARPANET grew into a loose collection of thousands of computer networks around the world and, after several name changes, is now called the Internet.

The 1970s

The decade of the 1970s was a heady time for the development and sale of small, powerful computers designed for individuals. Computers built during this time fit on a desktop and had more computing power than the earlier room-size computers. The advancements in technology were staggering. Alan Kay (1977) put the situation in perspective:

> The evolution of the personal computer has followed a path similar to that of the printed book, but in 40 years rather than 600. Like the handmade books of the Middle Ages, the massive computers built in the two decades before 1960 were scarce, expensive and available to only a few. Just as the invention of printing led to the community use of books chained in a library, the introduction of computer time sharing in the 1960s partitioned the capacity of expensive computers in order to lower their access cost and allow community use. And just as the Industrial Revolution made possible the personal book by providing inexpensive paper and mechanized printing and binding, the microelectronic revolution of the 1970s will bring about the personal computer of the 1980s, with sufficient storage and speed to support high level computer languages and interactive graphic displays. (230)

It started in 1970, when Alan Shugart, inventor of the computer hard disk (a mass storage device), developed the first floppy disk (eight inches in diameter) at IBM. The floppy disk allowed information and programs to be transported easily between computers, as well as stored safely for long periods of time. In 1971 the first microprocessor, the 4004, was offered by Intel. Computer chips replaced transistors, reducing the size of computer components dramatically. The first chips were not programmable; they could only perform the function for which they were designed. Intel's programmable chip could do several different functions. One chip could even contain the entire central processing unit of a computer. These programmable chips, now called microprocessors, became the heart of the computer revolution. This microprocessor was the size of a thumbnail. In comparison, Charles Babbage's analytical engine, had it been built, would have filled more than ten railroad cars and required several steam engines for power (Jespersen and Fitz-Randolph 1984, 18).

In 1971 Seymour Cray founded Cray Research and introduced the first successful commercial supercomputer, the Cray 1. At the other end of the spectrum, in the same year, The People's Computer Company, a populist public relations endeavor to promote computers and computing, was started in San Francisco by Robert Albrect.

The first public computer terminal was set up outside Leopold's Records in Berkeley, California, in 1973 by the Community Memory Project, an offshoot of Project One, an umbrella of "Bay Area groups fostering community activism and humanistic programs" (Levy 1984, 156). Led by Leo Felsenstein, the Community Memory Project wanted to provide hands-on computer access to "the people" for communication and information sharing. Computer technology was utilized as guerrilla warfare against the perceived developing threat of computerized bureaucracy. Community Memory sympathized with Richard Brautigan's 1967 poem "All Watched Over by Machines of Loving Grace." Brautigan's poem inspired a special name for Community Project's parent company: Loving Grace Cybernetics.

This sense of computers as counterculture was echoed by Theodor Nelson in his self-published (1974) two-part book. The first part, *Computer Lib*, is Nelson's view of the mid-1970s computers and the necessity to understand them. The second part, *Dream Machines*, deals with Nelson's thoughts about "new freedoms through computer screens."

The first commercial microcomputer in kit form was introduced in the January 1975 issue of *Popular Electronics* magazine. Built by Ed Roberts, founder of Micro Instrumentation Telemetry Systems (MITS), Albuquerque, New Mexico, this computer, half the size of an air conditioner, was named Altair 8800, after a destination in the popular television show *Star Trek* (Levy 1984, 184). This computer received input from switches on its front, and displayed output via LEDs (light-emitting diodes). Bill Gates, founder of Microsoft, wrote the first BASIC program for the Altair computer, and complained when people copied it.

The Altair was, undoubtedly, a topic of discussion at The Homebrew Club, which held its first meeting in San Francisco in 1975. Comprised of West Coast software and hardware engineers and computer hackers, The Homebrew Club, an outgrowth of the People's Computer Company, drew together people who liked to "homebrew," or build computers. From this club grew the microcomputer revolution that continues to change the world. According to Steven Levy (1984), one of the "articles of faith" of The Homebrew Club was to "[N]ever miss a club meeting. This is where it's at. The juicy little news bits, the how-to-fixits for the problem that has been bugging me the last two weeks . . . that is the real thing! Besides, they might have some free software" (232).

College dropouts Steve Jobs (age twenty-one, working for Atari) and Steve Wozniak (age twenty-six, working for Hewlett-Packard) attended many Homebrew meetings. In 1977, after six months of development, they were the first to build a computer with a television-like screen and a useful keyboard. Hewlett-Packard was not interested in their computer and gave its blessings to Jobs and Wozniak's outside work. Jobs and Wozniak called their computer the Apple II, and their company, the Apple Computer Company. Like many other computer and information technology developments at the time, Jobs and Wozniak's initial capitalization was small: $1,300 from the sale of

Steve Jobs's Volkswagen bus (Capron and Perron 1993, 556) and from the sale of Steve Wozniak's Hewlett-Packard programmable calculator (Levy 1984, 249). Jobs and Wozniak officially introduced their Apple II computer at The First Annual West Coast Computer Faire [sic], in 1977, in the San Francisco Civic Center. Almost thirteen thousand people attended. The Apple II computer became the most famous computer ever built and spawned a multibillion-dollar industry.

The decade of the 1970s was also an important time for the development of many of our notions of computer networks as sites for collaborative, community-oriented communication. Howard Rheingold (1993) says computer conferences emerged unexpectedly from the ARPANET because people adapt the original/intended purposes of technology to meet their own communication needs.

> Computer conferences emerged, . . . somewhat unexpectedly, as a tool for using the communication capacities of the networks to build social relationships across barriers of space and time. . . . [C]omputer conferences [were] quickly adapted to commercial, scientific, and social discourse. (7)

Dating the first use of computer conferences is subject to differing interpretations. Jacques Vallee (1982) says the first attempts at computer-network-mediated communications occurred during the Berlin crisis and airlift in 1948, when telex machines from several countries were wired together. Everyone attempted to communicate at the same time, in different languages, and the system didn't work.

Douglas Englebart, in 1968, gave a demonstration at the Augmentation Research Center at Stanford Research Institute in California, where he linked several people together using computer keyboards and screens. Participants in this conference were able to mix voice, video, and text together in real time (Rheingold 1993, 113).

Paul Taylor (1992) credits Murray Turoff with designing the earliest computer conference, in the 1960s, for the President's Office of Emergency Preparedness (138). In 1971, when President Richard Nixon ordered a national wage and price freeze, Turoff's prototype computer network, which borrowed from earlier work done by the RAND Corporation, became the Emergency Management Information System and Reference Index (EMISARI) and provided a way to collect information from computers at geographically dispersed offices (Rheingold 1993, 112).

Like computer hardware, network-based computer conferences were first used for government purposes. But a precedent had been established with the ARPANET, and perhaps drawing on this precedent as well as their own research of early computer network communications, Starr Roxanne Hiltz and Murray Turoff (1978) predicted that the medium would not be confined to think tanks or laboratories. Individuals would use computer networks to find and communicate with others who shared their interests, they said. Their prediction proved correct in the following decade, when computer conferencing began being used in writing classrooms.

The 1980s

During the 1980s, developments in computer technology occurred at a seemingly nonstop pace. IBM introduced its first personal computer in August of 1980, late in the game, as it had been with large computers. Making up for lost time, IBM soon captured 75 percent of the personal computer market (Trager 1992, 1085). In 1983 the computer was *Time*'s "Man of the Year." The Apple Macintosh computer was introduced in a television advertisement aired during the 1984 Super Bowl. The ad suggested that the Macintosh computer would provide release from the centralized control of information that George Orwell had predicted in *Nineteen Eighty-Four*. Desktop publishing was launched the following year with the introduction of the PageMaker program for the Apple Macintosh computer. And in 1987, Apple Computer's HyperCard program made hypertext available to ordinary computer users.

On a darker note, a nondestructive computer "worm" produced by Robert T. Morris, a Cornell computer science graduate student and son of Robert Morris, chief scientist at the National Computer Security Center, a branch of the top secret National Security Agency, replicated itself in thousands of computers connected to the Internet in 1988 causing massive shutdowns of computer networks and loss of information (Hafner and Markoff 1991, 251–341).

The 1980s was the beginning of our present introspective examination of computer technology. Whereas the emphasis of this introspection is now centered on the effects of technology on the ways we interact with each other, in the 1980s, writers concentrated on the people who built, programmed, and used computers. Pulitzer-prize wining author Tracy Kidder's *The Soul of a New Machine* (1981) chronicles the technology and human drama behind the development of the Data General Eclipse computer. Steven Levy, in his book *Hackers: Heroes of the Computer Revolution* (1984), reports on the first twenty-five years of the computer revolution and the efforts of young, nonprofessional computer programmers to develop programs that would turn early computers into useful, productive, and efficient machines.

This decade of the 1980s also saw the first use of computer networks in writing classrooms. According to Alan Feenberg (1987), David Hughes of Colorado College used electronic mail in a writing course in 1981. Whereas Hughes may have been the first to *use* a computer conference for teaching writing, Edward Jennings was the first, according to Gail Hawisher (1992), to *publish* an experiment in the teaching of writing within a virtual environment. Jennings conducted his paperless writing class in the spring of 1985. Trent Batson (1988) used a computer network to improve the writing skills of deaf students at Gallaudet University in Washington, D.C., beginning in January 1985, and stakes claim to the first use of this technology. Batson (1993) says,

> Steve Lombardo and I were the first writing teachers at Gallaudet and, as far as I know, the first *anywhere* to teach a whole semester of composition by communicating entirely in writing through a computer network in our classroom. (87, emphasis in original)

The 1990s

In 1991 George Bush became the first president with a computer terminal, but he showed no signs of using it. Under the administration of President Bill Clinton, however, the White House was connected to the Internet in 1993. Email addresses for President Clinton and Vice President Al Gore were widely distributed.

When Gore introduced his concept of an information superhighway, a high-speed computer network linking homes, schools, and businesses across the country to facilitate the rapid and efficient sharing of information and communication, many business concerns saw dollar signs in his vision and quickly began reinventing themselves in order to sell services over computer networks. For example, John Malone, president of Tele-Communications, and Raymond Smith, chairman of Bell Atlantic, proposed, in 1993, a merger of their companies' operations: cable television and telecommunications. The proposed deal promised interactive television in private homes offering videophone, shopping, on-demand movies, information, games and entertainment, sports, and concerts (Solomon 1993). Reports of similar mutations are now announced daily but the actual implementation of the promises still seems a long way off.

The examination of the effects of computer technology continued during the first half of the 1990s, spawning a publishing industry dedicated to producing magazines, books, and other publications related to the so-called computer revolution, the industry it created, and the computer entrepreneurs who ran it. Christopher Evans (1980) writes about computers bringing about the fall of communism, reinvigorating capitalism, transforming the third world, and putting an end to war. Jonathan Littman (1990) chronicles the business and legal machinations involved in starting ComputerLand, a computer company that sold computers for both business and personal use. And Robert Cringely (1992) humorously examines the human foibles compounded and perpetuated by computers. For example,

> PCs killed the office typewriter, made most secretaries obsolete, and made it possible for a twenty-seven-year-old M.B.A. with a PC, a spreadsheet program, and three pieces of questionable data to talk his bosses into looting the company pension plan and doing a leveraged buy out. (4)

In 1992 William Gibson, the godfather of cyberpunk and inventor of the term *cyberspace*, published, with Kevin Begos, a publisher of museum-quality manuscripts, and Dennis Ashbaugh, a New York artist whose canvases employ models of computer viruses, *Agrippa*, a text that self-destructed as it was read. Guy Martin (1992), reviewing the book before its publication, offers this description and explanation:

> The physical object will be a large, somewhat tortured bronze or graphite portfolio containing Ashbaugh's original copper-plate engravings of DNA codes. Under the engravings will be a floppy [disk], swaddled in its own niche. Gibson's story will be on the disk, along with a very slick little computer virus. If the reader boots up and commits to reading this work, the disk will scroll at a preordained speed, once, and then the virus will cause it to mutate and then disappear. Appropriately, Ashbaugh's engravings will be done in two kinds of ink, one that disappears after being exposed to an hour of light and one that appears on exposure to light. The five hundred or so editions of *Agrippa* will cost between $450 and $7,500, depending on how much of an "object" the collector wants to buy. (33)

Robert Killheffer (1993) says that *Agrippa* is "an elaborately conceived marriage of antique bookcraft and modern computer technology that may alter our conceptions of the immortality of artworks" [and] raise "issues about the shape of books to come, issues we'll all be confronting, like it or not, in the very near future" (14).

Speaking of marriage, Hugh Jo and Monica Liston were the first couple to exchange wedding vows in a computer-mediated virtual reality setting. Friends and family watched as the 1994 ceremony unfolded on the lost continent of Atlantis (Associated Press 1994). This computer-network-mediated marriage is only one example of the ways people have sought, during this decade, to direct the power of computer technology to desires of individuals and grassroots community organizations for communication and connection with others. Building on the original ARPANET science fiction discussion list, it is now possible to find an Internet-based discussion list for any conceivable topic of interest. MUDs and MOOs encourage role playing and synchronous interaction between people. And the growing capabilities of video conferencing promise a morphing of the telephone, television, and computer into a device with great potential for changing the way we interact with others, conduct business, and construct our culture.

The Future of Computers

Mathematician, philosopher, and Dartmouth College president John Kemeny (1972) looks to the future of what he calls a symbiotic interaction between humans and computers with cautious relish. Writing at the beginning of what we now call the computer revolution, Kemeny foresees that humans will experience significant adaptations to keep abreast of the changes rapidly occurring in computers and computer-related technology.

> My major concern is whether man can keep up with his symbiotic partner. Even today computers have more power than we know how to use. We can keep the machines busy, but many computer experts feel that we have not yet learned how to make full use of their capabilities. Therefore a rapid social and scientific evolution must take place if man is to maintain the role of a full partner. This, I predict, is one of the most exciting challenges facing mankind. (71)

Whether these social and scientific changes have, will, or can, occur is, of course, debatable. There is no debate, however, over the fact that *computers* have, and will continue, to evolve in the future. Two future areas of computer evolution are interactive multimedia and networks.

The notion of combining telephones, television, and computers was a hot topic of speculation and development in the early 1990s. Driven by technological advances, and fueled by the Clinton administration's stated commitment to a national, computer-network-based information superhighway, telephone, cable television, and computer companies competed, and cooperated, to secure a place for themselves, and their products and services, on television sets in homes all across the country. Philip Elmer-Dewitt (1993) asserted that the technology behind this explosive merger includes:

1. The ability to translate all audio and video communications into digital information that can be processed by computers.

2. New methods of storing this digital information and compressing

it so that it can travel through existing telephone and cable television lines.

3. Fiber optic wiring that provides virtually limitless transmission capabilities.

4. New switching techniques that make it possible to bring all this to a private home through existing wiring and cables. (51)

The interactive merger of the telephone, television, and computer promises, according to experts like Barbara Kantrowitz (1993a), the most important medium since television. Kantrowitz says, "it will put the world at your fingertips, changing the ways you shop, play and learn. . . . In the household of the future, all will depend upon your connections" (42).

How does all this translate into a scenario for the computer user of the twenty-first century? Mark Weiser (1991) says that computers will be ubiquitous, part of the fabric of everyday life, part of everything we do, everything we use. Philip Elmer-Dewitt (1992) says, "technology watchers foresee a world filled with multisensual media, smart roads and robots that are almost alive" (9). Computers will continue to get smaller, Elmer-Dewitt says, and will be insinuated into the walls of our homes, our furniture, even our clothes. Computer networks will become populated with special forms of software called "personal assistants, or agents" that will glean important information for us, track our appointments, and offer advice. As Elmer-Dewitt explains, "A travel 'agent,' for example, would be indispensable to a foreign traveler by doing simultaneous translations or pointing out sites of interest. A virtual lawyer could give expert legal opinions, a Wall Street agent timely investment tips" (40).

This new form of interactive multimedia is not here yet, not completely, but already people are voicing concerns. Astronomer Clifford Stoll presents a galaxy of objections in his book *Silicon Snake Oil: Second Thoughts on the Information Superhighway* (1995). Novelist Robert Coover (1993) cuts to the chase and asks, and answers, the fundamental question:

> Will everyone have equal and universal access to this magical new realm? No, they will not. But the gap between haves and have-nots, already almost unimaginably vast in our time, will not necessarily widen. Digitalization, like the Gutenberg technology before it, has so far had a democratizing effect on cultural exchange, greatly empowering the individual user, and it is easy enough to learn that small children can make full use of it. (16)

Richard Zoglin (1993) speculates on the effects that the proposed merger of the computer, telephone, and television will have on elements of the media: television channels "will multiply into the hundreds. . . . Advertisers will be able to target [commercials] to individual homes." Networks "might survive only as brandname suppliers of programming." For video stores "the prospects aren't bright," and our bills "could get bigger as pay-per-view options multiply along with such services as games and video conferencing" (56–58).

Cultural critic Neil Postman (1993) discounts the highly touted ability of the information superhighway to deliver untold amounts of information to the average American home, saying, "The fact is that information has now become a form of garbage. We don't know what to do with it, have no control over it, don't know how to get rid of it" (16).

How will these new services—be they useful or garbage—be implemented? John Keller (1993) reports on a secret two-year research project conducted by American Telephone & Telegraph Company to test interactive communication multimedia content and devices. Keller says companies hoping to capitalize on the multimedia boom are placing billion-dollar bets based on little more than intuition. "They don't know which products and services could make money," Keller says, and concludes that new services which are developed will have to be "mindlessly simple to operate and presented as an advanced form of television entertainment" (1).

In the meantime, sizable populations of people meet and interact through computer networks and electronic conferences. The September 1991 issue of *Scientific American* magazine devoted a large section to detailing the fusion of computers and communication technologies, and the resulting changes to civilization. The thrust of this fusion is seen as computer networks that will facilitate the flow and exchange of digital information (Cerf 1991). The amount of information exchanged will require new, more advanced computer networks. Lawrence Tesler (1991), seemingly disagreeing with Neil Postman, says new computers will be active collaborators in the getting and using of information. According to Alan Kay (1991), computer networks will be as important as the advent of privately owned books during the Renaissance as a medium for providing information and acquiring knowledge.

Computer networks will also influence the way we conceive and conduct work. Lee Sproull and Sara Kiesler (1991) predict that computer bulletin boards will help make employees more open, less conscious of hierarchies and status. The question is, however, can management adapt to a more flexible and dynamic environment? Thomas Malone and John Rockart (1991) are concerned with the changes computer technology will have on production and marketing. They say computer networks, by coordinating activities, will force decisions downward in the organization.

The power of these new networks, according to Nicholas Negroponte (1991), will be the wide variety of products and services available to users and new opportunities for work and play. Negroponte (1995) elaborates on these concepts in his book *Being Digital*, in which he posits that more and more information, in more and more forms (text, video, and audio) will be turned into digital data and made available for computer-based manipulation by more and more people. Speaking of being digital, Barbara Kantrowitz (1993b) reports on the "more than 12 million Americans [who] are living 'on line'—looking for love, stock tips and therapy on computer networks" (42).

Howard Rheingold (1993) says that the computer has created a new form of human social life: "virtual communities," groups of people linked by their participation in computer networks. Rheingold examines virtual communities in the United States, Japan, and France, observing that their advantages include a folksy sense of a place where participants chat and ask one another for all kinds of help. He implies that within a computer network everyone is equal, disembodied, without the usual markers of social status, class, race, gender, and sexual preference. The disadvantages include obsession as the virtual community becomes a substitute for reality and the possibility of despotic monopolization as extremists take over and push their views and preoccupations on others.

Whether an advantage or disadvantage, computer networks also point to different notions of literate interaction. One day, predicts Rheingold (1991), no longer limited to the transmission of text, computer networks, with their ability to send and receive digital information, will foster a sense of presence.

> Eventually, what we will send one another over the telecommunication lines will not be restricted to text, but will include voice, images, gestures, facial expressions, virtual objects, cybernetic architectures—everything that contributes to a sense of presence. We will be able to send worlds, and ways to be in them. (88)

This ability to "send one another over the telecommunication lines" will, according to John Markoff (1994), create posttextual literacy based on digital audio/visual rather than textual thinking. Markoff says this will offer us the opportunity to manipulate streams of images in order to share stories about our lives in ways never before possible using only words.

According to Rheingold (1993), a virtual community can be a highway or a trap. The central question is whether computer communications will end up centralized, despotic, controlled by big business and government, or decentralized, democratic, controlled by ordinary people. Who will have access? Rheingold asks. Who will be cut off? Will a new class-divided society develop around one's ability to connect and interact through computer screens with virtual communities?

These kinds of questions are certainly central to what we, as teachers and administrators, see as our roles in our classrooms and schools. Positioned squarely at the crossroads of the brewing debate over whether computer technology will foster the hegemonic interests of big business and government or whether it will promote more democratic concerns voiced by individuals and grassroots community organizations, we have, in our utilization of computer network technology in our pedagogy and curricula, the opportunity to affect the future. We have, as Michael Lemonick (1993) suggests, the opportunity to act as facilitators who "will inspire, motivate, and referee the human-to-human discussion that computerized instruction is designed to provoke" (60). Computer-augmented education may well become the key to educational activities in the future. We must, therefore, continue to examine critically and creatively the use of computer technology to facilitate the future of teaching and learning. One resource in this endeavor is an understanding of the roles computers and computer technology have played in the past. As students continue to arrive in our classrooms with no knowledge of a world before computers, we must be prepared to position the multiple roles of this technology in such a way that it encourages our students to develop a well-rounded view based on a critical examination of the world surrounding them.

Note

1. For an interesting speculation as to what might have happened had Babbage been able to build his computing machines, see William Gibson and Bruce Sterling's 1991 detective thriller set in an alternate nineteenth-century techno-Victorian world powered by steam-driven machines. Charles Babbage perfects his analytical engine, which the police use to keep track of citizens. When a box of punched program cards for the engine turns up, someone is willing to kill for them.

Works Cited

Associated Press. 1994. "Couple Gets Married in Cyberspace." *Asheville Citizen-Times,* 22 August, 2A.

Batson, T. 1988. "The ENFI Project: A Networked Classroom Approach to Writing Instruction." *Academic Computing* (February): 32–33, 55–66.

———. 1993. "The Origins of ENFI." In *Network-Based Classrooms: Promises and Realities,* eds. B. Bertram, J. Peyton, and T. Batson, 87–112. New York: Cambridge University Press.

Bell, D. 1982. *The Social Sciences Since the Second World War*. New Brunswick, NJ: Transaction.

Berk, E., and J. Devlin, eds. 1991. *Hypertext/Hypermedia Handbook*. New York: McGraw-Hill.

Berkeley, E. 1949. *Giant Brains, or Machines That Think*. New York: Wiley.

Bernstein, J. 1963. *The Analytical Engine*. New York: Random House.

Brautigan, R. 1967. "All Watched Over by Machines of Loving Grace." In his *All Watched Over by Machines of Loving Grace*. San Francisco: Communications.

Bush, V. 1945. "As We May Think." *Atlantic Monthly* (August): 101–108.

Capron, H. L., and J. Perron. 1993. *Computers and Information Systems: Tools for an Information Age*. 3d ed. Redwood City, CA: Benjamin/Cummings.

Cerf, V. 1991. "Networks." *Scientific American* (September): 72–85.

Clarke, A. C. 1986. *Arthur C. Clarke's July 20, 2019: Life in the 21st Century*. New York: Macmillan.

Coover, R. 1993. "We Are the Wired: Some Views on the Fiberoptic Ties That Bind." *New York Times*, 24 October, sec. 4, p. 16.

Cringely, R. 1992. *Accidental Empires: How the Boys of Silicon Valley Make Their Millions, Battle Foreign Competition, and Still Can't Get a Date*. Reading, MA: Addison-Wesley.

Elmer-DeWitt, P. 1992. "Dream Machines." *Time* 140 (27): 39–41.

— — — . 1993. "Take a Trip into the Future on the Electronic Superhighway." *Time* (12 April): 50–55.

Englebart, D. 1963. "A Conceptual Framework for the Augmentation of Man's Intellect." In *Vistas in Information Handling*, eds. P. D. Howerton and D. C. Weeks, 1–29. Washington, D.C.: Spartan Books.

Evans, C. 1980. *The Micro Millennium*. New York: Viking.

Feenberg, A. 1987. "Computer Conferencing and the Humanities." *Instructional Science* 169–86.

Gannett, L. 1959. Introduction. In *War with the Newts*, ed. Karel Čapek. New York: Berkley.

Gibson, W. 1992. *Agrippa*. New York: Kevin Begos.

Gibson, W., and B. Sterling. 1991. *The Difference Engine*. New York: Bantam.

Hafner, K., and M. Lyon. 1996. *Where Wizards Stay up Late: The Origins of the Internet*. New York: Simon & Schuster.

Hafner, K., and J. Markoff. 1991. *Cyberpunk: Outlaws and Hackers on the Computer Frontier*. New York: Simon & Schuster.

Hardison, O., Jr. 1989. *Disappearing Through the Skylight: Culture and Technology in the Twentieth Century*. New York: Viking.

Hawisher, G. 1992. "Electronic Meetings of the Minds: Research, Electronic Conferences, and Composition Studies." In *Re-Imagining Computers and Composition: Teaching and Research in the Virtual Age*, eds. G. Hawisher and P. LeBlanc, 81–101. Portsmouth, NH: Boynton/Cook.

Hiltz, S., and M. Turoff. 1978. *The Network Nation*. Reading, MA: Addison-Wesley.

Jennings, K. 1990. *The Devouring Fungus: Tales of the Computer Age*. New York: Norton.

Jespersen, J., and J. Fitz-Randolph. 1984. *RAMS, ROMS, and Robots*. New York: Atheneum.

Kantrowitz, B. 1993a. "An Interactive Life." *Newsweek* (31 May): 42–44.

———. 1993b. "Live Wires." *Newsweek* (6 September): 42–49.

Kay, A. 1977. "Microelectronics and the Personal Computer." *Scientific American* (September): 230–44.

———. 1991. "Computers, Networks and Education." *Scientific American* (September): 138–49.

Keller, J. 1993. "AT&T's Secret Multimedia Trails Offer Clues to Capturing Interactive Audiences." *Wall Street Journal,* 28 July, sec. B3: 1, 6.

Kemeny, J. 1972. *Man and the Computer*. New York: Charles Scribner's Sons.

Kidder, T. 1981. *The Soul of a New Machine*. New York: Little, Brown.

Killheffer, R. 1993. "The Shape of Books to Come. A Collaborative Book (?) Challenges Ideas About the Immortality of Art." *Omni* (January): 14.

Kurzweil, R. 1990. *The Age of Intelligent Machines*. Cambridge, MA: MIT Press.

Lemonick, M. 1993. "Tomorrow's Lesson: Learn or Perish." *Time* 140 (27): 59–60.

Levy, S. 1984. *Hackers: Heroes of the Computer Revolution*. New York: Anchor Press/Doubleday.

Littman, J. 1990. *Once upon a Time in ComputerLand: The Amazing Billion-Dollar Tale of Bill Millard's ComputerLand Empire*. New York: Touchstone.

Lubar, S. 1993. *Infoculture: The Smithsonian Book of the Inventions of the Information Age*. Boston: Houghton Mifflin.

Malone, T., and J. Rockart. 1991. "Computers, Networks and the Corporation." *Scientific American* (September): 128–37.

Markoff, J. 1994. "The Rise and Swift Fall of Cyber Literacy." *New York Times,* 13 March, sec. 4: 1, 5.

Martin, G. 1992. "Read It Once." *Esquire* (May): 33.

Negroponte, N. 1991. "Products and Services for Computer Networks." *Scientific American* (September): 106–15.

———. 1995. *Being Digital*. New York: Alfred A. Knopf.

Nelson, T. 1974. *Computer Lib/Dream Machines*. South Bend, IN: Theodor Nelson.

― ― ―. 1992. "Opening Hypertext: A Memoir." In *Literacy Online: The Promise (and Peril) of Reading and Writing with Computers*, ed. M. Tuman, 43–57. Pittsburgh: University of Pittsburgh Press.

Orwell, G. 1949. *Nineteen Eighty-Four*. New York: Harcourt Brace.

Postman, N. 1993. "We Are the Wired: Some Views on the Fiberoptic Ties That Bind." *New York Times,* 24 October, sec. 4: 16.

Ralston, A., and E. Reilly, eds. 1983. *Encyclopedia of Computer Science and Engineering*. New York: Van Nostrand Reinhold.

Rheingold, H. 1991. *Virtual Reality*. New York: Summit.

― ― ―. 1993. *The Virtual Community: Homesteading on the Electronic Frontier*. Reading, MA: Addison-Wesley.

Roszak, T. 1986. *The Cult of Information: The Folklore of Computers and the True Art of Thinking*. New York: Pantheon.

Shannon, C. 1949. "A Mathematical Theory of Communication." *Bell System Technical Journal* (July; October): 379–423; 623–56.

Shannon, C., and W. Weaver. 1949. *A Mathematical Theory of Communication*. Urbana: University of Illinois.

Solomon, J. 1993. "Megamergers: Big Brother's Holding Company." *Newsweek* (25 October): 38–43.

Sproull, L., and S. Kiesler. 1991. "Computers, Networks and Work." *Scientific American* (September): 116–27.

Sterling, B. 1992. *The Hacker Crackdown: Law and Disorder on the Electronic Frontier*. New York: Bantam.

Stoll, C. 1995. *Silicon Snake Oil: Second Thoughts on the Information Superhighway*. New York: Doubleday.

Taylor, P. 1992. "Social Epistemic Rhetoric and Chaotic Discourse." In *Re-Imagining Computers and Composition: Teaching and Research in the Virtual Age*, eds. G. Hawisher and P. LeBlanc, 131–54. Portsmouth, NH: Boynton/Cook.

Tesler, L. 1991. "Networked Computing in the 1990s." *Scientific American* (September): 86–93.

Trager, J. 1992. *The People's Chronology*. New York: Henry Holt.

Turing, A. 1937. "On Computable Numbers, with an Application to the Entscheidungsproblem." *Proceedings of the London Mathematical Society*: 230–65.

― ― ―. 1950. "Computing Machinery and Intelligence." *Mind* (October): 433–60.

Vallee, J. 1982. *The Network Revolution: Confessions of a Computer Scientist*. Berkeley, CA: And/Or Press.

Von Neumann, J. 1945 [1987]. "First Draft of a Report on the EDVAC." In *Papers of John von Neumann on Computing and Computer Theory*, eds. W. Aspray and A. Burks, 17–82. Cambridge: MIT Press.

Weaver, W. 1949. "The Mathematics of Communication." *Scientific American* (July): 11–15.

Wiener, N. 1948. *Cybernetics; or, Control and Communication in the Animal and the Machine*. New York: John Wiley.

———. 1959. *The Human Use of Human Beings: Cybernetics and Society*. Boston: Houghton Mifflin.

Weiser, M. 1991. "The Computer for the 21st Century." *Scientific American* (September): 94–105.

Weizenbaum, J. 1976. *Computer Power and Human Reason: From Judgment to Calculation*. San Francisco: W. H. Freeman.

Zoglin, R. 1993. "When the Revolution Comes What Will Happen to . . ." *Time* (12 April): 56–58.

3

The World Wide Web
Driving on the Information Superhighway in the Classroom

Donna Ashmus

"Every time I turn around, I see the World Wide Web mentioned—in magazine advertisements, in newspaper articles, on television commercials, and on business cards. But how can I use the World Wide Web in my classroom?" This is a question asked by many teachers as technology is forcing its way into the classroom. More and more, teachers are being encouraged to use technology in their classroom without knowing how this technology can be used. They often don't understand the full potential of the World Wide Web, don't know where to begin, and don't have the time to figure it out.

Instead of jumping onto the information superhighway and getting run over or left behind, teachers and students need some help in determining how they can use the World Wide Web to harness its power, potential, and numerous opportunities. This chapter will discuss these opportunities and provide specific examples of Web usage and locations on the Internet that demonstrate them (please note that, due to the fluid nature of information on the Web, addresses do change). First, let's look at why the World Wide Web is flourishing.

Why the World Wide Web
Is Appealing to Educators

The World Wide Web is a valuable resource for educators. Immediate access to global and multimedia resources can enhance educational objectives and motivate students. Telecommunications can connect teachers and students to "real world" events as they happen and encourage collaboration far beyond the classroom.

Not only does the World Wide Web provide exciting opportunities, it is also inexpensive and uncomplicated. The process is simple, and it doesn't require a fancy or expensive computer. Teachers can use most Macintosh computers or PCs to access the Internet, and creating Web documents is easy, as the many pages created by elementary students can attest. This simplicity, once it is recognized, should motivate and encourage educators to pursue integrating the Web into their classroom. However, educators often have very little understanding of the Internet and telecommunications and are apprehensive about integrating "the unknown" into their curriculum.

Many people do not understand the World Wide Web, for a good reason. It exists beyond the boundaries of time and place. The World Wide Web is more than just a global network of local, regional, and national interconnected computers. It is a massive collection of resources—business and government databases, library catalogs and files, and last but not least, human knowledge and experience. The World Wide Web is a diverse, everchanging, valuable tool. Therefore, teachers should know background information that will help them understand the World Wide Web and its potential.

What Is the World Wide Web?

The World Wide Web (also referred to as "the Web," "WWW," or sometimes "W3") is simply a system of linked and cross-referenced documents contained in computers across the globe. It was originated at CERN, the European Laboratory for Particle Physics near Geneva, in 1989 by Tim Berners Lee. Information available on the Internet was so overwhelming that finding, viewing, and using this information was very difficult. It was developed as a way for physicists in distant locations to exchange and share text and graphical information quickly and efficiently. By 1993 the Web included the ability to incorporate graphics, audio, video, and animation, which made the concept even more popular.

The World Wide Web provides a user-friendly interface or "front end" to many Internet services and allows users to navigate through the information jungle with little difficulty. Users no longer require knowledge of a computer command language. Through the use of hypertext links (which can be pictures or words), users can link to information in a manner that is clear and efficient. The Web creates an equality of access for technical and nontechnical users alike.

Much of the World Wide Web's tremendous popularity derives from the way in which it enables users to navigate from one document to the next. Hypertext links are embedded within the text of a document in the form of highlighted or underlined words or images and allow the user to easily follow the trail of an idea from one document to another. When the link is activated (usually by clicking on the word or image), the linked document is retrieved and displayed on the user's computer. The linked document can contain links to other documents and so on, thus creating a "weblike" environment.

Some Basics

The Web provides quick and simple access to a fast-growing, global information service. Because the World Wide Web provides a graphical way to navigate through information, most people find using the Web fairly easy and unintimidating. The Web allows users to concentrate on the content of information without having to think about the process of accessing it. Although the Web is easy to use, users need to know some basic concepts to get the most from it. (For further assistance, a glossary is provided at the end of this chapter. See Figure 3-3.)

Three Web Concepts: HTML, URL, and HTTP   Web pages are written with a simple language known as HyperText Markup Language (HTML). This language operates through a series of "tags" or "codes." For example, to make a word or phrase appear in bold letters, the tag <B> is placed before the phrase to turn the bold feature on, and the tag </B> is placed after the phrase to turn the bold feature off. All documents are written with these simple tags, which allow users on any kind of computer to share information.

The basis for identifying or addressing a Web document is the Uniform Resource Locator (URL). A URL is the "address" or "catalog number" for an Internet resource or Web page. A URL specifies the type and location of the document. For instance, http://www.clemson.edu/ specifies the type as a World Wide Web server and the location at Clemson University. The "suffix" after the location can provide users with a clue as to what kind of organization is being accessed:

- *.edu* indicates an educational institution
- *.com* indicates a commercial server
- *.gov* indicates a governmental server

The letters at the beginning of the URL indicate what kind of document is being accessed. *Http://* indicates a WWW document (graphics, text, audio); *gopher://* indicates purely textual documents on the Web; and *ftp://* indicates a document that has been transferred using a specific convention called File Transfer Protocol.

HTTP stands for HyperText Transport Protocol and is the consistent convention the Web uses to move hypertext files across the Internet. This protocol is a set of rules or standards for the programs at both ends of the network. Just as when two people meet and etiquette requires eye contact, a handshake, and a greeting, computers require a specific protocol that tells them how to talk to each other and what meaning to give the data they receive. Using HTTP ensures that the computer requesting data can "talk the same language" as the computer that receives the request.

How the Web Works   The Web is attractive to educators because it is simple to use and inexpensive to set up. Transaction of Web documents occurs in four basic stages (World Wide Web Consortium 1997):

1. Connection: the user's computer connects to a computer "server" that stores the desired information.
2. Request: the user's computer requests specific information from the server.
3. Response: the server on the other end responds to the request and sends data.
4. Close: the connection to the server is terminated.

Web sites are accessed with special software called browsers that are installed on the user's computer. A browser is a program that sends requests for information across networks and displays the information on the user's computer. There are many browsers to choose from, but two of the most popular browsers are Netscape Navigator and Microsoft Internet Explorer.

After a user has selected a hypertext link, the user's browser attempts to connect with the computer's server on the other end. The connection request can travel in any direction through many other computers or "routers" before reaching its destination. If the connection is made, the user's browser sends a request to the server for the specific data requested. The server then responds to the request by either "Reading file . . ." and sending the data, or by sending an error message, "Document not found . . ."

Once the data are transferred to the user's computer, the connection is closed, and the browser springs into action. It loads the requested data and displays the correct text, graphics, sound, and/or video information onto the user's screen.

The WWW transports data in pieces or chunks of information. Instead of dedicating a single line, such as a telephone call, for exchanging information, the WWW sends pieces of the data in "packets" or "envelopes" along with everyone else's packets. Every packet has a "coded address" that allows the pieces to be reassembled quickly once they have reached their destination. These packets of data are like pages of a book that are transported individually and then reassembled at their destination. Since the computer that is receiving the request and "serving" the data only deals with these short spurts or pieces of information, the computer does not take a constant and heavy beating. Educators don't need massive computers; just about any average computer can become a "server" with the correct software.

Web Pages   The term *Web page* can often be confusing or misleading. The Web uses a page metaphor to describe how it presents its information. Most people think of a document as a complete body of work (such as a book) and a page as a single element within that work. Yet World Wide Web pages are also called Web documents — the terms *page* and *document* refer to the same thing on the Web. Both terms refer to a single file that can be retrieved and formatted into audio, video, and visual information. When users access a Web page, they are actually accessing a file from another computer across the room or across the world. Once the file is transferred, the information is displayed on the user's computer. However, the complete file may or may not be fully visible on the user's computer screen. Therefore, what the user sees on the computer screen may not be the full "page." Users may need to "scroll" down the page so that they can actually view the complete file.

Growth of the Web   Evidence of the Internet is just about everywhere you look. You can't get away from it. Nowadays, advertisements in magazines and commercials on television list a WWW address on the Internet. The World Wide Web merits the attention of educators because no other technology, including the telephone, has grown so quickly and so captured the population's attention. The World Wide Web has grown exponentially and is proving itself not to be a temporary fad. Various studies have recounted different numbers, but one study reports a conservative measure of a sixfold increase (341,634 percent) in the Web during 1995 (WebCrawler 1996). Figure 3-1 shows the growth in the number of Web sites on the WWW from June 1993 to January 1997 (Gray 1996). With this rapid

Figure 3-1
Web Growth Summary

Growth of the World Wide Web has been exponential. This study conducted by WebCrawler measured an increase in the number of Web sites from June 1993 to June 1997 (http://www.mit.edu/people/ mkgray/net/web-growth-summary.html).

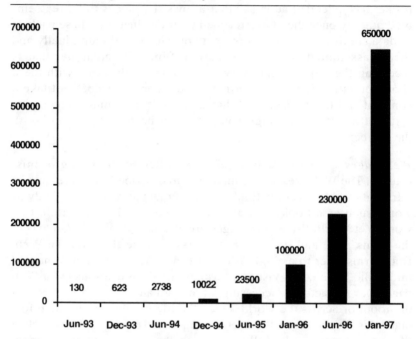

growth, the Web will have an effect on the way students access and assimilate information.

Using the World Wide Web in Education

The World Wide Web offers educators and students many opportunities to enhance and supplement education in the classroom. The Web can extend the learning experience beyond the textbook and the classroom walls. The World Wide Web is an exciting and easy way for teachers and students to:

- "visit" new places
- find information
- deliver class information
- communicate with others
- publish student work

Visiting New Places

The Web can help extend a teacher's curriculum by providing new content and experiences that go beyond the limitations of school schedules and structures. Teachers can now take their classes on "virtual" field trips or visit "virtual" museums. For example, English classes can travel to ocean, jungle, desert, or Arctic environments with real explorers and write about environmental problems or issues. Champlain Valley Union High School in Hinesburg, Vermont, uses a multidisciplinary approach to learning with at-risk kids. They have incorporated the WWW into their curriculum with a program called World Explorer (http://www.cvu.cssd.k12.vt.us/personal/jeffh/WEwebsite.html). Students travel around the world researching each country they visit. The students collect scientific, historical, and general data. At each stop, they make entries in journals and navigational logs. The students also create artifacts that represent some aspect of the country they are researching and post their project on the Web. Students become motivated as they gain a vested interest in their education.

Another exciting Web project is the JASON Foundation for Education (http://www.jasonproject.org), which sponsors an annual scientific expedition. During the expedition, students can take part in live, interactive programs that are broadcast using state-of-the-art technology to a network of educational, research, and cultural institutions in the United States, Mexico, Bermuda, and the United Kingdom. Primarily developed for grades four through eight, the project allows students to explore new environments, write about their experiences, and share ideas with other students around the world. For instance, Jason Project VII: Adapting to a Sea of Change allowed students to "tour" a submarine and to "visit" an undersea laboratory room by room via the Web. Students around the world participated in discussion groups, shared pictures, and submitted questions as well as possible solutions. For example, students were asked to design and build visual targets to attract sharks. Dr. Bob Hueter, director of the Center for Shark Research at Mote Marine Laboratory, tested the best of these targets in his research during the JASON VII expedition. Students in Florida also wrote and shared photographs about other related activities such as a visit from Dr. Robert Ballard, one of the scientists who discovered the *Titanic*.

Educators teaching American literature can supplement their presentation with a virtual field trip to Plymouth Plantation (http://media3.com/plymouth/vtour/). Students' experiences are extended beyond merely reading literature and descriptions about life in colonial America. Now students can actually view a reconstruction of the 1627 village occupied by the Pilgrims, people in historical period costumes, and other artifacts that depict the lifestyle of seventeenth-century colonial America. With this new perspective, students can gain insight and understanding about the literature they are studying.

Finding Information

The Web brings unlimited global resources to the classroom. From literary texts to interactive games, from educational grants to tours through European cities—the WWW has just about anything anyone would want to find. However, the Web offers so much information in so many different places, knowing how to find relevant resources can be a challenge. Aimless browsing may be fun at first, but it is not practical to sift through thousands of documents that exist on computers across the globe, hoping to find a resource that fits your needs. Fortunately, the World Wide Web has many search engines and subject-oriented directories that allow users to locate specific topics of information. It is wise to spend time learning how to use these research tools on the Web.

There are two methods used by search engines. One is spider-based searching, in which the search engines visit known Web sites and then index the Web pages they find into giant catalogs. Popular spider-based search engines are AltaVista (http://www.altavista.digital.com/), Hotbot (http://hotbot.com), and WebCrawler (http://webcrawler.com). The other method of searching is directory-based searching, in which the information is organized into subjects and compiled by humans rather than computer programs. Popular subject-oriented directories are Yahoo (http://www.yahoo.com) and the EINet Galaxy (http://www.einet.net).

Educator Resources   In addition to general search engines, the World Wide Web provides an abundance of other resources for educators. Teachers and educational institutions have created resources for curriculum planning for the benefit of other educators. These educational resources include lesson plans, classroom management ideas, electronic text collections, educational conference listings, and subject-specific information. Educators now have access to electronic course content as well as dynamic links to the variety of educational resources currently being developed online. (See Figure 3-2 for a sample resource page for educators.)

Teachers can use the Web to enhance the units they already teach by finding resources available on the Web. For example, educators teaching *The Diary of Anne Frank* can access the Web to let their students walk around Amsterdam, visit the Anne Frank Museum, tour the U.S. Holocaust Memorial Museum in Washington, D.C., and even correspond with Holocaust survivors. Classes studying Shakespeare

Figure 3-2
A Sample Resource Page for Educators
(http://tigger.clemson.edu/bnet/resources/)

Netscape: BLSE Resources

Location: http://tigger.clemson.edu/bnet/resources/index.html

Educational Resource Index:

Topics on this page:

✓ Composition   ✓ Classroom Activities   ✓ Grants
✓ Literature   ✓ Educational Technology   ✓ Student Interests
✓ Reference   ✓ Research Tools for Educators   ✓ WWW Starter Kits

Choose the one of the nine resource books you want to explore:

Composition

Topics on this page include general writing resources for teachers, electronic places students can write, as well as links to grammar and creative writing pages.

Literature

Topics on this page include links to general literature resources, fiction, poetry, British and American literature, Shakespeare, literature from other cultures, and other related sites.

Reference

You will find the information for which you would regularly go to the reference section of the library like dictionaries, factbooks, glossaries, quotations as well as how to find people on the Net.

Classroom Activities on the Web

Here is a list of curriculum ideas primarily for English teachers! It includes specific ways to use technology in the classroom through telecommunications as well as writing.

Educational Technology

Information especially for teachers! Topics on this page include teaching resources for educators, information about using technology in the classroom, and sites which contain lesson plans.

Research Tools for Educators

Intended to serve as a starting point to search for specific information on the Internet. Topics on this page include search engines, general resources, libraries and collections of electronic texts, and links to information about computers and the Internet.

Grants

Teachers are often looking for ways to fund projects. Here are a few links to places teachers can apply for grants.

Student Interests

This is a page designed primarily for students. It includes puzzles and interactive games as well as information about going to college.

World Wide Web Starter Kits for K-12 Schools

This page is intended to help you start your own web server and/or create your own Web pages. It includes links to software and tools to help you on your way to the Information Highway!

Created by Donna Adkins || Last Revised June 1996

can find complete electronic texts of Shakespeare's works, access a Shakespearean glossary, and view a collection of famous paintings and depictions of Shakespeare's plays including some explanation of the work, its origin, and the play/scene that is represented. Teachers can use these resources and many others to supplement their lesson plans and make course content more interesting to their students.

Teachers overwhelmed with new class preparations use the Web for ideas and generating lesson plans for their classes. For example, Allison Holsten, a rural teacher in Palmer, Alaska, who returned to teaching after a long absence from the profession, was faced with a daunting task of teaching for the first time a wide variety of English courses from debate to American literature, from ninth through twelfth grade. Having been away from teaching for ten years, she didn't have a reserve of information to pull from her files. However, with access to Netscape Navigator, Holsten conducted a search and found Robert Barsanti's English class (http://www.capecod.net/ ~bbarsant/class/) on the Web. She found an abundance of information for her American literature class and emailed Barsanti asking him about how he would organize the content or present information. Holsten said she logged on to his pages regularly and "every time he seemed to offer me something new." She used the Web to develop content for her other classes and found relevant biographical and critical analysis information that she could print out and hand to her students. She also found essays written by students and used them in her one-on-one student conferences so that her students could view a model literary essay.

The demands on a teachers' time are great, so teachers can't always look for creative new ideas and lesson plans. The Web can provide easy access to a variety of curriculum areas and levels. Some Web sites, such as ERIC Index to Lesson Plans (http://www.ericir.syr. edu/Virtual/Lessons), use a searchable index using keywords to allow specific searches. Other sites such as Teacher Edition Online (http://www.teachnet.com/index.html) and Teachers Helping Teachers (http://www.pacificnet.net/~mandel/) are locations where teachers exchange lesson plans, share new ideas and tips, and discuss teaching methodologies.

Student Resources   The Web is also a vast reference source for students. Instead of wandering through the library for information about particular topics, students can quickly access the World Wide Web for most of their needs. Because the Web incorporates graphics and audio as well as text, students are more motivated and excited about conducting research. The Web offers a surplus of information and can be easily accessed once users learn some basic electronic research strategies. The act of research can be an education in itself. Students often learn by exploring and are motivated by their curiosity to find answers about something in which they are interested. Students learn by completing a research cycle of questioning, planning, gathering, sorting and sifting, synthesizing, and evaluating information (McKenzie 1995). Students determine the questions to ask, access the Web and visit appropriate sites, collect promising information, sign off, sort and sift through the information, and then plan another visit to the Web. McKenzie (1994) refers to students performing this cycle as "infotectives, . . . a student thinker capable of asking great questions about data (with analysis) in order to convert the data into information (data organized so as to reveal patterns and relationships) and eventually into insight (information which may suggest action or strategy of some kind)." Researching on the Web opens the walls of the classroom by allowing students to find a variety of information not necessarily in their textbooks.

For example, students at Summit Parkway Middle School, a suburban school outside Columbia, South Carolina, researched information about Japan after reading and studying about World War II. The teacher, Doug Wood, was concerned that students had a negative conception of the Japanese after reading about the war. Given a specific task of researching Japanese culture, students enthusiastically used the Web to find information about Japanese festivals, Japanese schools that had Web pages, and the Japanese language. Students found pictures they could incorporate into their reports and a wide variety of information that wasn't available in their textbooks. The student interest in this research led to their communicating with Japanese students and eventually to visiting Japan (see Chapter 8). Following the visit to Japan, students created a Web page to showcase their experience and what they had learned.

Delivering Class Information

The World Wide Web offers an easy way to deliver information consistently to a large number of people. Teachers are using the Web to supplement instruction in classes and to distribute course materials or information. Teachers can disseminate course syllabi, class assignments, lecture notes, handouts, announcements, and slides or pictures. Instead of distributing pages of class information, teachers are publishing important information via the Web. The Web allows teachers to update class information and to add additional announcements as needed (see Chapter 5). Since the information is being published electronically, the time, cost, and effort of photocopying may also be reduced. The delivery of course information via the World Wide Web is consistent, and such information is easily published.

For example, students might access a Web page of a particular class and find a link to the class policies. When they click on the hypertext words, students would find information about course objectives, goals, prerequisites, homework assignments, and information about the teacher. When students access the online syllabus, they see that, like a paper syllabus, it provides them with an outline of the class. Included on the syllabus are topics that will be discussed in class, reading assignments, homework assignment due dates, and test schedules. Since the document is in hypertext, links to assignments and the lecture notes for each day allow students to see exactly what they need in preparation for each class period. Lecture notes can be published to provide students with a preview of what they will discuss or as a supplement to students' class notes. Handouts or homework hints can also be available via the Web to provide extra help to students who want it. The access to additional help is invaluable to students who are too timid to ask questions or who don't have questions until they try to complete their assignment.

Several teachers are already using the Web to disseminate information to their students. For instance, some high school teachers at Sidwell Friends School in Washington, D.C. (http://www.sidwell.edu/sidwell.resources/assignments/), provide assignment sheets for their students. Students can access class announcements, assignment deadline dates, and extra credit opportunities.

A variety of professors at Duke University (http://www.ctl.duke.edu/sulz/inspire2.html) are also offering course syllabi, handouts, and pictures/slides on the Web to make information more accessible to their students. Course syllabi can take on many forms. Teachers can convert the traditional syllabus into Web form or create a hypertext syllabus that allows students to see the syllabus according to the current date.

Handouts are another valuable resource that teachers can provide to their students. Purdue University's Online Writing Lab (http://owl.english.purdue.edu/), also known as OWL, provides students with a wide range of materials on topics such as commas, resumes, formats for citing sources, and nonsexist language. The University of Victoria's Hypertext Writer's Guide (http://webserver.maclab.comp.uvic.ca/writersguide/welcome.html) also provides students with handouts that help them with writing and studying literature. Students benefit from these online handouts since they can obtain the information when it is most helpful and when they need it.

Testing is another aspect of information dissemination for educators. Ed Tech Tools (http://www.motted.hawaii.edu/), a cooperative program of the National Science Foundation, the University of Hawaii Maui Office of Technology Transfer and Economic Development, and the Maui Community College ATE Project, provides a means to generate and correct online quizzes easily and quickly. Teachers can create quizzes on Web pages that provide instant feedback to students, and/or package answers in an email message that is sent back to the instructor. Testing on the Web can save time and paper as well as provide opportunities for students to test themselves.

Communicating with Others

Writing and exchanging ideas with distant classes motivate students strongly, enhance their communication skills, and can increase their geographic and cultural understanding. The WWW offers a broad range of online communication opportunities. Students can exchange messages and communicate with electronic mentors. The WWW extends beyond email communication, because students have the opportunity to communicate using graphics. For example, a second-grade Japanese class at Rinkan School, Yamoto, Japan, (http://www.st.rim.or.jp/~isamu/index.html) uses pictures on the Web to communicate with children in other countries.

The Web also provides a forum to communicate with well-known people. Students can write to authors, television stars, or government leaders. For example, Socks, the Clinton's cat, leads a tour of the White House (http://www.whitehouse.gov/WH/kids/html/home.html) while giving students a commentary about the history of the people and pets associated with the White House. Students then have the opportunity to write to the president, the vice president, the first lady, or Socks. Although the volume of mail received at the White House is enormous, Socks guarantees a letter in response!

Key pal exchanges are similar to pen pal exchanges, except the communication is conducted electronically via the Internet. Individuals communicate similarly to the traditional "pen pal," except they now can enhance their communication with photographs, images, and/or sound and video clips. This electronic communication can be teacher-to-teacher, student-to-student, or classroom-to-classroom. Exchanging messages provides students with the opportunity to learn about other cultures while participating in a "real" writing context. Students have a vested interest in the writing that they share with other students. They take responsibility and ownership of their communication as they learn another student's perspective. Classroom communication often begins with a biographical introduction but may wax into discussing issues important to teenagers, different perspectives on specific pieces of literature, or other themes. There are several electronic exchange programs such as Email Classroom Exchange (http://www.epals.com/) and Intercultural Email Classroom Connections (http://www.stolaf.edu/network/iecc/) which help teachers and classes link with

partners in other countries and cultures. KidsCom (http://www.
kidscom.com/) provides a forum not only for students to talk to
other students, but for teachers and parents to communicate relevant
issues with other parents and teachers.

The World Wide Web also offers students and schools the opportunity to work with electronic mentors. Electronic mentors are experts
on a specific topic or subject who volunteer to work closely with
classes or individuals online. The WWW has numerous advantages in
a mentoring program beyond simply removing distance obstacles.
The Web provides information of all types, which can be shared and
experienced by both parties. For example, the Science, Engineering,
and Math (SEM) Program (http://www.asel.udel.edu/sem/) strives to
increase the number of individuals with disabilities in SEM academic
programs and professions. The Web allows SEM participants to communicate, to work on projects together, and to build on others'
research.

Another mentoring program is Pitsco's "Ask an Expert" Web site
(http://www.askanexpert.com/askanexpert/). Students can find experts
to answer their questions about a variety of subjects. Ask an Expert is
a directory of links to people who have volunteered their time to
answer questions. These professionals give students one-to-one attention while helping to reduce classroom preparation time by helping
teachers leverage the educational material available on the WWW.

Publishing Student Work

Students can go beyond being information "consumers" to become
"producers" of their own information and participants in projects that
span the globe. Students can participate in collaborative projects with
other students around the world by publishing their work on the Web.
No longer is the audience just the teacher or even a class of thirty
other students. Now students are writing for an audience that is drawn
from around the world. Additionally, students also have the ability to
create their own learning environments and even present that learning
environment to the world.

The World Wide Web offers students innumerable possibilities
to publish their work. Electronic magazines, or "e-zines," are quickly gaining a presence on the Web. Some e-zines invite students to
submit strictly creative writing and are geared toward specific age
groups. CyberKids Magazine (http://www.woodwind.com/
cyberkids/CyberKidsIssues.html) and KidsPub (http://engarde.com/
kidpub/intro.html) encourage elementary students to submit stories,
poems, and artwork. Other e-zines, like Edge (http://www.jayi.com/

jayi/Fishnet/Edge/) and Cape Fear "Young Images" (http://yi.
wilmington.org), are geared more to journalism and encourage older
students to submit news stories and articles dealing with more
mature subjects.

Other publishing opportunities on the Web include home pages
and virtual museums. Home pages give students the opportunity to
show off their work as well as present a positive public image for the
school. The home pages of many schools typically include information about school history, academics, athletics, school activities, organizations and clubs, admissions, school publications, student life, faculty, and student and teacher projects. For instance, Lake Lehman
High School in Pennsylvania offers a wide range of information about
its school on the Web—from its handbook and school lunch menus to
a bulletin board where announcements are posted. For other examples, Webb 66 (http://web66.coled.umn.edu/schools.html) provides
an exhaustive list of schools on the Web.

The virtual museum is an exciting way for students to publish on
the World Wide Web. Not only can students go on virtual field trips
to visit a museum, they can create a virtual museum of their own.
The Bellingham School District in Washington defines its virtual
museum (http://www.bham.wednet.edu/bpsmuse.htm) as a "collection of electronic artifacts and information resources which may
include paintings, drawings, photographs, diagrams, graphs, recordings, video segments, newspaper articles, transcripts of interviews,
numerical databases and a host of other items." The Web's multimedia ability fully supports this concept. Students become "curators" in
these museums as they generate and produce text to accompany
graphics and pictures.

Several schools in the Bellingham district are already working
on virtual museums. Alderwood Elementary is collecting electronic
artifacts to create a virtual heritage museum called Ellis Island.
Students built several "wings" in the museum which lead visitors to
different projects students have created about their heritage.
Bellingham High School created a Career Pathways Museum to give
students information about planning a career. Students can access
information about typical jobs related to areas of interest and student
interviews of people in those jobs. Kulshan Middle School developed
a Pacific Rim Museum of Culture, which offers resources to assist
students as they compare and contrast Pacific Rim cultures. Students
research and present information about life in schools around the
Pacific Rim. They also give readers a virtual tour of the museum construction process, which is valuable to other schools interested in
designing a virtual museum.

Conclusion

The World Wide Web is clearly a powerful tool that educators can use in their classrooms. Using the Web—to assist with class instruction, to research information, to communicate and interact with a global audience, and to publish student materials and projects—can successfully motivate students and help them enjoy the learning process. Educators can also be encouraged that accessing and publishing on the Web is simple, inexpensive, and fun.

This chapter has discussed and provided specific examples and ideas of how teachers and students can use the Web. However, before embarking on the information superhighway, educators are wise to gain a comfort level with technology and the World Wide Web. Then, understanding and determining how to use the World Wide Web are the beginning to integrating the Web into the curriculum.

For specific information about how to gain access to the Internet in your area, contact a local Internet provider, which can provide details on cost, access, and connection requirements.

Works Cited

Gray, M. 1996. "Web Growth Summary." http://www.mit.edu/people/mkgray/net/web-growth-summary.html [sited October 1997].

McKenzie, J. 1994. "Grazing the Net: Raising a Generation of Free Range Students (Part One)." http://fromnowon.org/grazing1.html [sited October 1997].

———. 1995. "Beforenet and Afternet." http://www.fromnowon.org/oct97/research.htm [sited July 1995].

WebCrawler. 1996. "World Wide Web Facts." http://webcrawler.com/WebCrawler/Facts/Size.html [sited July 1996].

World Wide Web Consortium. 1997. "About the World Wide Web." http://www.w3.org/WWW/ [sited October 1997].

Figure 3-3
Glossary of Basic Web Terms

TERM	DEFINITION
browser	A client software program, like Netscape or Internet Explorer, used to examine various kinds of Internet resources, such as the WWW.
client	The user's computer, which has access to the Internet and can display Web documents.
home page	A Web page usually designated as the first or main page in a Web site.
HTML	(HyperText Markup Language) the coding or "tag" language that allows a client to interpret and display the document data on the computer screen.
http	(HyperText Transport Protocol) the standard convention that allows a Web server to transport Web documents across the Internet.
hypertext	Any text that contains links to other documents or resources.
interface	What the user sees and interacts with when using the computer.
Internet	A worldwide network of networks; often referred to as the information superhighway.
Netscape	A specific client software program, which displays WWW documents on a computer.
network	Two or more computers connected by telephone lines, satellites, or some other means for sharing information.
server	A computer where Web documents are located and can be accessed.
URL	(Uniform Resource Locator) the address of any resource or document on the Internet. The URL specifies the type of resource and its location.
Web site	A group of related Web pages belonging to the same organization, company, etc.

4

Hypermedia and the Future of Networked Composition
Inter/Disciplining
Our "Selves"

Tharon Howard
Jane Perkins
Clemson University

If we look back at the history of technology in writing instruction and consider how new technologies changed what and how we teach, certainly one of the major "moments" would have to be the desktop publishing revolution. Before the desktop publishing revolution in the 1980s, we didn't really have to think about graphic design, page layout, and printing techniques when we taught our students about writing processes. However, after the introduction of WYSIWYG (what you see is what you get) word processing/page layout software and high-quality laser printers which allowed writers to control the writing process all the way from the genesis of discourse through publication, writing teachers began to see the need to integrate new areas of instruction into their pedagogies. The new technology forced us to begin thinking about the "rhetoric of the page," the relationship between text and graphics, and the importance of visual literacies. As a result, we were forced to expand into other disciplinary traditions and learn the techniques and languages of graphic designers and print shop managers. Suddenly, we had to know about "symmetry," "halftones," "resolution," "kerning," and "leading." Today, we face a new revolution—a digital publishing revolution that promises to rad-icalize our understanding of writing processes. Once again, we are challenged to discipline ourselves in the techniques and languages of other media and traditions.

As more and more writing teachers and their students are compelled to write for the World Wide Web (WWW), hypertext, and CD-ROM publications, many familiar constructs like "the page," "the document," and even "writing" quickly break down, and English teachers are forced to depend on the languages and techniques of media other than print. Hypermedia makes us uncomfortable because it forces us to stretch beyond the familiar English or language arts curriculum into what might initially appear as an unfamiliar, uncharted, and even threatening expanse. However, for those who are willing to explore other disciplinary traditions, there *are* charts that will help us navigate the currents of unfamiliar media.

In this chapter, we will collect some of these charts in order to give purpose and direction to the exploration of the hypermedia authoring process and its potential impact on the ways we will teach "composition" in the future. Building on our experiences of studying the ways people use hypermedia and building on our work in helping students develop hypermedia projects,[1] this chapter articulates key areas of expertise that need to be integrated into our classroom pedagogies. The following traditional disciplines, representing areas of expertise, suggest the breadth of knowledge and skills necessary for teaching hypermedia authors:

Medium/Disciplinary Tradition	Expertise Needed
Rhetoric and Composition	→ Project Management
Software Design	→ Interface Design
Video and Theater	→ Video Production and Scripting
Graphic Arts	→ Color and Design Theory
Music and Sound Engineering	→ Audio Production and Editing

Obviously, we aren't going to argue that teachers need an exhaustive understanding of each of these disciplines, but we do need at least a rudimentary understanding of the concepts and approaches used by specialists in these areas. We need some basic navigational skills to approach different aspects of the hypermedia authoring processes, and we can find these in other disciplines. Rather than thinking of disciplines in terms of boundaries and turf that must be guarded and defended, the metaphor that we think best describes the inter/disciplining of hypermedia is that of an ocean on which explorers sail from sea to sea, carrying cargo of many ports. Of course, exploring and learning about other disciplines requires time, but because hypermedia encourages new collaborations and forces us to reconsider and to forge new disciplinary formations, it warrants the investment. Obviously, any journey begins from some home port, so we begin with a navigational chart from rhetoric and composition to explore the use of project management skills in hypermedia authoring processes.

Project Management and Writing

As English teachers, our background in rhetoric—appropriate and effective communication—provides a communicative perspective that focuses on the reader, audience, or user of a document; from our background in composition and writing processes, we conceptualize the production of any document as a collaborative, integrated, and usually recursive process. For hypermedia authoring processes, rhetoric and composition combine in the following areas of expertise:

- project management—our ability to invent, to plan, to coordinate, and to execute writing projects and our experience managing collaborative teams

- "writing"—our skill at accomplishing the many textual opportunities that guide and drive the hypermedia authoring processes, texts ranging from the development of all the concept papers, proposals, and other preplanning guides to the creation of the story lines and scripts

Besides being familiar territory for English teachers, project management is both the starting point for hypermedia projects and the ability or skill that integrates and coordinates all of the other disciplines. A critical skill in the development of any media, project management is even more important in hypermedia authoring because of the multifaceted and collaborative nature of the hypermedia authoring process. As writing teachers, we are experienced with the complexities of writing processes; yet hypermedia authoring compounds those complexities.

Although small hypermedia projects may be "singularly" authored effectively, many projects require collaboration. Therefore, while we may be concerned with growing and managing our own diverse interdisciplinary skills, we will almost assuredly need to coordinate the skills of colleagues in relevant disciplines and/or the skills of our students. In any scenario, we will need an idea of the many components we are managing and how they can fit together.

To manage their components, the graduate students in our program have learned from experience to value production documents that guide and "discipline" complex hypermedia authoring. Like most of us who are new to this medium, students find that hypermedia authoring is extremely demanding and that it has steep learning curves for everything from learning new interface software to shooting video footage to manipulating audio tracks. As a result, hypermedia authors are understandably captivated by the detail level of production and may lose sight of the big picture or perhaps fail to consider the full scope and purpose at the onset of a project. To avoid these dangers, hypermedia authors can adapt "charts" from rhetoric and composition to hypermedia project management, especially process documents such as preplanning guides for project invention and description and storyboards for project planning and implementation. There is, however, nothing hard nor fast about these process documents. Charts are, after all, merely guides drawn by adventurers who have gone before: they must be contextually interpreted depending on your sailing vessel (depth of hull, width of berth, speed and power, etc.). The terrain that charts depict is constantly shifting; and they must be adapted to the purpose of each voyage.

Preplanning Guides

Preplanning guides can take many forms: for example, concept papers, proposals for funding and support, or outlines developed from collaborative brainstorming sessions. Burger (1995a) explains that, as is the case with any written document, "a multimedia project begins with a concept—one typically driven by need," and that hypermedia authors should "try writing down a synopsis of the idea, describing the catalyst, goals, and what you see in your mind's eye" (96). A rhetorical approach—that is, a "user-centered design"—transfuses the entire authoring process with audience considerations and user feedback, starting with this early preplanning stage and continuing throughout storyboarding and implementation, and even in post-project review and analysis.

Reader- or user-centered questions, similar to those employed in teaching writing, are appropriate for guiding hypermedia preplanning. You will probably want to create your own list of questions to help generate ideas and establish common goals for each project—starting with those that describe your purpose for the production—that analyze your potential users and that evaluate your relationship to the users and the content of the production. However, as Burger suggests in his book *The Desktop Multimedia Bible* (1993), you will also want to ask some preplanning questions that are specific to hypermedia. Some of those questions will generate decisions about integrating nontextual components (54).

- What should the content or subject feel, look, and sound like stylistically to the viewer?

- How much motion will be effective? Will the product need to move? Will the user's perspective need to move?

- Which production elements—video, animation, 3-D, music, and so forth—are envisioned?

- Is the use of any particular platform, operating system, hardware, or software mandated?

- Do any usable source materials already exist, especially in digital form?

Some of your questions will elicit information about computer delivery systems (54).

- How will the production be delivered—e.g., local-area network, CD-ROM, Internet, floppy diskettes, etc.?

- What are the circumstances under which the production will be viewed?

- Do any existing materials, styles, and themes (such as logos, slogans, artwork, ads, photos, videos, and brochures) need to be carried over for continuity and synergy?

Even if we have a difficult time answering all of these questions, they can guide our preproduction decisions. Note also that one project does not need to be considered in isolation; documents and materials produced previously can be incorporated into hypermedia documents, and in the same vein, a document, or parts of it, can also be included in future projects.[2] Hypermedia documents are perhaps even more citable and conducive to boilerplating than hard copy documents because of the complex and work-intensive demands of hypermedia authoring processes.

Responding to these audience, purpose, and production questions and, perhaps, other project-specific ones helps hypermedia authors develop both the main thesis of the document and themes or metaphors—important techniques for document coherence. Although metaphor is useful in all phases of hypermedia authoring processes, it is especially significant in interface design and will be covered later when we discuss interface design in detail. Preplanning questions need to be articulated; however, they are seldom completely answered preproject. Instead, they become part of the ongoing process guides and move the project into the storyboarding phase.

Storyboarding

Storyboarding often guides the processes of print documents, especially in coordinating diverse efforts of collaborative projects or of making "visual" the complexities of a document's organization.

Storyboarding evolved as a production tool from the design process of Walt Disney and his animation staff. This origin is described by Fisher (1994): "Mechanically, the storyboard was a cork-covered wall of the studio, on which the artists and animators pinned sketches that represented their visual impressions of the dramatic visual images that would be taking place in the film" (54). For a presentation, a cartoon, or a film, storyboards manage the development of the story; for hypermedia authoring processes, storyboards fulfill that function, coordinate additional complex interdependencies, and merge many "disciplines." In this elaborated sense, storyboarding is especially useful for hypermedia authoring processes. Besides its capacity to coordinate diverse disciplinary aspects of text, visuals, sound, and computer functions, it provides, as Fisher emphasizes, the following capabilities:

1. The storyboard forces you to think in visual terms, to cast your document in the most dramatic, informative and clear images possible to convey your message.

2. The storyboard is infinitely flexible, allowing you to move ideas, images, even whole sequences of events easily across the entire range of the dramatic action (or descriptive flow) of the document. (55)

Additional advantages of storyboarding are even more specific to hypermedia production. Storyboarding allows authors to depict visually the links between information and to plot users' interactional choices. Fisher suggests, for example, color coding "bi-directional" and "uni-directional" links (61). Critical "transitions"—or hypermedia techniques that help users know where they are at all times—are part of hypermedia production storyboards, including visual and audio fades, repetition of visual features or sound tracks, and consistency of interface design. In the complex development of a hypermedia document, storyboarding not only facilitates overall timing and sequential production, it also makes possible the production of concurrent tasks because it illustrates task interdependencies.

Finally, because of the potential involvement of a diverse group of disciplinary experts, the advantages of storyboarding are further heightened in hypermedia authoring. Managing the people involved is as critical as managing the various technologies. The storyboard itself, according to Fisher, "becomes the common repository of the document's structure, the town meeting where all the disparate elements—writers, art directors, programmers, photographers, audio technicians, anyone who is involved with the document in a creative capacity—can meet to resolve questions about style, aesthetics, or even content" (70). Storyboarding can also be used as a tool for gaining buy-in or support from the project participants, as a prototype to test with users (Hackos 1994, 40), and as a selling tool with administrators and investors. For all of these purposes of persuasion, storyboards are effective, because they visually depict the entire document and yet connote flexibility.

Depending on our purpose, audience, and use for a storyboard and on our available resources, we can create hard copy storyboards or online versions. Hard copy storyboards—sketches and comments on paper tacked on a wall or taped against a white board to provide additional writing space—cost almost nothing. And, most importantly, they provide a total visualization, one contributors can live with daily. Available from several different companies, storyboarding software offers other advantages and a variety of features. An analysis of this software and its relevant attributes is provided by Salamone (1996): "If you have to keep track of many data files, a tool that provides thumbnails and a way to archive the elements would be a good bet. If you're working on an interactive training presentation that requires handling lots of conditional branches and juggling many forms of multimedia data, a storyboarding tool that integrates tightly with the authoring software is essential" (70). Because storyboarding software is relatively new, published results of user tests are not available. However, the development of storyboarding software indicates the awareness of hypermedia authors' need for such coordination tools. No matter which storyboarding medium we choose, the important thing is to invest the time in this key element of project management and then to be flexible enough to make the storyboard a working process document.

Normally, a project manager—or editor, or director, or producer—guides the planning and coordination of the entire project, time line, and people involved, balancing the big processes and the small details. These key people combine important expertise for hypermedia authoring processes: they "have a thorough understanding of the component media, as well as a talent for storyboarding, aesthetics, entertainment value, and balancing budgets. They must also be skilled at assembling the right team members to work on a project" (Burger 1995b, 3). While project management and storyboarding coordinate the entire hypermedia process, interface design provides additional cohesion as the vehicle that connects other disciplinary components.

Interface Design

Success in hypermedia authoring is often contingent on the design of a document's interface. Because it creates interpretive and navigational contexts, the design of an interface is a principle element in the hypermedia authoring process; it sutures diverse media formats together into a single, cohesive document. Just as good page layout is essential to a usable computer manual or just as transitions between paragraphs are needed for logical coherence, good interface design creates a context that allows users to locate and interpret information easily and quickly. In short, an understanding of interface design is critical, because the interface is the point at which the reader or user and the document coalesce.

Despite the fact that volumes have been written about how to design interfaces and computer engineers receive specialized graduate degrees in graphical user interface design, the most important concept behind interface design usually boils down to creating a "metaphor" that is appropriate for the document and its users. Indeed, though it may at first seem that English teachers and computer scientists could have much in common, we have a lot to teach and learn from each other because of our shared interest in thinking about the role of metaphors in interface design. An interface's metaphor is quite simply what allows users to predict what will happen as a result of their interactions with a piece of software. Metaphors make the "esoteric commands and formal logic" of the computer accessible to users by representing computing functions "through familiar and recognizable objects" (Coyne 1995, 250). For example, the icons found on the "desktop" of the Macintosh interface allow users to perform complex computing tasks without comprehending recondite machine language. Users don't have to understand the bits and bytes of data storage in order to delete a file from a hard drive. Instead, they simply manipulate familiar, metaphorical objects (like a file) and "throw it in the trash can" or "drag it to a new folder."

Yet these are merely simple, iconographic metaphors. The real power of the metaphorical thinking that governs effective interface designs can be seen in programs like word processing or personal finance software packages. In the program Quicken, for example, the software designers have constructed the interface around the metaphor of writing a check. Rather than requiring users to understand complex statistical and financial-analysis algorithms, Quicken users simply need to follow the familiar steps involved in writing a check or in filling out a bank deposit slip. The software then takes the data the users entered and, behind the interface scenes, performs statistical and financial functions that in the "real world" would require the specialized technical knowledge of a financial expert. Thus, through the power of the interface's metaphor, users are able to complete sophisticated tasks that would otherwise require training in a specialized area of study.

Interface design takes advantage of a metaphor's ability to explain an unknown object in terms of the commonplace and familiar.

It allows designers and their users to "map" an unknown cyberspace in terms of previous, socially shared experiences. In the metaphorical space created by the interface, users may forecast or predict the results of clicking on a particular button or selecting a particular menu option because they have preexisting schema or mental models that suggest appropriate behaviors for particular contexts. In other words, through its graphical or verbal cues, the interface sets the stage for dramatic interaction between the computer and its users. Perhaps the best-known advocate of this dramatistic approach to interface design is Brenda Laurel, who, in her book, *The Computer as Theatre* (1993), suggests that the role of an interface designer is analogous to that of a producer/director. Like a director, the interface designer constructs a set, selects props, chooses the musical score, contrives a wardrobe, and places the lighting in order to establish a context or create an interpretive framework for an interaction between the action on the stage (or screen) and the audience (or user).

Design metaphors and the theater analogy are powerful tools which teachers can use to help students understand factors that have to be taken into consideration in designing an interface for a hyper-media document. In fact, even if you aren't going to have your class actually produce their own hypermedia documents, you can use these concepts as heuristics for critiquing other interface designs. For example, we mentioned earlier that an interface's design takes advantage of a metaphor's ability to explain an unknown object in terms of the commonplace and familiar, but it's also the case that interfaces suffer from their metaphors as well. Metaphors can be mixed, inconsistent, or simply ill-conceived, thereby misleading their users. Or the graphical and visual cues designers use to set the stage for a metaphor may fail to achieve the desired result, so that users don't "get" the metaphorical context and fail to understand the software's logic (or plot structure). Finally, students may critique metaphors because they carry cultural or ideological baggage that may affect the interpretative context the interface creates. Selfe and Selfe (1994), for example, discuss how the desktop metaphor depends on an understanding of office environments and, thus, participates in the values of corporate culture. Microsoft Corporation's BOB interface is another example of an interface that could be critiqued because its metaphors are based on the model home of 1950s white, middle-class America. BOB uses rooms in a traditional middle-class home to orient users to the electronic space they will "inhabit." Young boys, for example, can have their own furnished "bedroom" filled with familiar objects that will link them to particular tasks they wish to perform. Clicking on the picture of a calendar in the room will, for example, launch a personalized scheduling program that will allow the user to keep track of holidays and other special events. However, the very thing that makes BOB appealing to one group of users—i.e., its use of familiar objects found in suburban homes—is also what makes it open for cultural critique by students. Students could, for example, be assigned to describe how their experiences with BOB would differ if they were from a different nationality or culture. As a follow-up assignment, they could be asked to play the role of a producer/director and redesign the interface for a user of a particular nationality, race, gender, and/or economic group. Assignments such as these not only provide students with analytical tools that will enable them to use computer interfaces more effectively by helping them to better understand the logic behind interfaces, they can also make students more computer literate by helping them understand the ways technology involves them in larger socioeconomic concerns.

Digital Video Production

Writing, producing, and digitizing video as part of a hypermedia document is, next to designing the interface, perhaps the most interesting and engaging portion of the hypermedia authoring process. Unfortunately, it is also the most technologically challenging and difficult to fund. Digitized video is extremely resource-intensive, and technology is only just now becoming powerful enough to support it. In fact, it may well be that your school will decide to postpone investing in the resources required for digital video until the costs and complexity of the technology involved become more standardized and accessible. In order to understand why this process is so resource-intensive as well as to understand how to digitize video clips for hypermedia documents, we need to consider what's required in order for a computer to display one frame of video on a monitor.

The display a user sees on a computer monitor is actually composed of tens or hundreds of thousands of little dots called pixels. Now, as one might expect, getting a higher-resolution image on a computer monitor involves adding more pixels, so one way of expressing the resolution of a display is to count the number of pixels across the top and down one side of the monitor. On most SVGA monitors available today, the typical resolution would be 640 x 480 pixels. Thus, on the same size screen, an 800 x 600 resolution would produce a higher-quality image because it would use a larger number of pixels to display the same image. Conversely, a 320 x 240 resolution would produce a poorer quality image because it would only use 76,800 pixels, while a 640 x 480 would use 307,200 pixels in the same space. This, of course, leads one to question why anyone would want to use a low resolution like 320 x 240, and the answer is memory consumption. Consider that in order to draw a single pixel on a display, the computer first must "know" its location. This takes roughly one byte of the computer's memory. Of course, location is only part of what the computer has to know; it also has to know what color to make the pixel. Now, color can be particularly tricky, since the number of available colors on most systems today can range from 256 to 16.4 million, and the more colors available, the more memory it will cost you (two bits/pixel for four colors, four bits/pixel for six-teen colors, eight bits/pixel for 256 colors). Just for the purpose of example, let's say that we're dealing with a typical system that uses twenty-four-bit color to display sixteen million colors. This would mean that the amount of memory that our computer requires would be three bytes per pixel. Thus, an image at 640 x 480 resolution requires 921,600 bytes of memory while a 320 x 240 resolution requires 230,400 bytes (Ozer 1995, 8).

So far, we've only been talking about displaying a single image on the computer's monitor, but video obviously isn't a single, still image. Video is composed of many still images or "frames" displayed one after the other in rapid sequence, and the speed at which the images are displayed is measured in the number of frames per second (fps). Normally, the video that runs on your home VCR plays at thir-ty frames per second, but video playback can be slowed down to fif-teen fps without the motion appearing too "jerky" and distorted. Consequently, most digital video clips available today play back on the computer at fifteen fps. Now, if we take what we know about the amount of memory required to display still, color images at the low resolution of 320 x 240 and combine it with a frame rate of fifteen fps, it's easy to see why digital video is such a "resource hog." At 320 x 240 and fifteen fps, one second of raw video would consume 3.456 megabytes of memory. One minute worth of this jerky, low-resolution video would require 207.36 MB of memory—and we're only talking about the video image here; the digital audio to go with the video would require even more memory to store.

Obviously, the size of files involved in digital video are larger than text files by orders of magnitude, and simply storing digital video and audio will require a system with an enormous hard drive. However, data storage isn't really the limiting or most problematic factor involved in digital video. The more significant problem is "bandwidth," or the number of bytes per second at which data can be transferred from one component to another. In the example of the one-second, 320 x 240, fifteen-fps raw video clip above, the band-width required is roughly 3.5 megabytes per second (MB/s). Unfortunately, an older 486 PC (one with an ISA bus) can only trans-fer data across its main bus at a rate of 2.5 MB/s, over a megabyte-per-second too slow for our low-resolution, jerky, silent video clip. A dual-speed CD-ROM player has a bandwidth of only 300 kilobytes per second and would need to be 11.52 times faster to keep up.

Yet, we've probably all seen older 486 PCs playing back audio/video clips stored on a dual-speed CD-ROM—so given the bandwidth issue, how is this possible? The answer is software compression. Without compression, digital video would still be well beyond the bandwidth capacities of almost all our current technologies. However, there is a variety of compression algorithms available today that compress raw video clips by factors of 10:1 to as much as 200:1, thereby making it possible for low-bandwidth systems to keep up with digital video's demands. There are two principle ways through which compression algorithms can achieve these file size reductions, and at least a basic understanding of them is important if hypermedia authors are going to produce quality digital video.

The first compression method is to use a "lossy" standard to strip out data that is not critical to viewing the overall image. One of the most commonly known lossy standards was developed by the Joint Photographic Experts Group (or JPEG), and it basically takes advantage of the human eye's tendency to interpolate the information that makes up an image. In other words, just as the French impressionist painters were able to paint with "dots" of color and still produce a recognizable image, lossy standards like JPEG trade fine detail for data savings. To hypermedia authors producing digitized video segments, this is important, because it both limits the kind of information students can deliver in their videos and the ways they can set up their shots. For example, several of our students created a hypermedia document that explained different methods of installing tile on floors, in baths, on walls, etc. Initially, the students wanted to use line-art diagrams to illustrate the installation process. Specifically, they wanted to videotape different diagrams at different stages of the installation process in order to produce a video clip that would appear to animate their diagrams. Now, if the target audience for this clip were using standard VHS analog tape, this approach would have worked well. However, in a digital video compressed with a lossy standard, the loss of detail and the small size of the playback screen made this approach impractical. The lossy compression made watching the line-art diagrams like trying to read a telephone book from across the room—you could tell some shape was there, but you couldn't quite make out what it was supposed to be. Thus, because of lossy compression, hypermedia authors need to develop scripts that call for shots of large, easily recognizable objects and close-ups in high-contrast settings.

The second major compression technique hypermedia authors need to consider as they plan their digital video productions has to do with the lack of motion in most video. As a general rule, there's usually a fair portion of an image in a video clip that doesn't change from one frame of video to the next. Consider a typical interview clip, for example. Usually, the background doesn't change at all during the course of the shot; only the facial expressions and body gestures of the person being interviewed change from frame to frame. In spite of this fact, however, normal analog video completely redraws the background for every frame, whether it needs it or not. A much more efficient approach would be to redraw only those parts of the video which actually change from one frame to the next, leaving the remainder unaffected. For a notable percentage of video clips, this results in significant data saving, because it allows you to eliminate redundant information. Thus, hypermedia authors who wish to take advantage of this type of compression need to develop scripts that limit camera motion as much as possible. Panning, push-ins, zooms, and other techniques that move the camera are "expensive" in digital videos because they require that almost every pixel of a display change from one frame to the next. Hypermedia authors can avoid this expense and improve the final quality of their hypermedia documents by carefully planning around these types of shots during script development.

Since we've mentioned script development several times now, it's perhaps appropriate to turn our attention to this critical part of the digital video production process. As Figure 4-1 indicates, scripting is the first stage in the video production process. The script effects all the subsequent stages in the process, which is why it is so important for hypermedia authors to understand how each of those stages, in turn, should influence the script's development. As we've already seen, understanding video compression influences the script's development by limiting the camera's movement, angles, distance from the action, and so on. Yet, though compression plays a significant role in script development, probably the single most significant influence on a digital video's script is the resource consumption problem with which we began this discussion.

Because digital video is such a resource hog, hypermedia authors have to write scripts that plan for: (1) clips that are very short, ten to thirty seconds in length, (2) clips that will usually be played back at slow fifteen-fps frame rates, and (3) clips that will appear in a screen window that usually takes up only 25 percent of the display. During script development, authors must always be conscious of the fact that each second of an audio/video clip is going to cost them roughly one MB worth of space in the final hypermedia document. Also, they have to consider that the small size of the display, the low resolution, and the jerkiness of the playback are all going to limit the types of shots the script can require.

Figure 4-1
Producing Digital Video

Producing Digital Video

create script

record video & audio

digitize & compress
video clips

digitize audio clips

store all files

edit clips, synch audio
to video, and output
to final file format

For example, hypermedia authors need to plan for close-up shots so that the objects displayed are large enough to be easily recognized in a small display window. Rather than panning from one object to another in a shot, digital productions need to depend more on simple, direct cuts from one object to the next, thereby reducing both background motion and time. Instead of panning the camera along with a moving object in order to give the viewers a sense of motion, scripts should be written to try to keep the background still—not just because of the compression savings, but also because moving, poorly focused background images disorient viewers during a low-resolution, jerky playback.

During scripting, authors have to pay attention to their transitional techniques. When hypermedia authors do call for a "dissolve" from the scene in one shot to the next, they need to be sure that the dissolve is being done in order to achieve the maximum effect on the user. Slowly dissolving from one image to the next not only increases the amount of motion that has to be updated, it also lengthens the clip, and this resource consumption needs to be justifiable. This is also the case with "fade-ins," where the screen slowly lightens until the image comes clear, or "fade-outs," where the last image slowly grows darker until it "fades to black." Fades can usually be replaced with much faster "wipes." These are transitional devices where, starting on one side of the screen, the image is ripped off the display to reveal either another image or some solid color underneath. The effect is almost as though a squeegee wiped across the face of the screen, taking the image with it, and its shorter duration can save one MB to one and a half MB over a slow fade to black.

However, keeping track of shot transition techniques is only a small part of script development, and the real limitation on scripts for digital videos is the fact that the clips are usually limited to ten- to thirty-second durations and rarely exceed seventy to ninety seconds. Such short time frames make it very difficult for authors to build their scripts around a story. Consider the following excerpt (Figure 4-2) from a sample script that was intended for an interactive CD that introduced graduate students and industry professionals to usability testing research methodologies. The script is for the opening segment of the CD and is the first thing the users would see once they launched the program. In its entirety (we have excerpted only the first page), the clip is intended to welcome users to the document, give them an overview of what the document is about, and help them understand how to use the buttons and navigation features of the document. On the left side of the page, the text inside the lozenges describes the on-screen action for each shot in the script. In the right hand column is the text which the narrator or "talent" speaks for that shot.

Figure 4-2
Opening Clip for Usability Testing Interactive CD

SHOT 1

Black screen; music up
Usability Testing Lab Logo fly-in to center of screen
Music upbeat, something like Fresh Aire's "Toccata"

4 secs.

SHOT 2

Orange tiger paws walk across black screen (footfall sound for each step.
Paw prints begin to fade out, and "Usability Testing" title fades in simultaneously. Music down.
There's a tiger roar. Then rip sound and wipe to black.

8 secs.

SHOT 3

Dr. H walks out of dark background and steps into single pool of light. Addresses camera.	Hello, I'm Dr. Tharon Howard, director of the Clemson University Usability Testing Facility. On this CD, we're going to take you on an interactive tour of usability testing methodologies. Just by pointing and clicking, you'll see . . . *12 secs.*

Obviously, it takes a fair amount of visualization and imagination both to read and to write a script like this (particularly if the reader hasn't ever seen the Usability Testing Lab logo or the tiger paw graphics required by the script). In spite of these difficulties, however, hypermedia authors must to be able to visualize the events taking place in the script as though they were stories unfolding before them. They must be able to close their eyes and see a black screen with upbeat music becoming progressively louder, while a tiny dot in the center of the blackness grows progressively larger as though it were "flying" toward the user, until it is finally large enough to stop and be recognized and interpreted. Next, in shot two, they have to imagine that the music continues playing while the screen cuts abruptly to black again. Across the blackness, an invisible tiger walks from the left side of the screen across to the right, leaving behind four orange paw prints that begin to dissolve back into blackness. As the paw prints dissolve, the blue letters of the CD's title, "Usability Testing," grow brighter and brighter, until they are sharp and clear. The same music that has been playing since the opening grows quiet, then the tiger roars loudly and the blue "Usability Testing" is wiped off the screen from left to right and, simultaneously, a ripping sound is heard. Then out of the silence and darkness, a man walks in from the back right edge of the screen, growing lighter and more visible with each step. He walks, head bowed, into a pool of light in the center of the screen, becoming plainly visible, stops, raises his head, and begins to speak directly into the camera.

Teaching students to "see" the kinds of "stories" required to make some point in a hypermedia document and then teaching them to develop their scripts in the fashion exemplified above is perhaps the most challenging of the pedagogical goals we have to accomplish. However, storyboarding the entire hypermedia document can help the students see where they need to supplement the content by providing a video clip. Once they see the need for the clip and its rhetorical purpose, it's much easier for them to create short stories that will make their points vividly. Also, providing students with sample scripts, asking them to write prose descriptions of the action they visualize from those scripts (i.e., asking them to write a description like that in the preceding paragraph), and then showing them videos of the actual, final productions is a useful technique for helping hypermedia authors to develop visualization skills and to gain control of the script-development process.

Once students have become competent in the development of scripts like that in Figure 4-2, they can learn to edit their shots to make them appropriate for digital video productions. For example, the Figure 4-2 script excerpt represents only twenty-four seconds of a script that ultimately ended up requiring almost seventy seconds worth of digital video. Seventy seconds is far too long, even for an opening where, as an author, you want to generate user interest and establish your document's tone and credibility. Nevertheless, asking a user to sit passively and to wait for a seventy-second clip to finish playing before they can actually begin using the hypermedia document is probably not an effective design technique, particularly when you consider that many repeat users will already have seen the opening clip and, therefore, will not need or want to see it again. However, armed with the script and a willingness to edit—which isn't easy for students—a hypermedia author can make decisions before going to the trouble and expense of developing the graphics, creating the special effects, choosing the audio, syncing the audio to the video, setting the lighting, shooting the video, and so on. To say it's heartbreaking to go to all the time and trouble to develop these elaborate shots, only to have them dumped, is a serious understatement. In this particular case, it was decided to eliminate the first two opening shots from the script, saving not only twelve seconds of digital video, but also, and perhaps more importantly, about three hours worth of graphics development and AV editing.

Writing a script; negotiating special effects like dissolves, wipes, and fades; and contending with the novel technological challenges of digital video are all skills not traditionally considered essential for English teachers. Yet, if your hypermedia authoring experiences are going to include digital video production, these are all initial areas you and your students will need to explore.

Color Theory

Like interface design and video production, any attempt to cover the whole of color and design theory, even in an introduction, is a foolish undertaking in a book of this scope. Again, you could get a graduate degree in these areas. We simply want to give a sense of direction here which will serve as a navigational aid for hypermedia authoring. Given this limited goal, perhaps the best place to start is to begin discussing the color theory that informs most imaging and graphic-production tools hypermedia authors will need to use. There are, in actuality, several different theories of color, but in order to understand how to use software packages like Adobe Photoshop, Corel Draw, or FreeHand, it's important to understand the most common way these tools deal with color, or what is often called the RGB (red, green, blue) color model.

The RGB color model begins with the observation that visible white light actually contains all the colors humans may perceive, or more specifically, that white light is composed of red, green, and blue wavelengths. When we see the green color of leaves on a tree, for example, we perceive the leaves to be green because leaves are absorbing most of the red and blue wavelengths in the white light striking the leaves, and only the green wavelengths are reflected back to our eyes. Of course, there are a number of factors influencing the actual color of the leaves we see, but in theory, since not all the red and blue wavelengths are absorbed by the leaves, the mixture of the three wavelengths yields different shades of greenish colors. So mixing different values of red, green, and blue, you can produce an entire spectrum of colors. As the circles in Figure 4-3 illustrate, mixing blue and green produces cyan; red and blue produces magenta; green and red produces yellow; and mixing all three primary colors produces white. It's also perhaps worth noting that the cyan, magenta, and yellow generated by mixing any two primary colors make up the first three colors of the "secondary" or CMYK (cyan, magenta, yellow, black) color model.

The cathode-ray tube (or CRT) inside a computer monitor takes advantage of the fact that the primary colors RGB may be mixed in order to display colors on the screen. As we saw in the section on digital video, each pixel in a digitized image is assigned color values. More specifically, each pixel will have a red, green, and blue value, and each of those values will range from 0 to 255, with 0 indicating the absence of the primary color and 255 indicating the most intense level of the color. Thus, as the numbers in the circles of Figure 4-3 illustrate, students can obtain the particular colors they want in an image by assigning a number to red, green, and blue. A dark purple, for example, would be 19, 5, 59, light tan would be 247, 179, 87, pure black would be 0, 0, 0, and pure white would be 255, 255, 255. In other words, there are 256 x 256 x 256 or over sixteen million possible colors, and when students understand the RGB color model, they can then take advantage of programs like Photoshop to control them all.

Once students understand this basic color theory, teachers can build on that foundation to help them understand how scanners and other input devices digitize images. Indeed, we've observed that many of our students, curiously, regard scanners as enigmatic, mystical devices; they are daunted and intimidated by them because the technology seems so abstruse and alien. Students (particularly older students) often require a great deal of encouragement and nurturing just to get them to start using a scanner. Yet, when students realize that digitized images are little more than a set of instructions about how to display each pixel on a screen and that scanners are little more than photoelectric cells that measure the levels of red, green, and blue light reflected off an image being scanned, then they seem to lose

Figure 4-3
RGB and CMYK Color Values

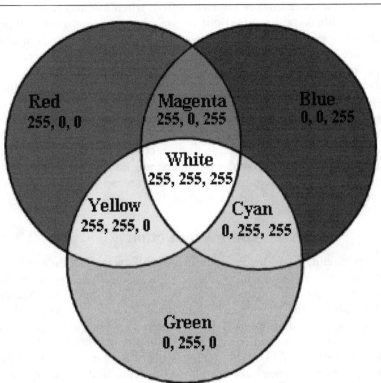

some of their inhibitions regarding scanners. What's more, understanding color theory and its relationship to pixel displays is very
useful as students attempt to deal with the color correction needed as
a result of bad scans or poor photographs.

One of the major problems hypermedia authors have to overcome
when they are dealing with documents containing multiple images is
developing a consistent "look 'n' feel" throughout the hypermedia
document. The problem here is that images (particularly scanned photographs) don't have the same white balance or contrast level that
other images in the document may have. Unless hypermedia authors
edit their images for consistency of hue, color balance, sharpness,
and contrast, the result is almost always an erratic, sloppy-looking
hypermedia document. In other words, the visual consequence of not
editing for consistency in color is analogous to the effect that gram-
matically incorrect verbal texts have on readers. Just as hypermedia

documents must be proofread in terms of their textual grammar, they must also be edited to ensure that they meet a consistent "visual grammar." When some images are red-shifted, when humans look green, when the blacks are washed out or greenish-gray, or when images are badly "pixelated" so that the "dots" that make up the image appear as square blocks of color, then the document's overall meaning, clarity, *ethos*, and *pathos* may suffer. RGB color theory is the first step toward developing a sophisticated visual grammar, and it provides students and teachers of hypermedia with the same explanatory power for visual grammars that knowing the parts of speech enables when they have to edit a complex sentence. Just as an understanding of nouns and verbs allows students to correct for agreement, an understanding of RGB helps students understand that they can correct a yellowish-looking image by increasing the values assigned to blues or by decreasing both red and green.

Audio Production

Most beginning hypermedia authors are well aware that they need to develop expertise in dealing with video; however, developers consistently overlook and undervalue the importance of audio production and editing in the hypermedia authoring process. As explanation, Burger suggests that audio is undervalued as a learning media and that students are not uniformly encouraged to participate in music curricula (1995b, 253). Another possibility is that, with all of the other facets of hypermedia production to learn and to incorporate, hypermedia authors take shortcuts and make do without audio enhancements. The absence of audio may also be the result of careful analysis: audio too must be appropriate for users and their purposes; some productions, designed perhaps to be used in busy classrooms, may need to be soundless.

When audio is appropriate, we need to think in terms of spoken narration, music, and sound effects, all of which can be used individually or mixed in hypermedia documents. Audio adds variety, impact, mood, atmosphere, and additional information that cannot be expressed visually. Planning for audio and its integration with other hypermedia components is part of hypermedia storyboarding processes and techniques. Therefore, as teachers of hypermedia production, we first need to help our students analyze the appropriateness of audio in the production, specifics about kinds of audio, and where that audio can be most effectively incorporated. We need to help our students create hypermedia plans that include the audio equipment and resources needed for capturing and for editing digital (as opposed to analog) audio.

In simple terms, we need to understand that sound in the world around us is described as a series of analog waveforms, vibrations in the air. In analog devices like microphones, amplifiers, and speakers, sound is represented as fluctuations in electric or electromagnetic current. And in computers, sound is represented as a stream of digital information. Audio processing thus involves capturing a sound, converting it to digital information for the computer, and then reproducing it back as analog again for our ears to interpret as sound waves. In other words, each end of the process comprises analog electronics, but in the middle, audio is digitized for the computer so that it can be edited and stored. An analog-to-digital converter (ADO) transforms the electrical fluctuations of a microphone or analog sound source into bits and bytes. On the other end of the process, a digital-to-analog (DAC) converter changes those bits and bytes back into an electric signal that can then be amplified for speakers (Burger 1995b, 254–56.) With a basic understanding of these production and conversion processes, hypermedia authors can investigate specific audio equipment and computer compatiblities, including sound cards—the hardware that gets audio in and out of a computer.

Although most sound in hypermedia documents is digitized, another consideration in computer-audio production is Musical Instrument Digital Interface (MIDI). MIDI jacks are included with most computer sound cards. Although MIDI does not carry audio, it provides performance information; the computer serves as a musical "composition tool, conductor, notation printer, and virtual multitrack recorder" (Burger 1995b, 258). MIDI cables connect, for example, a keyboard to a computer sound card; musical components can communicate with each other as a kind of local area network.

Sound editing software is of course needed to manage sound files. Sound editing, much like textual or visual editing, involves cutting and pasting material (trimming empty silence at the beginning of a document) or adjusting emphasis (adding fade-ins for transition or increasing volume in a specific section). Sound editing can include equalization to enhance clarity, and mixes of several sound files to combine spoken narration, music, and sound effects. Additionally, sound editing software allows similar kinds of processing such as those performed in professional recording studios: "processing can be as simple as optimizing levels and tonal settings or as complicated as altering the sound dramatically for special effects" (Burger 1995b, 282). Special effects capabilities include a wide range of features, from delaying and copying a sound to replicating a chorus, to creating echoing effects.

Although audio production is often mentioned last or frequently overlooked in hypermedia production, the equipment necessary for near-professional quality is available at reasonable prices. As with the other disciplines of hypermedia authoring, audio production can involve the creative involvement of music and sound specialists and/or the challenge of learning new techniques.

Other Important Concerns

In addition to teaching our students about production management, interface design, graphic editing, and digital audio/video production, we have found that our students have encountered other important areas that require explicit attention when we teach hypermedia authoring.

Delivery Systems/End-User Access

Hypermedia is almost always a serious "memory hog" and places intense resource requirements on a system. As a result, delivery is a complex and, usually, system-specific issue, one that can waste all the money and effort you put into your hypermedia document if you and your students fail to address it. Even if primary users have systems capable of reading CD-ROMs and of displaying the hypermedia documents, the cost of shipping commercial viewers/browsers on your CDs can make the project less desirable. It doesn't make sense, for example, to create a hypermedia tutorial in PowerPoint or Framemaker if the intended users can't view the tutorials because they lack the software needed to open the files. Thus, if hypermedia authors haven't considered and accommodated the delivery systems available to their end-users or "audience," other media (i.e. videotapes, print documents, audio cassettes, etc.) are almost always a better choice.

Intellectual Property/Content Acquisition

Traditionally, professional communicators have understood print-based intellectual property issues; however, hypermedia radicalizes many of the practices acceptable in print-based media.[3] For example, if you use an image from a commercial clip art package in a print publication, you and your students are not violating any copyright laws. However, if you use the same clip art image in a digital publication, it is often not clear whether or not you would be violating the software license for the clip art by redistributing it (i.e., copying it). Also, if you edit a scanned image of a painting, how much editing do you have to do before you can claim that your use is covered by the fair use clause of the *U.S. Code?* And audio files are even more problematic for students. We have found that students who fully understand that copying someone else's text is plagiarism and a violation of copyright laws nevertheless fail to transfer that understanding to the music clips they digitize from commercial audio CDs and attempt to include in their multimedia programs.

Technological Expertise

The lack of a sophisticated understanding of operating systems, file formats, compression algorithms, input devices, and system architectures is, of course, the most obvious stumbling block that hypermedia authors and the people who train them must overcome. Technological expertise, though not a sufficient condition of the ability to develop hypermedia, is certainly a necessary condition.

Media Appropriateness

The number of hours that go into the development of a hypermedia document far exceed those required by single-media documents, and as a result, it is critical that hypermedia authors are able to justify the costs in terms of the document's impact and purpose. Also, hypermedia authors need to know which types of content can be presented most effectively in which media. All too often, developers try to use video for material that might be better suited to presentation in text. Students and teachers alike are often seduced by the "gee-whiz" aspect of digital video in particular and, consequently, they will spend inordinate amounts of time integrating it into a production just because they *can*. As teachers, we need to ensure that our students understand the old axiom, "Just because you *can* do something doesn't mean that you *should*."

Conclusion

As we have attempted to show, hypermedia authoring represents a serious interdisciplinary and interdisciplining challenge for anyone who wishes to learn it and especially to teach it. It takes both teachers and students on a journey across disciplinary traditions and, without some charts to "discipline" you, it can leave an unprepared classroom adrift in an ocean of confusing currents. And yet, this danger is also the source of hypermedia's promise. We believe that, as hypermedia becomes an increasingly familiar instructional technology in our classrooms, it promises to restore the discipline of rhetoric and composition to the respected position it once held—i.e., Quintilian's "Queen of the Arts."

In our introduction, we noted the apprehension English teachers might feel when confronted with the challenge of incorporating hypermedia into their classrooms. However, because these new authoring processes begin with what we already know well about writing and managing documents, hypermedia authoring—when supported by some basic charts from other disciplines—offers links to new areas in which English teachers and students certainly *can* develop expertise. When computers were first introduced into composition classrooms well over a decade ago, there were certainly teachers and administrators who contended that computers were "mere tools" and that writing instruction and rhetorical theory did not have to change significantly. This is also the case for hypermedia authoring. However, as Hawisher et al. discuss in the history text *Computers and the Teaching of Writing in American Higher Education* (1996, 149–50), there were others who argued that these tools create significant opportunities for change—changes that affect writing, writing processes, textual conventions, means of communication, and even new ways of learning and knowing. The essays in this book are certainly examples of the changes envisioned by those early computer adopters.

Hypermedia teachers and students are the next generation of change. In addition to learning and incorporating new areas of expertise such as we have outlined above, English teachers will also learn about similarities and differences in the texts that they produce, format, and integrate with other media. In other words, studying hypermedia promises to enrich our understanding of traditional print media "since it allows researchers to situate themselves on the boundaries between various media where the meaningful play of differences becomes most clear" (Howard 1997, 25). As such, hypermedia will force our discipline and our classrooms to change and evolve. Hypermedia authors will create new ways for guiding users through documents and for helping them understand the connections and relationships among the authors' ideas. Hypermedia will challenge authors to consider their users in new ways, to provide opportunities for new forms of interactions, to support learning and ways of knowing with means other than text. Hypermedia is not just another new tool into which authors can copy text as it was written for the printed page; it is a *re*contextualization of both message and meaning. Yet, for us, as English teachers, the most important issue may be whether we will remain ensconced in the tradition of the printed page or whether we will also incorporate new media and with them sail in new directions, developing new expertise, new collaborations, and new disciplinary traditions. Hypermedia authoring challenges us to ask if we are truly willing to "cross boundaries and create communities."

End Notes

1. We would like to thank the graduate students in Clemson University's Master of Arts in Professional Communication program for their work and evaluations of their hypermedia authoring projects in our classes.

2. See our comments on citation of documents and materials in the subsection on intellectual property.

3. For a discussion of the ways current copyright law is challenged by changes in emerging digital publishing technologies, see Howard (1996).

Works Cited

Burger, J. 1993. *The Desktop Multimedia Bible*. Reading, MA: Addison-Wesley.

———. 1995a. *Multimedia for Decision Makers*. Reading, MA: Addison-Wesley.

———. 1995b. *Multimedia Studio for Windows*. New York: Random House.

Coyne, R. 1995. *Designing Information Technology in the Postmodern Age: From Method to Metaphor*. Cambridge, MA: MIT Press.

Fisher, S. 1994. *Multimedia Authoring: Building and Developing Documents*. Boston: AP Professional.

Hackos, J. 1994. *Managing Your Documentation Projects*. New York: John Wiley & Sons.

Hawisher, G., P. LeBlanc, C. Moran, and C. Selfe. 1996. *Computers and the Teaching of Writing in American Higher Education, 1979–1994: A History*. Norwood, NJ: Ablex.

Howard, T. 1996. "Who 'Owns' Electronic Texts?" In *Electronic Literacies of the Workplace: Technologies of Writing*, eds. P. Sullivan and J. Dautermann. Urbana, IL: National Council of Teachers of English.

———. 1997. *A Rhetoric of Electronic Communities*. Greenwich, CT: Ablex.

Laurel, B. 1993. *The Computer as Theatre*. Reading, MA: Addison-Wesley.

Ozer, J. 1995. *Video Compression for Multimedia*. Cambridge, MA: Academic Press.

Salamone, S. 1996. "Make Multimedia Happen: What's the Story." *BYTE* (March): 65–90.

Selfe, C., and R. Selfe. 1994. "Politics of the Interface." *College Composition and Communication* 45: 480–504.

5

Webbing the Universe of Science Fiction

Elisa Kay Sparks
Clemson University

I've been teaching a junior-level course in science fiction in pretty much the same historically organized format since 1980. Over the years, I'd been struggling with several pedagogical issues in the course: I liked for my students to write journals, but with thirty-five enrolled in the course, I had a hard time keeping up with grading my traditional assignment of three pages per week. I wanted to tap some of the enthusiasm and expertise students had about particular authors and genres by having them work on projects in groups, but I had never been able to get group oral reports to work consistently. I wanted students to do some kind of individualized research project on a particular author or book, but my enrollees, mostly non-English majors, were not used to writing traditional literary analysis papers, and I could see their creativity and energy drain away when forced into a conventional scholarly mode.

In hopes of solving some of these problems, I "webbed" my science fiction course in the spring of 1997. I decided to devote eight to ten of the forty-five one-hour classes that make up the semester to teaching my students to surf the Web, to use a listserv, and to write Web pages with HTML. To my surprise and delight, this experiment with introducing computers into my course actually transformed my classroom in ways I had never expected or intended. It decentered the learning experience so that the focus was no longer on the podium at the front of the room. Now, learning spread out to the desktops students worked at in the lab or at home and even to the point of engagement with a whole world of other people pursuing passions and doing research on the Internet. The class became a collaborative workshop, and learning became active rather than receptive. The students produced work for themselves and their audience on the Web and only incidentally for me, continually updating and improving assignments, even after the work had been turned in and evaluated, sometimes without even telling me.

I think I worked harder on this class than I have ever worked on one before, but my students worked harder too. And what we had produced when the semester was over was something more lasting and more public than the product of any other course I have ever taught: a Web site displaying more than one hundred documents, which I will continue to use and develop over the years as I teach the course, and which my students will always be able to access and explore through the Web, long after they've left Clemson University. More intangible but equally valuable was the sense of empowerment and participation in a community of expertise that students gained from learning how to publish on the Web.

The Listserv

Although it was somewhat complicated to set up and get operating, a list server proved to be such a giant leap in class connectivity that I can now hardly imagine teaching any course without one. Simply a computer address set up on a network so that anyone on the list can write to the one address and everyone on the list will get the message, the listserv allowed me to communicate with students efficiently as a group and as individuals. But most importantly, it allowed the students to communicate directly with each other without me as a mediator. This democracy in our class' communication ensured that every voice in class got heard with nearly equal clarity.

On the most basic level, of course, the listserv allowed me to monitor students' reading for the class. Each student was assigned to write three pages or 750 words a week for fifteen weeks of the semester. Some did this as three short entries, some as one long one; most wrote over their quota. A few did not keep up, and they got lower grades on that 25 percent of the course requirements. I use journals extensively in my other classes, and students are always asking if they "have to do one this week"; I never got that question with the listserv journal. Also, because of the email time stamp, I knew exactly when entries were turned in, and I never had to worry about misplacing entries handed to me in the parking lot.

Still, I admit I cursed the listserv for the first few weeks of class. Since computers are very, very stupid, the list server wouldn't operate unless you had its complicated address exactly right, including spaces. It wouldn't let anyone—including me—write to the list from any address except his or her main university account, even when I followed directions carefully about adding new user addresses. But once we all got straightened out, I discovered that the initial setup time and anguish was worth it. Through the listserv I could clarify assignments for students, post notes about schedule changes, make comments I had never gotten to in class, provide handouts that just hadn't gotten finished in time. And I only had to send the message/handout once. (You can cut and paste any document you have on your computer into most email programs with two key-strokes.) The listserv also provided me a nicely distanced method for praising and prodding students. I could deliver ultimatums to students whose absences were piling up; praise to students whose class comments had been especially smart; encouraging reminders to those who were neglecting their journals.

But the most important aspect of the listserv was the ongoing class discussion it created. I decided early on not to enter the listserv discussion publicly; this was, at first, just a matter of time constraints, but it turned out to be another empowering decision for the students. Occasionally in class, I would bring up points from someone's entry as a prompt for class discussion or refer to someone's journal as being particularly good. And sometimes, I commented to students privately. But mostly I just left them alone to talk. This resulted in students' deciding which topics were interesting and meant that the discussion sometimes went into areas I would have never foreseen. Some students who never spoke in class wrote very capable and engaging journal entries and so began to create class presences for themselves, while others created alter egos, the most elaborate being an alien from the future named Blessedm'n, who periodically took over one of the student's minds in an attempt to learn more about our culture through analyzing science fiction.

How Technology Changed the Course Content

Having committed to using approximately one-fifth of my class time to teach computer-related skills, I of course had to eliminate some literary material from the course. I took out one novel, going from nine to eight. But instead of cutting out additional short stories, I decided to cut out the lectures I usually gave to introduce each historical unit of the course: Space Opera, Utopias and Dystopias in Science Fiction, the Golden Age, the Age of Acceptance, New Wave Science Fiction, Women in Science Fiction, Cyberpunk, and the New Hard Science Fiction. From the beginning, I felt that the computer literacy skills my students would gain would more than make up for the loss of one novel. In the end, I was sure that the commitment engendered by having their research published on the Web meant that students actually read more than what was assigned.

To provide the background material I would have given my students in lectures, I made *The Science Fiction Encyclopedia*, edited by John Clute and Peter Nicholls, a required text for the course. (If you are interested in SF, the thirty-dollar cost of this book is a great investment.) Its information is accurate, up to date, and presented with flair, humor, and a sophisticated knowledge of this highly variegated field. (Those who couldn't afford to buy the book discovered that chunks of it were available at various places on the Web.) Students were also required to do Web searches on various historical topics to prepare for class.

This turned out to be one of my most fateful and empowering decisions. Putting the *Science Fiction Encyclopedia* in the students' hands gave them their own access to the definitive reference source for the field, the ur-source, if truth be told, for many of my own insights and references. That, plus turning them loose on the Web, made *them* responsible for gathering and synthesizing historical background. Meanwhile, I retained my role as teacher and resource by having access to the whole realm of academic criticism not covered in the encyclopedia or on the Web.

On the day that we would begin a new section of the course—for example, the unit on the Golden Age—students would come to class having read some entries in the encyclopedia and having searched the terms *golden age* and *science fiction* on the Internet, as well as having read a couple of short stories. We would then have a discussion about developments in the field, using the short stories as illustrations of important historical trends. I would usually assign two or three entries. For example, for the Golden Age of SF, they searched the authors Isaac Asimov, Arthur C. Clarke, and Robert Heinlein. The *Science Fiction Encyclopedia* is so efficiently and thoroughly cross-indexed that students would often have read other related entries that I had not thought to assign. Add to that what students might have found on the Web and my folders of notes on academic research, and class was a rich mix.

The other thing I did to make room for computer days was to squeeze the time spent on discussing novels down from three days to two. This, too, had a surprisingly salutary effect. I found that with less time, I didn't waste it meandering about the first day. In addition, in the interest of getting the maximum out of class time, I began to create Web pages for our reading and discussion questions for each novel, partially to teach myself HTML, partially to serve as design examples for the students, and partially because I had become

obsessed with how easy and fun the process was. In my lecture notes,
I had always kept lists of questions to ask about the novels as setups
for the next day of class or for journal entries. I simply extracted
these and typed them up. Sometimes, I handed these questions out in
class. Sometimes, if I was running late and couldn't have things ready
by class time, I posted the study questions to the class listserv. As I
got better and faster at HTML, I began to compose study guides as
Web documents. Having the study questions available to the students
intensified the focus of discussion on the class listserv, easily making
up for the relocated class day.

Completing the study guides did take a considerable amount of
time, but I am convinced that it was time well spent. Now that those
pages are up on the Net, they will be there for future classes. I won't
have to run them off for class or remember to write them on the
board. I'll never again be panic-stricken because I misplaced my folder of notes on a novel. And I can actually start reducing the amount of
paper that clogs up my life, my house, and my office.

I also found that formalizing the study questions as Web pages
caused me to formulate a number of important thematic unities in the
course. It was as though the visual parallelism in the spatial design of
the pages began to help me think in terms of thematic parallels as
well. (I confess I now think about almost everything in terms of bul-
leted lists.) The pages began to take on a coherent, repeated organization: questions about the novel's generic structure (conventions of
the romance form, of science fiction, of verifiability); questions about
the structure of the hero's quest (we graphed out all novels and some
stories according to Joseph Campbell's *The Hero with a Thousand
Faces* and the feminist version of Campbell's categories contained in
Carol Pearson and Catherine Pope's *The Female Hero in American
and British Literature*); questions about plot and thematic elements
particular to each book; questions about utopian dimensions of the
novel; questions about gender issues and the role of the Other in the
novel; and questions about the relationships between humans and ani-
mals on the one hand, and humans and machines on the other. (See
Figure 5-1.)

A final benefit to having the study questions up on the Web is that
they can now serve as the basis for different kinds of community
building. One of my inspirations for putting my science fiction course
on the Web in the first place was my discovery that a colleague I had
met years ago at a conference, Paul Brians, had put up an extensive
Web site for his science fiction classes, including a tremendously useful list of basic reference and critical works on science fiction and
reading questions for all the books and short stories he taught. I knew
I wanted to use his materials in a couple of cases, and I wanted to pay

Figure 5-1

A Sample Discussion Web Page for The Left Hand of Darkness (http://hubcap.clemson.edu/~sparks/lhdstud.html)

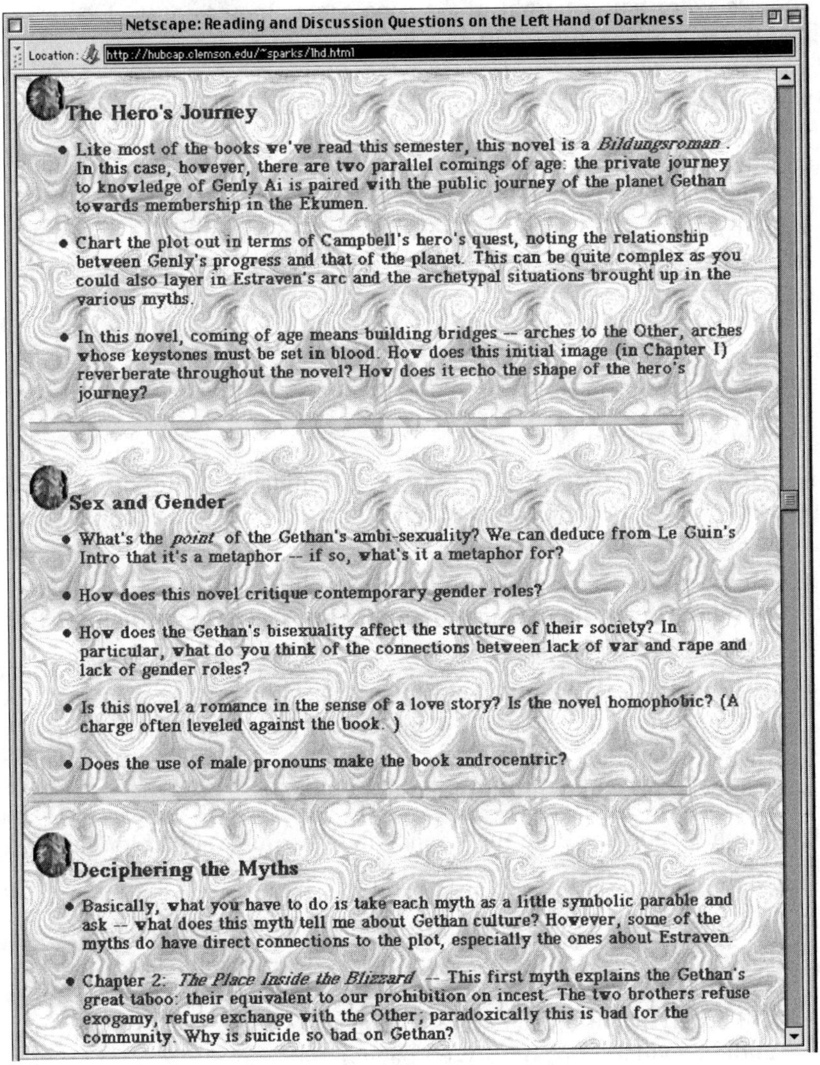

Netscape: Reading and Discussion Questions on the Left Hand of Darkness

Location: http://hubcap.clemson.edu/~sparks/lhd.html

The Hero's Journey

- Like most of the books we've read this semester, this novel is a *Bildungsroman* . In this case, however, there are two parallel comings of age: the private journey to knowledge of Genly Ai is paired with the public journey of the planet Gethan towards membership in the Ekumen.
- Chart the plot out in terms of Campbell's hero's quest, noting the relationship between Genly's progress and that of the planet. This can be quite complex as you could also layer in Estraven's arc and the archetypal situations brought up in the various myths.
- In this novel, coming of age means building bridges -- arches to the Other, arches whose keystones must be set in blood. How does this initial image (in Chapter I) reverberate throughout the novel? How does it echo the shape of the hero's journey?

Sex and Gender

- What's the *point* of the Gethan's ambi-sexuality? We can deduce from Le Guin's Intro that it's a metaphor -- if so, what's it a metaphor for?
- How does this novel critique contemporary gender roles?
- How does the Gethan's bisexuality affect the structure of their society? In particular, what do you think of the connections between lack of war and rape and lack of gender roles?
- Is this novel a romance in the sense of a love story? Is the novel homophobic? (A charge often leveled against the book.)
- Does the use of male pronouns make the book androcentric?

Deciphering the Myths

- Basically, what you have to do is take each myth as a little symbolic parable and ask -- what does this myth tell me about Gethan culture? However, some of the myths do have direct connections to the plot, especially the ones about Estraven.
- Chapter 2: *The Place Inside the Blizzard* -- This first myth explains the Gethan's great taboo: their equivalent to our prohibition on incest. The two brothers refuse exogamy, refuse exchange with the Other; paradoxically this is bad for the community. Why is suicide so bad on Gethan?

him back by creating materials that his students could use in turn. Since the pages have been up and registered, I have received email from as far away as Australia, commenting on my study questions and asking for information and ideas about various aspects of science fiction. Some of these contacts are academics, such as the professor who wrote to ask for suggested discussion questions for a conference panel on gender issues in fantasy. Some are nonacademics, such as the man who wrote me from Tempe, Arizona that my questions on Heinlein were interesting enough to make him want to check out what courses were being taught at Arizona State. Increasingly, I believe that Internet connections will also develop between students, allowing universities, faculties, and students to cooperate in completely new ways. For example, in building their Ecological Issues group site, my students set up a form for visitors to fill out in order to add books to the site's master bibliography. I have a colleague at Guilford in North Carolina who teaches a composition course centered around environmental issues, and I have invited his students to submit book summaries to my students' site.

What I Knew and What I Had to Learn

When I started I knew:

1. My way around Windows 95.
2. How to do basic email: I was on a couple of professional listservs and wrote and received notes to and from various colleagues on and off campus.
3. How to make a very basic Web page using HTML—I had taken two hour-long classes, had bought a book, and had practiced by making about five pages for our Women's Studies Program.
4. How to FTP or load the pages onto the server.
5. A lot about PhotoShop: I had taken a full semester course on Art in the Computer, had bought my own copy of PhotoShop, and had been playing with it for about two years.

In setting up and teaching the science fiction course, I had to learn:

1. More ins and outs about email and listservs.
2. Another level of HTML commands, including about ten to fifteen more "tags" or command codes, and how to use an HTML editor to help me make tables and then Web pages more quickly and efficiently (I did not attempt to master frames, Java, or loading audio or video clips onto Web pages).
3. A lot more about plug-in filters for getting special graphic effects in PhotoShop. This was complete self-indulgence—not at all necessary except to make prettier Web pages.

The main thing you have to know to make Web pages is HTML—HyperText Markup Language. HTML is a little off-putting

Figure 5-2
Home Page for Science Fiction Literature Class at Clemson
University (http://hubcap.clemson.edu/~sparks/sfindex.html)

because it is written with strange-looking tags. However, HTML is
very easy. It was written to be the simplest, most transparent possible
computer language, so that any computer in the world could read files
written in it. To make a basic Web page, you only need to know a
handful of these tags. For example, the home page for my entire science fiction site was written using only twelve different tags. (See
Figure 5-2.)

Learning and teaching HTML is very cost effective in terms of time and money. I taught my students everything they needed to know to make their first Web page in two one-hour sessions in the computer classroom. This process was made even easier by the fact that about a quarter of the class already knew HTML and were able to act as coaches. (In fact, there were several students in my class who knew more about building Web pages than I did, who had already mastered Java and frames, and who had animations and banners running across their sites.) The varying levels of computer literacy in the class actually served as a boon, additionally decentralizing my role as the only authority and further increasing collaboration and the sense of community.

Financially, making Web pages requires no investment. You write the code for Web pages in the text editors (Notepad, Word Pad) that come standard on every computer, so you don't have to buy anything special to make HTML documents. And once you make Web pages, you view them with the same browser you use to look at Web pages on the Internet—Netscape or Microsoft Explorer. (Most browsers will work on computers that aren't connected to the Internet, so you can build and edit your Web pages without actually being online.) Of course, you *can* spend money; for example, you can select from a proliferating variety of HTML editors—menu-driven programs that allow you to write Web pages without knowing any code. (At the time this book is going to press, one of the best if not easiest of these, Microsoft Internet Assistant, can still be downloaded for free from the Web, and Netscape Gold also has a free HTML editor.) I started out trying to use free versions of several of these editors but soon learned my "code-crunching" friends were right: In the beginning, it is actually easier to learn HTML tags. Without them, you don't know what you've done wrong or how the editor has messed up. I have only returned to using Web-page editors recently, after thoroughly mastering the basics for myself. There are some tasks they do make much easier: setting up initial page attributes, building tables, and finding and replacing pieces of text. Some HTML editors, such as Web Author, will also allow you automatically to transpose text from a word processing program such as Microsoft Word, preserving formatting elements such as italics and font sizes. (Windows 97 now has this feature built in.) However, since you can copy text out of any program or off any Web page into HTML documents, you don't need any of these, either. The things I had to buy were books to serve as reference guides for new tags I wanted to learn. A list of these books is included at the end of the chapter.

Breakdown of Lab Classes

My class of about twenty-five students met three days a week. We gathered in a multimedia authoring classroom on what turned out to be about eleven Fridays during the semester. This classroom had flatbed scanners and twelve IBM Pentium workstations—loaded with Windows 95 and Microsoft Office as well as PhotoShop—which were connected to the Web with Netscape, and an LCD projection panel attached to an overhead projector, which allowed me to project the computer screen of my machine onto a large screen for demonstration purposes.

Here is a schedule of what we did in the lab for the semester:

- Week 1. *Net-Surfing and Email*: basic introduction to Netscape Navigator, URLs, buttons, search engines; negotiation of problems with listserv
- Week 2: *Lab I on HTML*: basic HTML commands (head, body, heading levels, paragraphs; setting colors for background, text, and links)
- Week 3: *More HTML*: lists, inserting images, making hypertext links
- Week 4: *Lab Workshop Day*
- Week 5: *Intro to Graphics*: scanning, adjusting image-file size and format
- Week 6: *Intro to Graphics—PhotoShop I*: Tool Bar and Basic Menu
- Week 7: *FTP-ing and HTML Editing:* loading files onto the server; META tags; site registration with major browsers
- Week 9: *Intro to Graphics—PhotoShop II*: Image Menu, adjusting colors; basic filters
- Week 10: *Intro to Graphics—PhotoShop III*: making background GIFs; advanced filters
- Week 12: *Lab Workshop Day* (for group projects)
- Week 13: *Lab Workshop Day* (for group projects)
- Week 14: ***Site Presentations *** (2 days)

All the sessions on graphics are icing on the cake. You can download all kinds of graphics from the Web, so you don't have to make your own. (For lists of sites with HTML resources of various kinds see links at http://hubcap.clemson.edu/~sparks/HTMLindex.html and http://hubcap.clemson.edu/aah/mmug/mulinks.html.)

The Computer Assignments

Aside from a class journal sent to the listserv weekly, I created two main assignments for class: one individual and one group-oriented. (There was also a final essay exam.) Students thus did not do traditional papers for this course. I decided that weaving Web pages was a new form of literacy, involving not only traditional writing skills but also skills in computer programming, graphic design, and research.

Assignment 1: Web Page on an Author
(Due About the Fifth Week of the Semester)

This was just a basic test to show that everyone had mastered the first level of HTML. I asked each student to pick an author and create a Web page about him or her. Not making any demands for originality, I established a model for comprehensiveness with sample pages I put up on the Web about H. G. Wells and Charlotte Perkins Gilman (see Figure 5-3).

Each student was required to list the author's most significant works and demonstrate the ability to do the following things in HTML:

- establish colors for background, text, links, active links, and visited links

- display at least one image, either in-line or as a background for the page

- link to at least one other relevant site on the Web

Every student in class completed this assignment successfully, some going far beyond the stated requirements by incorporating biographical research, annotations of different works, extensive internal and external links, and a huge range of images including everything from scanned book covers (they emailed publishers or authors for permission, which provided an opportunity to discuss the ethics of copyright) to animated rotating eyeballs. (see Figure 5-4.)

Assignment 2: Group Web Site on a Thematic Topic
(Due at the End of the Semester)

By the second week of the semester, I began asking students to start forming research groups, linking up with people in class who were interested in the same SF subject, author, or area. Groups consisted of three to six people. (This actually didn't happen until about the fifth or sixth week.) I asked each group to go through several stages in

Figure 5-3
Sample Web Page Focusing on a Particular Author
(http://hubcap.clemson.edu/~sparks/gilmbib.html)

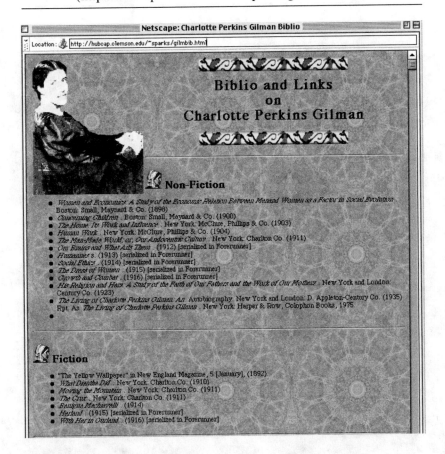

preparing, presenting, testing, then publishing their Web site. Here is the original plan:

Parts of the Assignment
Proposal (Turned in to Teacher for a Grade)

- Explain what kind of a Web site the group wants to build and narrow the task to a feasible level of specificity.

- Review what's already on the Web.

- Tell what the site is going to contribute to the SF and Web community, especially in terms of content (this involves doing some research of print sources at the library).

Figure 5-4
Students' Web Pages on Alan Dean Foster and Robert Heinlein
(http://hubcap.clemson.edu/~sparks/foster2.html

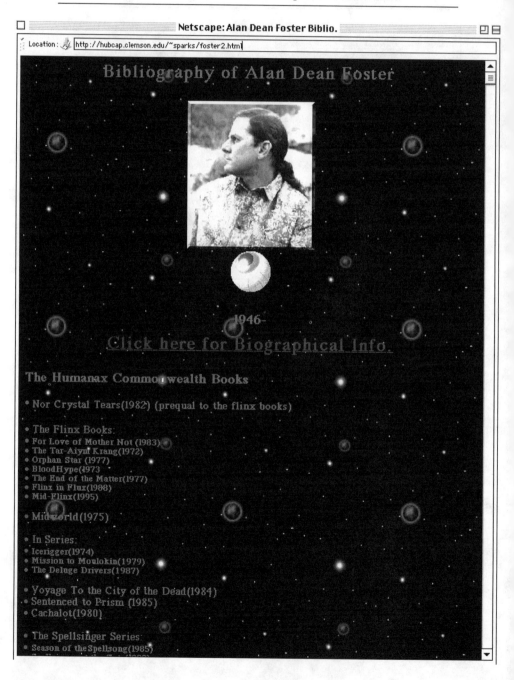

Figure 5-4
continued

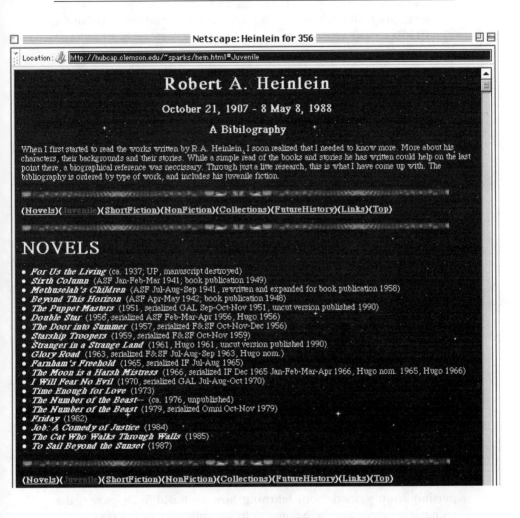

Presentation of Site Concept to Class
(in Lab Using Computer Projection; Five Minutes)

- Show the general content of the site.
- Give the class some idea of the visual/design concept of the site (colors/images style).

Site Installation/FTP

- Load site onto the server and check all pages to make sure graphics and links work.

Browser Testing

- Test how the site looks on a variety of different browsers (Netscape 3.0 vs. 4.0 vs. Microsoft Explorer or Mosaic), monitors, programs (Windows 95 vs. 3.1) and platforms (Mac vs. IBM).

- Make necessary changes in colors, heading sizes, etc., to enhance/assure legibility on as many systems as possible.

Final Presentation of Site to Class
(in Lab Using Computer Projection; Fifteen Minutes)

- Present the site to the class for evaluation, including all the pages and all the links.

All five groups completed their Web sites: Hive Worlds; Ecological Issues in Science Fiction; Gender Crossings: Science Fiction and Fantasy; SF and Horror; and SF Literature and Film. All the sites were presented in the computer classroom, with those who viewed the presentation filling out evaluation sheets that assessed not only the site design and content, but also the quality of the oral presentation. Each of the sites had different strengths. Those who had the least computer expertise tended to compensate by doing more reading and research, while the really flashy site relied mainly on research I had provided. As regularly happened in this course, some sites were impressively elaborate. The Science Fiction and Fantasy group not only created pages describing different subgenres in which science fiction and fantasy combine but also compiled a list of academic criticism on genre issues and made pages for twenty different authors; the SF and Horror group constructed links to 128 different writers. (See Figure 5-5.)

Having spent so much of my own time building Web sites, I have a very accurate idea of the hours of work that went into constructing these Web sites. In no other course that I have taught have I seen such productivity and such creativity. My only explanation is that empowerment of the decentered classroom, the sense of mastery and participation gained from learning how to build Web pages, the enthusiasm generated by belonging to a community of learners working together to make something to share with others, and the responsibility of actually publishing on the Web all created a level of motivation that I had never been able to achieve before.

The Web Site Now and in the Future

Please visit the class Web site at http://hubcap.clemson.edu/~sparks/sfindex.html. As of October 1997, it contained over one hundred Web pages. Course Info includes the syllabus and links to old materials

Figure 5-5

Science Fiction Literature Students' Project: Science Fiction and
Fantasy Web Site (http://hubcap.clemson.edu/~sparks/sff/sffint.html)

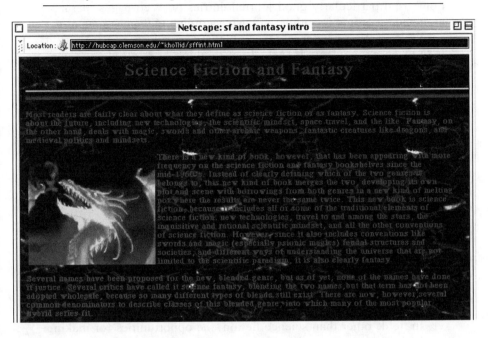

which show my initial ideas for the course. Study Guides and
Bibliographies is the richest category, containing not only reading
lists and lists of links for various authors and themes, but also a growing number of charts and reports of class or listserv discussions. The
section on HTML Materials provides templates which can be copied
to construct elementary Web pages, links to sites on the Internet of
particular use for constructing Web pages, and a library of the graphics I created for the site conveniently set up to be copied. Although
there are particular link pages for many authors, a more popular set of
links for SF in general is available at the Links Index. The Film List
organizes classic SF films according to the syllabus of the course,
providing students with a guide for checking out videos that coordinate with the course week by week.

Like all Web sites, this one is subject to change at any time. Now
that I have much of the basic groundwork laid, there are many
improvements I am imagining. The next time I teach this course, I
would like to do more to incorporate student work into the Web site. I
have plans to post some charts of discussions we had in class. For
example, students made outlines comparing the stages of the hero's

journey in both the movie and novel versions of Philip K. Dick's *Blade Runner* to present in class, which I am currently transforming into a table to be included on the Web site. I also want to post selections from particularly good journal entries on Web pages, perhaps arranged according to author, but also according to themes such as the hero's journey or gender issues. Now that I have learned how easy it is to teach my students HTML, I am thinking of reintroducing conventional modes of writing back into the course, at least a little — perhaps asking that the first Web page contain some kind of written summary/discussion of the writer's career.

It was a very obvious choice to try to introduce computer literacy into a science fiction course. Discussions of science fiction were among the first messages sent on the Internet, and there is a huge, almost overwhelming amount of material out there about it now. At the same time, what is available on the Web is mostly commercial and popular rather than academic. There are vastly more resources available on science fiction films and TV series than on books. Bibliographies available even for the most prominent writers are often inaccurate and/or incomplete, and many significant authors have little or no coverage. In addition, there is hardly any acknowledgment or awareness of the entire body of scholarship about science fiction and fantasy. Thus, there is a great deal for students and teachers to contribute: stories and books to annotate, articles to list, themes to identify and discuss.

In fields other than science fiction, the opportunities for making the Web a true community of exchange are even more wide open. When people complain about lack of content on the Web, I always think, that is the role of schools and universities: to provide content and knowledge to those who seek them. Since webbing my science fiction course, I have tried similar experiments in a contemporary literature class and a class in feminist literary criticism. (You can link to these Web sites through my home page.) In these academic areas, the situation is the same. There are a few pioneers introducing some academic content, a few enthusiasts pursuing personal interests and obsessions, and lots of basically irrelevant commercial sites. All along the information superhighway, the frontier is open, waiting for students and teachers to build virtual communities that offer more than the fast food of advertising-driven content, to build a Web of libraries full of shared scholarship and knowledge.

Computer Books

Basic, Introductory

Branscomb, H. E. 1998. *Casting Your Net: A Student's Guide to Research on the Internet*. Boston: Allyn and Bacon. A student's introduction to doing academic research on the Internet, how to find information, how to evaluate it, how to use it. The text assumes that students already have some general knowledge of how to use the Internet and how to write a research paper, and provides information on how to do effective Net searches using Boolean logic, which search engines to use for various tasks, and how to evaluate the veracity/reliability of information found on the Internet, discussing not only World Wide Web as an information source but also email, listservs, newsgroups, Telnet, Gopher, and commercial online services including subscription and pay-per-search sites.

Castro, E. 1996. *HTML for the World Wide Web*. (Visual Quickstart Guide). Berkeley, CA: Peachpit Press. A good, inexpensive, easy-to-follow introduction to HTML.

Clark, C. L. 1997. *Working the Web: A Student Guide*. Austin TX: Harcourt Brace. A guide for students who know absolutely nothing about electronic communication, this little book clearly and concisely explains what the Web is, how to access it, how to use browsers to Web surf, and the basics of email, as well as providing a tour of interesting sites on the Web, describing how to use search engines to do research on the Web, and outlining the basics of HTML, with a useful section on Web page design. Also includes extensive lists of useful Web sites in various disciples and student reviews of popular Web sites.

McCanna, L. 1996. *Creating Great Web Graphics*. Mis Press. A good introduction to Web page design.

More Advanced

Weinman, L. 1996. *Designing Web Graphics*. Indianapolis, IN: New Riders Pub. This book and disk provide an excellent, detailed introduction to all aspects of creating graphics for the Web. For more information, visit the author's Web site at http://www.lynda.com/dwg/dwg2.html.

6

Beet Farmers, Bombs from Baghdad, and the Northern Lights
Crossing Cultures, Sharing Stories

Anna Citrino
Brian Gentry*

I remember when I was about six years old. I used to come from school heading straight to the living room and hide beneath the table. Then my dad used to pretend as if he was looking for me. Even though I knew he saw me, he usually said, "Now where's my girl? I miss her. I want to eat her." He sounded angry and cruel, which made me very anxious. Then he would crawl under the table, put me on top of his shoulders, and run across the room. I loved it when that happened. . . .

It's not like today when I come home from school. I usually sit in my room by myself. I can still remember every single thing that happened when I was six.

Sama Al-Sane
Eighth grade, Kuwait

Many of us live in flux between the past and the present, between traditional ways of life and modern ones, uncertain of how past tradi-

------

*John Morse, who attended the Bread Loaf School of English as a DeWitt Wallace–Reader's Digest Fellow, participated in the following project and contributed significantly to the outline of this chapter.

tions might help us address today's problems. Sama, an eighth grader in Kuwait, draws attention to this dilemma when she undercuts her story's nostalgic mood with the statement "It's not like today . . ." Her words emphasize how quickly the world is changing, and this sense of loss is one reason we asked our students to begin telling their own stories and the stories of the communities in which they live. While we may not want to live in the past, preserving and understanding it seems important. Our project is about remembering and forgetting. We believe our lives are saturated with stories, but our breakneck lifestyle rarely allows us to share the stories that shape us, and if these stories remain untold long enough, they can evaporate and disappear. We may lose part of what we are. Stories reside at the center of life. They allow us to both imagine and negotiate reality. They help us appreciate the value of our diversity while simultaneously reminding us of shared human experiences. Remembering our stories helps us document changes in society, and aids us in growing deep roots that can withstand the storms of modern life.

We don't pretend to have all the answers for those who might want to try a project that uses stories as a way of making meaning. We can say, however, that allowing our students to share these stories reminded us of some significant truths about learning. We rediscovered the energy and enthusiasm for writing that can come when students tell or write stories for an actual audience. Most students were used to analyzing literature in some form, but interpreting culture by looking at narrative was foreign to them. By writing our stories and sharing them with each other, we came to see ourselves and the world in new ways. We experienced the power of meaningful discovery. We began the project wanting to learn how story preserves and reflects culture, how it teaches us to face the future. We came away understanding and learning much more than that. We've stood like miners panning for gold in the waters of story and culture, sifting pebble, sand, and silt, looking for nuggets that might lead us to the mother lode. We are still trying to understand and articulate the meaning of what we did.

Setting Up Camp: How We Began

We planned our project during the summer of 1994, at the Bread Loaf School of English in Vermont. The learning environment at Bread Loaf is unusual because it brings together teachers from widely varying cultures and provides them with opportunities and technical support for collaborative projects that transcend traditional cultural barriers. In one of our classes with Dick Harmston, we had been investigating the uses of writing in a small community near the campus, Bristol. We explored and documented the various kinds of literacy in Bristol by observing and interviewing people living there. We were specifically aiming to understand how people in that community used writing, what they said about their use of writing, and what implications these findings might have for what we did as teachers in our own communities. We were not members of the Bristol community. We could not know Bristol the way a member of that community did, and this distance between the observer and the observed made us consider how the gap between what a community knows and what it chooses to share with the outside world could help us to better understand our own communities.

During our study of Bristol, Dick suggested that we might create significant learning opportunities for our students through an online exchange. It took time for us to understand the significance of his suggestion, but when we began to think about the possibilities of connecting research in our own community with communities elsewhere, we felt we had an idea worth pursuing. Through our work in Bristol, we knew that the pictures of our communities that we would discover and describe would be incomplete, though we saw the value in collecting stories to enable people to see a collective picture of themselves in a place at a particular point in time. Noticing the rate at which traditional ways of life are falling by the wayside in the name of technological development and "progress," and observing how people's connections to particular regions are severed by a growing mass uniculture, we thought it might be valuable to collect both modern and traditional stories, exchange them with each other using telecommunications technology in our diverse locations, and determine what this process might show us about ourselves, our connections to particular regions, our uniquenesses, our common needs. We wanted to understand how stories offer insight and wisdom and guide our future. Before we (Brian and Anna) left the Bread Loaf campus, we contacted and enlisted the help of John Morse at the Bread Loaf campus in Santa Fe. While he was already involved in at least one other telecommunications project with his Native Alaskan students in Bonner Mission, Alaska, he agreed to join us and contribute to the project. His contributions added a further cultural richness and diversity to the project. With a grant of five hundred dollars each from the Bread Loaf School of English and the confidence of those who had helped us envision the project, we moved forward.

As we planned the project, we began to realize how geographically isolated our three communities were from one another and from much of the rest of the world: Bonner Mission, Alaska; Fahaheel City, Kuwait; and Clark, Utah. Bonner Mission, located on the edge of the Bering Sea, far from any major city, was the most isolated of the three. Our schools were also very different from one another. The school in Bonner Mission is a public school, set in a small Inupiat village of about 250 people, with about fifty young people attending the school. John's classes were small, with eleven students in their midteens. Two of his students were parents of young children. Located in Kuwait, Fahaheel City International School of Kuwait is a private school with a student body of about 1,200 K–12 students housed in one overcrowded concrete U-shaped building. The school has existed only since 1991, after Kuwait's liberation from Iraq. Approximately one-third of the students are Kuwaiti; the other two-thirds are a mixture of other nationalities, mostly Arab: Lebanese, Syrian, Egyptian. A few students come from Eastern European countries. The school's curriculum is mostly American, though faculty members hail from the United States, Canada, Europe, and Arab-speaking nations. All but a handful of students speak a language other than English as their native tongue. Brian's school in Clark, Utah, is a suburban public high school in the greater Salt Lake City area with a student body of mostly white, middle-class students, influenced by the Mormon community in the area.

Between the three locations, there were significant differences in how people within the community had tried to preserve the past. In Kuwait, for example, people don't generally appear interested in historic preservation. The discovery of oil catapulted Kuwait from poverty to immeasurable wealth, from a traditional lifestyle to a modern, westernized one in less than fifty years. Many people in Fahaheel City want to forget the poverty of the past and move into the future without looking back. Few students knew traditional tales. In Alaska, John unearthed cultural stories, tales that had been preserved by oral tradition for generations. However, even Bonner Mission had begun to absorb mainland attitudes that didn't leave much time to talk, and no one was writing these stories down. The stories were being lost. In Utah, Brian noticed some attempt to preserve cultural stories, but mostly in the context of gathering genealogical information. These stories were often cataloged in family volumes, but rarely were they shared with wider audiences. Accommodation of modern Western ways of life threatened to swallow up all three cultural groups.

Literature arises from the imagination of a people. The traditional and personal stories of a society help shape the future. As members of a particular culture, we pass on stories about what it means to be a man or a woman, what it means to be a member of a particular clan, tribe or group, how to face a challenge, how a wise person acts and how foolish people act, how a person gains honor or respect. These stories create a version of reality, an explanation for the way things are and why they are that way. We use these stories to imagine and reimagine the way we live.

In much of modern society, however, people no longer live in one region their whole lives, and the power of a place and its stories to shape the lives of people is diminishing. Cultures commingle and changes happen so fast that many of the stories connecting us to the past are lost. "All that matters is now," a parent of one of Anna's students told her, a Syrian who makes her home in Fahaheel City. "We do not need to know about the past. We do not think of those things. It has nothing to do with our lives now. We have not been back to our country for twenty-five years. My daughter cannot get her grandmother's story about the past. The past is a shame to her grand-mother. Why do you bother about it? Now is what counts." Perhaps family stories are not meant to be passed on publicly, or to be written down; yet, because many children in Fahaheel City, for example, are raised by maids, it's uncertain how much oral history or how many traditional tales are passed on to children. If only a few randomly chosen stories are passed on to children, how will young people learn who they are, their place in the world, their connection to those that have gone before them, and their responsibility to those who come after? If it's true that we create our world out of the stories we hold in our hearts and minds, how do we live, we wondered, when the old stories get lost? What kind of stories will we tell then?

We left Bread Loaf with a written proposal outlining our ideas for this project, and we used this proposal to introduce our idea to admin-istrators at home. At each site, school administrators were willing to help. In Utah, for example, Brian was successful in getting an addi-tional one-thousand-dollar grant from Jordan School District. He used that money to pay for a modem and long-distance telephone costs. In Fahaheel City, Anna's administrators assisted in covering the costs of connecting online. Anna also received a one-thousand-dollar fellow-ship from the Orion Society and used the money for necessary com-puter hardware. In Alaska, John's principal allowed him to use the phone at her house to access BreadNet, the telecommunications net-work of the Bread Loaf School of English. Though telecomputing is now becoming more convenient, linking remote sites like ours still requires resourcefulness and determination.

Arriving home, we were immediately confronted with technologi-cal difficulties of various types. We anticipated some of the difficulties we faced while others continued to haunt us throughout the year. All of us had some difficulty getting computer access. "I only have one com-puter in my room," Brian wrote, "and everything has to flow through that very tiny opening. My students can only see what I have seen first. While I would prefer to have students at their own computers sharing stories with their counterparts in Alaska and Kuwait, that just isn't pos-sible: I have to download what comes across the wires, photocopy and distribute it for students to read." Anna had computer access only at her home. At first, she typed all documents online. Later, students came to the school's computer lab after school and on weekends during the only time when the lab wasn't already occupied by students doing other schoolwork. Anna then took the disks home to upload the information online. Living abroad presented Anna with additional problems. During the first three months, she spent several hundred dollars on adapters and modems because transformers wouldn't adequately adjust electrical cycles for the modems she used. Computer parts and repairs are not as available overseas as they are in the States.

We each interpreted the original plan of how to select stories to exchange and how to organize them. Our varied approaches, in fact, seemed to be a strength. John incorporated the project into a speech class of eleven students at the junior/senior level and sent the students out to interview elders in the community. Anna collaborated with another eighth-grade teacher in Fahaheel City, and together they organized their seventy-five students into groups. Students wrote about their own lives, interviewed members of their community, and collected oral histories and traditional tales. Brian's eighty tenth-grade honor students wrote poetry, gathered ancestral stories, and wrote descriptions of places in the community.

Seeing this project take form was like watching electrons circle an atom under an electron microscope. The seemingly empty space that exists between subatomic particles makes it difficult to understand how an object can appear so substantial, so solid, but there's all that light woven together, swinging around a core, and it is the energy there, buzzing around in attraction to the center that keeps the object together. There were times when we felt lost in the empty spaces between what we knew and what we needed to learn. Our students' continued enthusiasm and energy pulled us in many directions. They informed us of fund-raising ideas, started their own magazine to raise money for the project, told us of people in the community we could interview in class, and bought cameras to take videos of the project activities. There were many activities zooming about, many requests, and the thinking and writing we did early on were crucial to the overall success of the project. While we didn't know a lot about online communications before we began, we kept focused by pursuing the ideas we had outlined in our proposal. One success followed another; student enthusiasm grew, and we found ourselves caught in the gravity of powerful ideas.

Breaking the Ice: What Students Wrote

Online communication shrinks the world and makes history come to life. When we realize we are part of history, that we are watching it happen, we pay close attention. Students at all three sites shared information that would never have made it into the history books, and this information made the events they discussed seem real. Here, we share some of what was written to create a context for what we will say later. The pieces include both original pieces written from firsthand observations and experience, oral histories, and pieces written from oral histories, as well as student responses to each other's writings. Students' names have been changed.

The Hardware Store

Paint peels
like sunburned skin
splintering boards
pleading
to be nailed down
but
left alone
independent

Aged and faded
it stands
out of place
in a world of new
threatened
to be erased
by time.

Donna Dix, Utah

Northern Lights

My grandma, Molly Ruben, is seventy-two years old. She is an Inupiat Eskimo. She speaks our language very well, but hardly speaks English. She said she never went to high school because her parents always moved around. They went camping to hunt for seal and fish. During August, they picked berries and stored them away for the winter. She once told me a story about the Northern Lights. She said a person was out dog-teaming during good weather. The moon was out and there were lots of Northern Lights and that person whistled at the Northern Lights. They came down and took his head off and played basketball and other games with his head. The dogs ran off and they never saw him or his dogs ever again. Our elders tell us never to whistle at the Northern Lights when we're traveling alone.

Darla Ruben, Alaska

Response

Dear Darla Ruben,

Your piece titled "Northern Lights" is a very unusual, yet interesting piece that shows me a lot about your culture. It is very interesting how your grandma used to pick berries and stored them for the winter. However, it is unusual that your elders tell you never to whistle at the Northern Lights when you are alone. Is it a way of respecting a god, or respecting your culture? It was a very clear piece, which made me wonder about the Northern Lights.

Kamil Al-Reyes, Fahaheel City

Mom's Story

My name is Sharon Al-Ghareeb and I have been asked by my son Khalid to elaborate about my life a little. There were these two or three questions about my interview that I hesitated to answer. . . . I just didn't know how to answer them. . . . My son asked me, 'Why did you come to Kuwait'? I didn't know if I should say I came because I liked it or what, so I said I thought Kuwait was beautiful, and besides it's where my husband's family lives. OK so I'm saying to myself, I'm doing pretty good with this talking about my life thing. . . . I hope he doesn't ask me . . . if I like living here or something. [He did.] I told Khalid I love living here in Kuwait, but it has its pros and cons. Sometimes I wish I was back in old Maryland. The people here don't care about the cleanness of this country. I mean they still throw trash in the streets and pollute the ozone by burning oil. After that, I asked Khalid, 'Do you have any more questions you'd like to ask'? 'Yes,' he said. 'One more. What could make Kuwait a better country?' I said, 'Some laws would be nice.' About forty-five minutes later, Khalid came to me and said, 'Thank you for letting me interview you on such short notice.' I said 'You're welcome.' I gave him a hug and said, 'Go to bed because you are never going to wake up tomorrow.'

Khalid Al-Ghareeb, Fahaheel City

Gulf War Diary

August 22, 1990
Dear Diary,

Today is the scariest day of my life! Iraqi troops invaded Kuwait. Tanks and busses were everywhere. People were running like crazy, looking for a safe place to hide. After the Friday prayer (in the afternoon), I saw troops taking men and boys and putting them on busses going to Baghdad. . . . I was alone in my house. My wife and kids were vacationing in London. I was to go to them in two weeks. They were probably worried about me. I was going to call them but the lines were dead. I couldn't communicate with them. We were totally cut off. I heard loud machine guns and bombs exploding. The Iraqis came into my house. They didn't hurt me, but they took all my valuables like the TV, my wife's gold, and the stereos. I prayed that night for God to help us and protect us.

August 31, 1990
Dear Diary,

The rumor was true. We were going to be rescued at last. I was so glad. I felt sad because of what the invaders did. They tortured our men. They raped our women and wounded our children. The Kuwaitis helped each other in every way they could. . . . There was a lady, Asra Idris. She was thirty-six years old. She went in and out of Kuwait bringing in weapons, and important documents. The Iraqis caught her and stabbed her to death. I also heard the story about Ahmed Mohammed. He was one of those people that would fight the Iraqis back. He was captured and they electrocuted him.

Shahad Al-Marzook, Fahaheel City

Response

. . . I realized what a sheltered world I seem to be living in. The war in Kuwait was frightening here, but after reading a firsthand view on the inside, fear is replaced with horror. . . .

Karen Talbot, Utah

From an Interview with Mother

Growing up as a child, my family never had a lot, but we always had plenty to eat. We all learned the importance of work. My father was a farmer so we worked out in the fields thinning beets. It was a backbreaking job and required a lot of work. We would have to weed, top, thin, and pile the beets in all kinds of weather. When it was windy, the dust would get into our eyes and if there was bad weather we would have to work out in the snow. Our only income was the beet check that we got in the fall and when it came my sisters and I would each get a new dress, otherwise my mother made all our clothes. Saturday was our day off and we never worked on Sunday since we went to church. On Saturdays my father would take us downtown and we would go to dinner and a show. The dinner cost only thirty-five cents, and we were served a full-course meal. On the days we worked, dinner was at five o'clock. Afterwards, we would sit and do our lessons. My mother was a teacher and was well educated. I began school at the age of six and every day I had to walk a mile and a half to school. During the Depression, times were hard, but there was always food on the table.

Amelia Rasmussen, Utah

Response

Dear Amelia,

I feel very sorry for your mother. Is this piece true? She really worked in a field? And meals were thirty-five cents? I wouldn't want to see people suffering like that! I would like to help all the poor people and families in need. I really like your piece. It made me think about what I take for granted like my education.

Shahad Al-Marzook, Fahaheel City

Grandma's Stories

When I was little, my grandma told me that if we played with strings to make figurines after midnight, an old lady would sit by the door and play with our guts.

A long time ago my grandma used to dog-team to Teller, a village eight miles southeast of here to buy groceries because Bonner didn't have a store. The first snow machine came to Bonner about twenty to thirty years ago.

A long time ago when my grandpa was a reindeer herder, some Chinese people were staying at our camp, and when they cooked their food, the flounders were still flapping inside the pan.

Carly Orleona, Alaska

"It's interesting to me," Brian wrote online in April, "how we are so similar and so different at the same time. It seems like there are parts of culture that we somehow inherit just because we're part of the human family, and other parts that we possess because of the place we live. . . . As I read some of these pieces . . . I felt as if this project had reunited me with distant members of my family, and I found myself craving these stories in deep ways that I don't have the words to describe."

Surveying the Landscape at Harvest: What Students Learned

We aren't who we were when we began this project. We know more about our students and the cultures we live in. We're also more aware of our own blindnesses. We know many things we didn't know before, but as we try to sift through the writing we have collected, questions still swirl around us like desert winds. We have only uncovered fragments that are part of a larger, more significant whole.

Before our project began, students knew little about each other's cultures. Many devalued the past; some just ignored it. Modern life was better, more comfortable. The past was too painful or shameful to recall, and they thought people would do better to leave it behind. "The value of our culture to me is almost nothing," one student said. "It is better to leave our personal or family stories to ourselves," another commented. Some students wondered if they were even part of a culture. Their past seemed boring, and they preferred to have it buried in an unmarked grave.

By the end of the year, many students had begun to speak about the past with pride. Somehow exploring other cultures had made them feel pride in their own. While it's difficult to explain exactly how this change occurred, it did. The students' hard work brought them rewards as they began to see both similarities and differences in the other cultures they studied. Their comments say it best.

It (the project) opened my eyes and made me realize that other people aren't so different. . . . When they wrote stories about the Gulf War . . . we got to see a side that wasn't shown on the news.

Hanna Durham, Utah

We have lost a certain culture (bedouins) so we lost knowledge about the desert but we gained modern ways of life, but they cause a lot of pollution.

Amal Nejm, Fahaheel City

If I could have the opportunity to do this again, I would do it in an instant. Next time it would be easier for me to know what questions to ask and how to embrace another culture.

Jeremy Toklas, Utah

In a very real way, this project put students and teachers on the same level. As teachers, we had never tried anything like this. Our students rarely had the opportunity to learn firsthand about other cultures. Most of their knowledge came from reading carefully edited history books. In this project, students had access to raw textual material that hadn't been sifted through an editor's hands. Knowledge gained from this project came from students' own experience of going out in the world to observe and get information, which they brought into and reflected upon in the classroom. After reflecting on and discussing the information and stories, students shaped and shared their stories with others online. Together, students and teachers searched for meaning. As a result, the classroom dynamics changed. The unexpected could occur, and you couldn't always chart classroom activity on a predictable time line. Students and teachers worked as a team to uncover truths in the stories we received and sent.

Because this kind of activity was new to us, it was often difficult. The material from each of the cultures seemed quite different. Students began the project with cultural misconceptions that all people in Alaska lived in igloos, for instance, or that people in Kuwait rode camels as a main means of transportation. First, we had to educate one another and provide a more accurate picture of what each culture looked like. Then we tried to understand that picture, integrating it into a new concept of reality. We all struggled to see connections between the online exchanges we were reading, and it wasn't always clear what the connections were. With time, this became easier, and we began to see that the stories fell into general categories. Some students told strange stories about interesting events in their family's history. Other students told stories of displacement caused by having to move from one location to another. Some students wrote about fearful experiences, while others shared stories about how cultural traditions were passed from parents to children in the past. In the end, we were all fascinated by the rich tapestry these stories had woven and were surprised to realize that, even in the midst of our diversity, we had much in common. Several students noticed this and commented on it at the end of the year.

It's amazing how, by attempting to show our differences . . . we inevitably end up telling each other how we are . . . the same. . . . There is a universal need for a place to fit in, friends, and families that love us. The thing that is making the world a more peaceful place to live in is that we are all recognizing that we share the same spirit, that human nature knows no cultural or racial boundaries.

Bill Tyson, Utah

During this project, I learned that these people are . . . similar to Kuwaiti people and their ways of life . . .

Sezen Dzafic, Fahaheel City

The lives I've read about, lives surrounded by strange places and even stranger circumstances, seem at their core to be my life, or the life of someone I know very well. While I've never tracked a wolf or lived through a bombing attack on my neighborhood, the excitement or fear caused by those situations are as common in my life as in yours. What it all boils down to is that there is an "us" and a "them" because we choose it to be that way, not because nature intended it so. Although it is human nature to segregate and divide yourself from what you don't understand, it is our common basic fear, our survival instinct, that makes us believe that slight differences create a gap too wide and deep to be bridged. I hope we have evolved far enough to see how very wrong that is; this project turned hope into belief, one that will last long after the computer link is severed.

Joanne Thresher, Utah

Students began the project by sharing stories of diversity but finished the project by recognizing what they shared in common. This recognition of commonalities at the end of the project moved beyond the surface questions students began with in their search for how to connect, such as "What do they eat?" and "Do they have shopping malls?" to a recognition, at least for some of the students, of each other's humanity—the hopes, loves, and fears all people share.

As we watched our students collect and share cultural stories, we sometimes met resistance. Some parents, for example, wondered about the value of collecting stories. Students at each of the sites questioned our motivations for pursuing this project. "We've never done anything like this in English before," they reasoned. "Why should we be doing it now?" Some parents even suggested that grammar drills should be taught in place of an effort like this. Most of these criticisms were not new. We realized that parents were expecting that their children would be taught using the same methods of past generations. When this didn't happen, they began to ask questions. By learning to interview, observe and revise, students became more than passive classroom participants. Learning often grew in twists and turns rather than in a straight line and, therefore, was not as easily quantifiable. Students were creating their own texts. They edited their own grammar and spelling errors. They transformed pieces from raw transcripts to focused drafts. They revised with their online audience in mind. They performed their pieces, talked excitedly about them, and gained confidence. Those who criticized the project were few, and by the time we finished, most skeptical students and parents had found their own reasons to believe in collecting and sharing stories. At the end of the year, students commented on what they had learned.

> One of the best things I learned was how to interview someone. Before we started this project, I was so nervous about interviewing. Now, I know how to organize my questions and clearly discuss an issue with another person. We can learn that all cultures are being dissolved into each other, and it helps us understand the world and ourselves. . . . Our picture of the other cultures that we've gotten from the media changes.
>
> Mohamed Al-Mazeedi, Fahaheel City

> Sharing my writing with other people gave me a whole different audience . . . to write for. . . . The one thing I will take from this experience is a respect and admiration for the people living in different places throughout the world. I admire people who aren't afraid of who they are and where they come from.
>
> Amelia Rasmussen, Utah

As students responded to one another, they frequently expressed themselves with clarity and grace.

Pearl Diving: What We Learned as Teachers

The project has changed us as teachers. We've done things we never would have tried before, because we weren't alone. While we clearly feel the project was a success, there are some things we will do differently the next time around. We learned how important it is to create visual images for students. They want to see the people they are writing to and the place where they live. In this project, visual images seemed especially important because students' communities were half a world away from each other and in diverse cultures, with different landscapes and different physical realities. Students' interconnection with each other via their writing sent online by computer made them curious to know one another more fully and as real people. They wanted to understand the way one another lived, how it was related to or different from them. Over the year we exchanged postcards, maps, published photo books of our communities' architectures and natural environments, as well as videos, slides, and still photos we took of the students, the school, and the communities in which we lived. The photographs we sent each other certainly assisted in providing a context for the students' verbal exchange and in enabling the exchange of ideas to be grounded in tangible events and places. We would make visual information even more of a priority with future projects, and with the rapid development of telecommunications and multimedia computing, the visual representation of cultural knowledge will be more convenient.

Students often wanted to write to specific people, and we encouraged them to do this through the mail, but we wanted to avoid creating groups that included some and excluded others. It seems natural for students to be drawn to one another, but sometimes their motivations get in the way of the focus we had set before us for the exchange between the group as a whole.

As the year drew to a close, we realized the need for time to reflect on the learning and the writing. While we included reflection and discussion, we felt that we didn't allow enough time for this, and in fact, this necessary part of learning often gets shortchanged in curricula. The discussions seemed most effective when coupled with outside reading about the geography and traditions of the areas being studied. Students sometimes misread the writing they received and developed misconceptions about the other cultures. We now see these misconceptions as a normal part of the growth toward understanding unfamiliar cultures. More literature read alongside the writing exchanges and more frequent interaction online might have discouraged these misconceptions.

While we planned year-end presentations for the communities where we lived, they didn't always come off the way we would have wanted. Students were generally willing to participate, but sometimes school politics disrupted plans and made things more difficult than they needed to be. One of Anna's administrators had committed to giving her a specific percentage of support to help send students to the United States, but then redefined what that meant one week before her students were due to leave, making it impossible to send the number of students originally planned.

Many things can slow the momentum of a project like this. Sometimes our time schedules prevented us from interacting with the community as we had hoped. In Anna's case, the local press didn't show up to publicize the project as they had promised. Parent and community turnout for events were small. In Utah, Brian asked to have his project included in a program to commemorate the arts. This promise was broken late in the year, and school schedules made it impossible to overcome the problems this caused. This experience reminded us of the importance of finding people in our school and communities who are committed to assisting the project. Looking back, we think we should have kept administrators better informed and invited them into our classrooms more often. Next time around, we would work for more community involvement and support. We would also continue to work to make computer facilities more accessible to students.

Learning experiences of high quality usually require significant time commitments. During this experience, we all gave significant amounts of personal time to this project, time that would otherwise have been spent with our family members or friends. While we anticipated some of the time constraints we experienced, we did not realize how much time we would have to give up. This was one problem we never adequately solved. It would have been ideal to have more time in the school day, such as an open period, in which to work on planning for, organizing, and reflecting on the project, but in our cases, this was not a possibility. New technology that produces new ways of learning will require school administrators to allow for flexibility in scheduling and school curricula. If teachers are encouraged to experiment with curricula and technology, schools must also provide them with opportunities to study and reflect on the process.

In the schools where we did our project, most student access to computers was located inside computer labs. This setup tends to separate computing from the curriculum. We would advocate for telecommunications technology in all classrooms. Placing this technology in classrooms encourages collaboration among teachers and students across the various academic disciplines as well as greater communication across cultures. Moreover, increased access to the computer as a tool for learning makes learning more direct, personal, and timely. Improving students' and teachers' access to computers helps to ensure that a project like the one we describe will be successful. While we will continue to work for improvements in our schools' computer technology and access, we know that changes take time, money, and understanding. Before necessary changes can occur, the school community and the community at large need to witness the benefit to students' learning that can be brought with online exchanges.

Though access to technology certainly increases convenience, perhaps even the chance for success, in online exchanges, low-tech resources shouldn't be discounted. Sometimes teachers will decline an opportunity for such a project because they have only one computer. While having a computer for every student would be ideal, that wasn't possible for us. In fact, each of us had access to only one computer. Although that clearly made it more difficult to gather and send material, it wasn't impossible. Where we could, however, we asked students to help us manage the logistics of transmitting their ideas from notebooks to computer monitors to diskettes.

Throughout this project, we provided opportunities for substantive student conversation. While all of us would have liked more opportunity for online exchanges, lack of additional computer equipment and the press of other curriculum obligations forced us to limit our responses. It took months to set up the project and to send our first pieces of writing. We didn't feel obligated to send everything students wrote. Instead, we tried to select what was best or most representative of the whole, and students participated in making these choices. This selection process helped students to analyze the elements of good writing and the power of narrative in their own writing, and their attention to these concepts was greater than when we simply pointed them out in anthologized literature.

Like our students, we didn't always know how to respond to the writing that came across the wires, but we were all searching for meaning in the experience. One of Brian's online entries captured the importance of this kind of study: "Each year I try and do new things—to unsettle myself a little bit. It helps me understand some of the feelings my students have as they face reading and writing tasks that aren't familiar. . . . It keeps my blood pumping . . ."

New Frontiers: Suggestions for Creating Similar Projects

The proposal we wrote at Bread Loaf looked reasonable in July, but after we returned home, we realized adjustments were necessary. These modifications resulted from the differences in the communities where we lived, and the differences in the student populations we were trying to serve. While the proposal gave us a clear vision of what we wanted to do, the paths we followed and the things we discovered could never have been predicted in July. During the project's first months, we worked through a variety of logistical details. Through the rest of the year, we fine-tuned. This project became much more than we had ever imagined it might be. At various points in the year, we had to make conscious choices to limit the scope of the project, since it could have become an entire class by itself.

Initial Outline (Goals) Preparation in Summer

- Decide on an area of interest relevant to the area where you teach and that personally interests you.
- Describe and define the project.
  - What do you want to do? (Goals)
  - Why do you want to do it? (Purpose)
  - How will you judge its success? (Evaluation)
- Create a general plan or time line.

Elicit District and Administrative Support

- Make an appointment with administrators to discuss your proposal.
  - Propose the idea in the summer before school begins.
  - Go to the meeting with a clearly written proposal.
- Sell your idea.
  - Name the benefits specifically as you currently see them.
  - Ask for verbal and/or written support.
  - Mention the benefits to them.
  - Mention outside backing and support that you have.
  - Allow them to ask questions.
- Have an alternative plan in case things don't work out.

Elicit On-Site Collaboration

- Find ways your work connects with other subject areas.
- Approach teachers and describe how your project might supplement and enhance what they do in their classroom.
- Propose a formal meeting where interested teachers can decide how to work together on the project.
  - Come to the meeting with several concrete suggestions of your own.
  - Remain open to other ideas.

Preparing the Students to Write

- Propose the project to students.
  - Explain its basic elements.
  - Explain the reasoning behind it.
  - Sell it to them.
- Generate a list of guest speakers and background reading material.
  - Use these sources to help students think about the issues of the project.
  - Use them to help develop a context for future writing and discussion.
- Exchange audiovisual materials with other sites.
  - Begin this early in the project.
  - Include pictures and introductions of student participants to promote bonding.
  - Include other relevant visual material that relates to the topic.
- Teach and practice the following skills in class.
  - Finding knowledgeable people to interview.

- Questioning.
- Note taking.
- Transcribing.
- Selecting relevant sections from interviews to manipulate.
- Experimenting with different genres.
- Organize students into groups.
  - Have students work on interviews together or individually.
  - Encourage young students to work with partners.
  - Make a chart listing topics and interview subjects, to balance the number of students in each topic area.

Exchanging Student Writing

- Provide training so that students know how to access necessary computer files.
- Provide general guidelines on how to respond to the writing.
- Provide time to read and discuss pieces in class.
- Allow students to read a variety of pieces sent online.
- Allow students to respond to those pieces that strike them.
- Find ways to connect project writing to the larger curriculum.
- Promote enthusiasm for the project by regularly sharing writing.

Evaluation of the Project

- Provide an opportunity for students to evaluate and reflect on the project halfway through and at the end of the year.
- Assign several students to record the project's progress.
- Share periodic online messages with administrators to make them aware of progress; at key moments invite them into the classroom to share student writing.
- Invite parents, community members, and the press to observe, participate in, or report on class activities.
- Invite students to speak to others (administrators, parents, businesspeople, other teachers, classmates) about the project and what they are learning and doing.
- Invite students often to make and discuss connections between the work they are doing, what they are discovering through the online exchanges, and the larger questions and issues the exchange suggests.
- Provide a culminating activity or a tangible product where the work and writing can be shared with the community at large.

Other Possibilities

- Create online "auditoriums" and "chat rooms" where experts in areas related to your project's topic or concerns can inform students and respond to questions.

- Partner students with experts for online exchanges in the field your project explores.

- Create an online "gallery" of student-generated photos, drawings, and videos of objects relevant to your project's topic.

- Create a "sound room" where recordings significant to your topic can be heard.

- Using writing from the project, have students create a magazine or book to send online.

- Create a brochure designed by students to notify community sponsors of project activities or equipment needs.

- Raise money to send your students to meet the students you have been communicating with online, and then send messages and photos online of their activities on the trip so students at home can follow.

- Organize a live conference including video shots sent online during the conference.

- Invite parents and community members to a dramatic storytelling presentation of pieces your students have written. Videotape it. Send excerpts online.

- Make computer software as compatible as possible to help save you and your students' time in transferring data.

The very nature of this project changed our classrooms. It forced us to cross traditional classroom barriers such as culture, age, and language. Students wrote, thought, and spoke in ways that were new to the classroom. They discussed issues and ideas with new enthusiasm. This experience raised the specter of stereotype and prejudice, yet also encouraged students to see themselves as citizens of a global community. Although there were difficulties and challenges, we gained valuable experience and confidence in several areas. We learned firsthand about computers, and we now see how this kind of communication can significantly enlarge the learning world of our students. We became familiar with—and in most cases successfully negotiated—the politics of administrative decision making. We discovered much about the communities and cultures we were studying, but more importantly, we learned how much we have in common with people in other places. While this project allowed us to cross many barriers, its most important contribution came from the serious questions it forced us to ask ourselves about the nature of culture. It changed the way we see the world and posed questions with which we are still wrestling.

Heading Home: Conclusions

The project produced several significant benefits. Because of the real audience of peers at the other end of the line, students wrote things they likely wouldn't have written otherwise. The context of the writing became as important as the content. The project changed our classrooms and changed us as teachers. It made our classrooms less lonely. We felt supported by colleagues in other places. By sharing other cultures, we became more aware of our own. By opening ourselves to the world, we became more introspective. We saw ourselves more clearly because we had the help of those who were not like us and did not take the daily life we live for granted. As Brian described in one of his online letters to John,

> If [the students] have difficulty responding to the cultural stories we've shared, it may be because they need more time to read and think and experience the world. . . . One of our major purposes of this project isn't to get students to come up with an analysis similar to ours, but rather to invite them to begin reading real-world writing with a focus. Since this is the first time my students have probably been asked to do something like this, I expect many of them to poke at the project like they would a dead fish. That's why I see that the project's purpose and focus will change with time. I've enjoyed the opportunity to bat ideas around with you and Anna, and I believe that whether my students can articulate what they see or not, they will come away with an expanded vision of the world. . . . Maybe this is too idealistic, but I believe that learning takes time—sometimes more time than we want to give it. . . . Technology is a powerful tool that can open up doors and tear down walls. It can help us remember a time when the world was smaller, a time when we could share stories over the back fence and know that those stories connected us. I've felt a need in myself to hear those stories again, and I've seen the lights in the eyes of my students as history and language and culture have become real.

As we began this project we had a tendency to look for exotic stories that fell into our traditional stereotypes of what culture should be. Now, we are beginning to see that all human activity carries a culture and a story. In a message Anna sent online, she describes this thought.

> I drive down the highway now and see simple things: a worker with his head wrapped in a turban operating a huge tractor, a woman in a long, black *abaia,* hurrying down the roadside in tennis shoes, get-

ting her exercise. I stroll through a mall and notice three women with *abaias,* veils, and gloves, holding out bright red and black cotton spandex dresses with plunging necklines. These are stories, I tell myself, about an entire culture at this moment in time. When I first came to Kuwait, I thought it strange to see people in traditional dress standing at a Hungry Bunny (Burger King) counter, ordering a Super Bunny with cheese and fries. Now I see it as a story and think, why not? But I still wonder what this story means, what are its implications for Kuwait, and what will happen next.

In April, Anna sat in her room, reading computer messages the day after receiving the financial gift from a sympathetic sheikh that would make her students' trip to the United States possible. Anna described her feelings about this moment to the rest of us online: "Much tension surrounded the days of waiting," she wrote. "And then, afterwards, we did not know if one of our students could get a visa because the embassy in Fahaheel City wasn't sure that the U.S. recognized the country she held a passport from. Messages are waiting online from John, Brian, and other colleagues from the Bread Loaf School of English, people I didn't even know were following our project's stories, interested to know what the sheikh decided, expressing support for our efforts. I read the words, excited, pleased, knowing I am not alone in my efforts. For the first time, I sense the power to create community behind this kind of online interaction, although I couldn't find the words for it at the moment." With our project, we have begun a journey, uncertain of where it will take us. While some of our plans didn't materialize the way we envisioned them, we believe we made a significant beginning. As Sama Al-Sane says in the quote at the start of this chapter, few things are like they used to be.

This project helped us to frame the past, to live in the present, and to imagine the future. It helped us participate in and predict a world where diversity is celebrated. It changed the classrooms we teach in, and helped us see the common threads that bind all of us together.

7

Our Way or the Highway?
Perceptions of Self and Other on the Electronic Frontier

Tom McKenna
With an Afterword by Robert Baroz

This morning I am on vacation in Vermont, and as I look out across the already sunlit lawn, I'm thinking of my students back in Alaska. I'm wondering whether this Vermont, of jays and crows and hazy morning light, could possibly resemble the Vermont that my students created in their minds during a telecommunications project they initiated with a group of Vermont students in 1996. In February of that year, my tenth- and eleventh-grade students at Egalik High School in a remote coastal location in southwest Alaska, and Robert Baroz's students of the same age at Champlain Valley Union (CVU), a regional high school in rural Vermont, decided to collaborate through telecommunications across the same distance that I try imaginatively to bridge this morning.

Our goal was to publish a series of collaborative, student-edited literary magazines. Rob and I agreed that the first of the monthly publications would be edited by a team of Egalik students, since they had a semester's experience with the process. While my students were beginning their second semester of a writing-for-publication course which centered around a weekly literary magazine, Rob's kids had just convened for the semester.

The memories of my student editors, four girls, sitting in a circle on the floor, passing papers around, debating merits of one piece or another, reading aloud, and occasionally giggling, are still vivid for me; yet, they are already beginning to blend into a single memory of what this class was like. And I still have only the most vague idea of what Rob's classroom and his students might have looked like in action. The English teacher in me can't help thinking about the difficulty of trying to construct even the immediate physical world through language, let alone trying to reassemble the thoughts and ideas of others with so slippery a tool.

I have decided to revisit the events that we shared this past year—events that my intuition tells me are important for many of us who both thrill to and worry about the impacts of telecommunications in our classrooms. If our collaborative literary magazine project is to be judged on its original assumptions—that our online collaboration might create a diverse supportive *community*, and an *authentic* audience for writers developing pieces for publication—it was a startling failure. By May, students in both schools had come to resent one another at various phases of the project, and my students ultimately opted to drop out of the project. Rob and I also had experienced tensions during the exchange and at its ultimate breakdown. At the close of the school year, we had completed only one monthly publication and students in both locations had been frustrated with the process of communicating.

On one level, this is a very simple story. Our oversights were many. In a perfect world with better foresight and more time, we might have more clearly articulated what each of our visions for the project was. And we might have more carefully structured time for our students to come to know one another initially, and matched our schedules soon thereafter. But the story quickly becomes more complex, the moral less accessible, when we ask whether it was worth the risks to young writers' developing senses of identity, gender, and confidence to have their work evaluated in the impersonal forum of a telecommunications exchange. To what extent, I wonder, do we unwittingly position students to create partial and distorted representations of their partners in a telecommunications collaboration?

Within this book's collection of narratives and essays about "online communities," I would like to make a case against the facile use of that term. Our exchange did not, initially, impose especially formidable barriers to developing community. The geographic separation between the Vermont and Alaska students was greater than the cultural gap. Most of the participating students at Egalik had lived elsewhere in the States, and one of the editors had in fact lived in Vermont for some time. Yet, our experience suggests that we need to look carefully at the resistance to any kind of generic community, resistance that comes from local identity, local classroom norms, and from disagreement within our own classrooms, before we can appropriately see ourselves in an online community. Several breakdowns in the movement toward completion of our "objectives" invite a critical look into these students' patterns of representation of self and other throughout the exchange. While this chapter will be grounded in the assumption that telecommunications can create empowering relationships among students and teachers located in remote locations, it will highlight moments where these relationships were hindered or threatened, often in spite of students' own best intentions.

And so I wish to weave a narrative of an attempt at collaborative publication between our two classrooms—or, more accurately, some odd *representation* of those classrooms as it evolved through the language of our online discourse. But if this meditation is to be of value, it must be more than just a cautionary tale about obstacles in creating online communities. I must acknowledge that this story is, also, an exploration into the problematic realm of representation itself. In telling this story, I invite the reader along to help me locate myself in my own subjectivity, to keep me aware that I am *reinventing*—as I attempt to narrate—the place where I lived and the relationships that ensued. I have no doubt that there are different, and equally problematic, accounts of the same story from the perspective of students in Rob's classroom. Some names of people and places have been changed to protect individual's identities.

*　　*　　*

If you were to arrive at Egalik for the first time, you might arrive in the same way I like to imagine the eagles coming here, flying for hundreds of miles along the volcano-strewn Alaska coastline. You would fly from Anchorage, for two or three hours, over 875 miles of mostly treeless land and sea. You would find that you had landed in a complex nexus of culture, history, and economic activity.

A geographically isolated village, Egalik has been the center of bustling economy for centuries. Twentieth-century settlement patterns, much influenced by the American presence there during World War II, have bifurcated the community; the more industrial area is connected to the older, original village of Egalik by a bridge, and by a recently paved road, the latest in a flurry of new capital projects. A city of less than four thousand people, it is one of the busiest, and usually the most productive, fishing ports in the nation. In addition to the Native Alaskans (people whose families have lived in Egalik for thousands of years as well as people who moved from outlying villages after the economic and social dislocations of the past half-century), Egalik's population comes from all over the Pacific. Significant numbers of people who come from the Philippines, Vietnam, Japan, Russia, Korea, and Mexico join a Seattle-based, largely transient labor force. A few years ago, a twenty-year resident of the community commented, upon retiring and moving from Egalik, "The longer you live here, the fewer people you know."

Nowhere is the cultural complexity of Egalik realized more fully than in the school. The student population at Egalik represents an inordinately small percentage of the general population (less than 10 percent), because of the high numbers of single, transient workers who live there. Still, those who are students in the K–12 school of approximately three hundred usually come from families who plan to spend some time in the community. As a result, students in general have significant ethnic diversity, yet a relatively high sense of shared history with their peers and teachers, and thus a high comfort level with the intimate and isolated social climate. Most students in the tenth/eleventh grade class that participated in the exchange had spent at least two years in the same school together, and many of them had spent most of their childhood and adolescent years together.

In my high school at the time of our collaboration, tenth and eleventh graders took English classes together. Any tenth or eleventh grader could choose from three English classes, one of which was called simply Publications. The Publications class, initially modeled after a graduate class I had taken with Ken Macrorie at the Bread Loaf School of English, centered around the production of a literary magazine, titled *Winter Bay*. In this class, students examined and revisited the question of what is good writing, and they worked in collaboration and negotiation with one another to produce it. The process of developing pieces, as I had adapted it from Macrorie, began with intensive freewriting. Students wrote five freewrites per week and chose one of those each week to refine and shape into a crafted piece of writing. These pieces were then submitted to a group of three student editors who would choose the most promising submissions. The editors would then, under my supervision, begin to negotiate with the writers to make changes in the work. Each issue took two weeks to produce, so at any given time the class was busy in the production of two magazines, one in an early stage of development, another in the final stage.

On Fridays, our students "released" the magazine after our whole-group meeting, in which editors discussed the process, and we checked the publication against the list of qualities of good writing that we had developed and posted on butcher paper on the classroom wall. At the time of our collaboration with Vermont, *Winter Bay* had enjoyed two years of very good reception in the school community. Students often greeted me enthusiastically in the hallways to con me out of extra copies, and teachers often wrote to students about their work, and occasionally used pieces as models for writing in classrooms of younger students. Thus, the publication worked in modest ways to identify a community of writers in the school.

By midyear, many in this particular group of students had begun to tire of our routine, and the learning curve flattened. At the semester break, Rob and I decided to link our classes via BreadNet, the telecommunications network of the Bread Loaf School of English. Participants in BreadNet are, I believe, especially well positioned to build online community among students for several reasons. First, they know one another. Most exchange partners on BreadNet have met one another on one of Bread Loaf's campuses during a summer of study. Second, their participation is often embedded in the supportive academic community that teachers experience during a summer at Bread Loaf. While the school is only in session in summer, in every academic year since 1984, college professors, secondary and elementary teachers, and students have been using the BreadNet telecommunications network to collaborate on issues of teaching. The result is that there's a significant amount of accumulated wisdom among BreadNetters about what makes a successful exchange.

At the outset of this exchange, Rob and I had a lot going for us. A Bread Loaf student and an activist for student-centered writing contexts, Rob had been a student of Ken Macrorie's publishing class as well. Rob and I each had a significant amount of experience with composition-based exchanges between students, and so we both believed that a collaborative publishing venture would reinforce the awareness of audience that was central to both of our notions of "real" writing. Students from each school would function as editors to negotiate with authors in the process of creating a collaborative monthly literary magazine.

*   *   *

I would like to center the story of our collaboration around a single incident that occurred in preparation for our first publication, *Inside Line*, issue one. The incident, which Rob and I now call "the Dodge Ram incident," contains many of the tensions of the entire project. Although we had initially hoped that the first issue would be coedited by a small group of student editors whose members came from each school, Robert suggested that my students in Egalik, who had a semester of editing experience in my class already, should take the responsibility for the first issue. Rob's Writing Prose class, a semester class offered in the spring, had just begun when we began to conduct the exchange. As a result, three of the four Egalik students who chose to be editors for the first issue figure in my version of this central incident. Let me begin to reimagine them.

Fiercely determined Andree, home-schooled in a conservative family, conducted herself as if she knew, always, what she was thinking. She wrote in much the way she carried herself. Her language was terse, the silences frequent and intense. Cara was more overtly playful. She brought an effusiveness to almost every situation, and she listened to other writers with the same kind of passion and sense of possibility. As a result, she often appeared to think by verbalizing. Sandra quietly mused. I sensed that she viewed herself as a writer slightly more than the other three editors did, and she assumed that both writing and editing were social processes; often she wrote me letters about her independent reading even when she knew that I'd be too busy to respond fully. By the middle of this past school year, I came to see all three of these young women as extraordinary editors of their peers' work. Kelley, a fourth editor and the only sophomore, was the organizer of this group of four, an equally vital role in the entire publication process, but she did not directly compose any text related to the story I'm about to tell.

*   *   *

Many levels of misunderstanding underlie comments about a single submission to the Egalik editing team, from a student named Todd at CVU. Some early confusion about process turned an exchange between a writer and editors into a fairly hostile encounter. We, as teachers, felt (and at times perhaps perpetuated) the confusion and anxiety as we shared our half-articulated assumptions with students and each other. While the volume of transcripts from the project testify in many places to a healthy exchange of perspectives on writing, I have selected several key documents where the language resonates with tension. I would like to refer to the following short pieces of text to illustrate the chronology and to explore the implications of this episode:

- a letter from Egalik editing team to CVU students, following the first round of submissions (document 1)

- an exchange of comments between teachers about the process (document 2)

- Todd's "Dodge Ram" piece (document 3)

- Cara's (of Egalik) handwritten, faxed response to Todd's piece (document 4)

- Todd's response to Cara's response (document 5)

- another exchange of comments between teachers about the process (document 6)

- a letter from Sandra (Egalik) representing the Egalik editing team (document 7)

The chronological sequence of the development of these texts began with CVU's submission of a batch of writing to the Egalik editors. Correspondence before the submission included many documents that I have not reproduced here. Among the early correspondence were the Egalik editors' brief descriptions of their notions of "good writing" and a few references to how their editing process worked. Much of this had also been "worked out" on- and offline by Rob and me. Since we had each taken Macrorie's course at Bread Loaf, I made the assumption that both classrooms would employ a roughly similar composing and editing process.

The Egalik editors divided the stack of submissions from CVU and took them home. (I would later discover that each editor had her own complete set of responses and that several Vermont students received very different comments written by different editors.) Each girl read through her stack of papers outside of class. On the following day, the Egalik editors expressed real disappointment and disbelief in the *form* of the CVU pieces. The consensus among the Egalik group was that only one or two from the stack were ready for submission. The rest, in their words, "were only freewrites." The students gathered, talked about each piece, and decided which of them would write comments. Then the Egalik editors, led by Andree, wrote a general letter, addressing the problem, as they understood it, with the entire batch of CVU submissions.

Document 1

Wednesday, February 7, 1996 10:21:30 AM
From: Tom McKenna
Subject: note from editors
To: Champlain Valley

Dear CVU students,

We just received and reviewed your pieces. Thank you very much for sending us so many pieces. It really helps us in the editing process. We may not have been clear on our process. Usually we bring a rough draft in, read it out loud in small groups, comment, and make some changes. After the changes are made we give them to the editor—for this edition, that is us. *The pieces that are turned in to the editors are FINAL DRAFTS!!* Final draft to us means that you have done everything you know how to do to make the pieces the best they can be. There should be no spelling errors. Pieces should be shaped much as the writer would like them to be in published form. We have had pieces turned in from our class that did not follow these guidelines. We turn them back the same as we have yours. We hope that you can try and work with us to create a great publication. It's going to be fun.

Most of the pieces we received seemed to be freewrites. We did feel Carl Nathan's piece on snowmobiles was fairly well developed. We plan to edit it and send it back to him to make some changes. If any problems come up with our comments, we can discuss them with Carl by email. As for the rest of the pieces, we would like to suggest that the whole class reads the chapter "Creating

Form" by Ken Macrorie. It really helped our class out. After you
have read the article, maybe you could take a good look at your
pieces and rework them so they follow Ken Macrorie's guidelines.
This will make your freewrites into nice drafts so that we can continue on our editing process. As editors, we feel our job is not to
compose the pieces; we hope to only add comments on what could
be added or cut or changed with sentences and punctuation. The rest
is up to the author, until it is time to publish and put it in the proper
format.

Please understand, while there are many interesting images in
the pieces, we need them to be further developed before we can
work with you.

Thank You,
Egalik Editing Team

Before I had time to really think through the implications of this
note, I allowed the editors to send it. Not surprisingly, the Egalik letter created tension through both its challenge to the expectations of
student and teacher, and through its tone. The letter gives a clear
example of how students' intentions to make the exchange function
according to their expectations actually functioned to alienate the two
groups from one another. A close look at its language shows several
tensions embedded in the text. Abrupt transitions and oddly placed
sentences throughout the document give a good indication that more
than one mind was at work here—I do not recall how the group came
to consensus on the final form of the letter. Note the friendly gestures of the first two sentences, and then the sudden change to
thoughts about process. In this section of the letter, the Egalik students alternate between describing the process as they have experienced it themselves, and giving directives with no personal pronouns:
"Usually we bring a rough draft in, read it out loud in small groups,
comment, and make some changes. . . . Pieces should be shaped much
as the writer would like them to be in published form." The italicized
directive *"The pieces that are turned in to the editors are FINAL
DRAFTS!!"* is unambiguous in tone and, indeed, underscores the tone
of the whole letter, but it is also followed by statements aimed at
establishing a friendly atmosphere and encouraging cooperation: "We
hope that you can try and work with us to create a great publication.
It's going to be fun." Whether from a problem with their own collaboration or from miscommunication about the composition process,
the Egalik editors are already struggling with forces of divisiveness in
the project.

In the second paragraph of their note, the Egalik students boldly
suggest that the CVU students read a chapter from one of their central

texts, Ken Macrorie's *Writing to be Read*. They are obviously applying their own classroom norms to those of the CVU students. Under the auspices of refining the process and keeping high standards for publication, though, they are setting up an adversarial relationship that will continue for the duration of the exchange. This letter closes with "we" and "you" clearly held in opposition: "Please understand, while there are many interesting images in the pieces, we need them to be further developed before we can work with you." Although I'm sure that the editors' intention was to fix the misunderstandings in the exchange, I suspect their message came across to Vermonters as something like "our way or the highway."

Several documents ensued from this one, including another note with suggested steps in the editing process from Egalik, and a reply to the February 7 note above (Document 1) from CVU's Carl Nathan, the author of the only piece that the Egalik editors had "accepted." Meanwhile, in behind-the-scenes conversations with Rob, I made allusions that the tone problem may have been the results of one of the editors' communication style—Andree often expressed her insights very directly.

Document 2

2/7
From: Tom McKenna
To: Rob Baroz

A pair of my kids is responding more personally to some of your students because they feel they as editors (specifically one) are being too harsh in their tone. Stay tuned.

2/9
From: Rob Baroz
To: Tom McKenna

My student Carl stopped by to see me at the end of the day. He had drafted a letter with comments from my students freewrites on their reactions to the student editors' letter. I showed him the letter that I had received with the steps, and he will look it over and make revisions to his. His first impression is that it sounded like your students were sorry. It could be that the harsh tone is indeed coming from just one of your students. So it would be good to hear from other students.

2/10
From: Tom McKenna
To: Rob Baroz

Today, two students worked for at least an hour together writing personal notes to as many of your students as they could. It was fascinating to watch out of the corner of my eye as they vicariously participated in a whole new range of extracurricular activities. They

(Cara and Marla) were saying things like, "Oh yeah, she's really nice. We're developing a real personal attachment with these guys." Of course your kids probably feel exactly the opposite right now, but I think that should come back on level. Cara and Marla, aware of Andree's tone, are trying to fill in to develop rapport. This is completely unprompted on my behalf. Interesting to watch. . . .

In hindsight, I see that my assumption that one of my student editors was responsible for a series of misunderstandings was, perhaps, a serious error, because letting that assumption slip into my February 10 note to Rob may have influenced Rob's interpretation of the events. This, in turn, may have contributed to a scapegoat notion implicit in Todd's and others' response to the editing process.

Sometime after, or simultaneous with, the process of clarifying expectations for submission, Todd's piece came over the wires.

Document 3

2-8-96
Freewrite: Dodge Ram

Hopefully, someday I'll get a Dodge Ram (1500 Sport) truck with a 350 V8 engine. I have wanted this truck ever since the first ones came out around three years ago. The truck I want is four wheel drive and black, with chrome wheels and a roll bar. It is amazing standing next to it because it makes you feel like an ant. This is also the truck that costs 25,000 dollars. After I get it, if I were to get it, I would put a RANCHO 6" suspension lift and 36" x 14.5" SUPER SWAMPER mud tires on it. This series of changes would add an extra three feet to the height of it. The next problem would be affording that. The lift would cost around 3,000 dollars, and the tires are another 3,000 to 4,000 dollars. The truck is rated best in its class by all of the Truck magazines. It comes in a wide range of sizes and styles, suspension packages, 4wd or 2wd, etc. There are also many different engines you can get in your Ram, six, eight, and ten cylinder engines, as well as the Cummins Diesel. I would love to have a V10, but unfortunately the smaller Sport truck that I want only comes with an eight-cylinder engine. My reasons for having this truck are, it looks really cool, women love guys that drive mean trucks, and I can drive over people in traffic if I'm in a hurry. I also like to go off-roading and romp through the mud. There is nothing that I couldn't do in this truck, it is great for hauling, and for pulling things as well. All I can do for now is save my money, and keep dreaming of someday winning the lottery.

The Egalik editing team's frustrations grew as Todd's piece added to a quickly growing stack of pieces that were in their eyes not yet well enough developed for an audience of peer editors. The girls were taken aback by Todd's hyperbolic claims, and they wanted my reaction to

his statement that "women love guys that drive mean trucks." I recall
chuckling with them, but mainly asking them to focus on the issue of
audience. I asked the editors to explore why Todd's piece didn't reach
them as his audience, and what he might do to change that. Cara wrote
the response to Todd's piece, and I believe I glanced at and—perhaps
shortsightedly—approved it before she faxed it to him.

Document 4

TODD:

So, I take it you like trucks. Here are a few of our suggestions: We
feel that your story would be more interesting if you could put it in a
context your audience would be more familiar with. Maybe tell us a
story about how you first saw this truck, and more of why you want it
besides all of the truck jargon I personally do *not* understand (Dodge
RAM 1500, 350 V8 engine). *Show* me what it looks like, color, size,
etc. Maybe write not that you need the money, but how you are going
to get it. Ask Mr. Baroz for some more suggestions. I'm sure this
could be much better if you kept your audience in mind. The sentence
I have underlined ("I also like to go off-roading and play in the
mud.") sounds funny (HA! HA!) if you think of it as getting out of
your truck and playing in the mud. Use description to keep the reader interested—a reader who knows *nothing* about trucks.

Cara's reply to Todd contains evidence of many of the tensions
that ran throughout the entire exchange. Significantly, Cara chose to
write the response in her own hand and to fax it to Vermont rather
than use the telecommunications system. Through the course of the
exchange, the editors found that email was an imperfect medium for
specific comments on the text, especially when the project required
responding to many separate pieces. Handwriting comments and fax-
ing them allowed students to compose responses at home, to emphasize portions of the text by underlining or marking without removing
them from the context of the piece, and to suggest their tone with
doodles and smiley faces in ways that the more limited format of
email text did not.

Here again, it is revealing to look closely at how language works
in one of the key documents. The use of personal pronouns in Cara's
response shows a distinct syntactic pattern for the different functions
of negative evaluation and constructive suggestions. Cara tends to
use the second person "we" only to describe general observations and
reactions, while she reserves her first person "I" for more incisive
critique. And she casts most of the constructive criticism at the
implied "you" of the imperative, thereby making it clear whose
responsibility change would be in this piece. Some examples:

- "*We* feel that your story would be more interesting . . ."
- "*I* personally do not understand . . ."

- "*I'm* sure this could be much better . . ."
- "The sentence *I* have underlined sounds funny . . ."
- "If *you* put it in a context . . ."
- "(*You*) Maybe tell us a story . . ."
- "(*You*) Use description to keep the reader interested—a reader who knows *nothing* about trucks."

This last example points to a minor but possibly significant confusion of audience implicit in Cara's response to Todd as well. Who is Todd's audience? Is it a set of three or four student editors and possibly a teacher who live at an inconceivable distance? Is it the vaguely imaginable readers of the not-yet-created publication—some people in this distant school as well as people in Todd's own school? I had not considered the multiplicity of the audience when I coached the Egalik girls to focus on audience. The audience for our own local version of this publication was, in hindsight, not an obvious mix. It included high school and middle school kids, school staff and administration members, elementary teachers who often read pieces to their students, as well as anyone else with whom any of the primary recipients shared the publication. So the result here shows up as ambiguity in Cara's reply. Cara alternates between referring to herself as his audience, and using the phrase "your audience" (Could Todd possibly have imagined Egalikans as "his" in any helpful way at this stage of the exchange?), and once as a generalized audience, "the reader . . . a reader who knows *nothing* about trucks."

My critique here is not to suggest that Cara's editing instincts are unsound. They are insightful and potentially helpful. The problem, rather, is in the context that the telecommunications exchange created for her. Because of the indistinct notions of audience for the student writing, and perhaps because of the "firm" tone of written text (as opposed to the more flexible nature of talk), Cara's editorial guidance adds momentum to the increasing centrifugal energy of the exchange. Todd's reply makes clear what Cara's selective use of personal pronouns and her reliance on imperative comments subtly hinted at: the polarization of the online community of writers and audiences into a local "us" and an alien "them," or the "right self" and "misguided other."

Todd's response, several days later, was an angry letter, addressed to "Egalik Editors/Andree" and sarcastically signed.

Document 5

Dear Egalik Editors/Andree:

To be perfectly honest with you, I really don't care what you think about my story about Dodge Rams. It is a story that I wrote for myself, not for you, and I really don't feel like explaining my truck to you. My suggestion to you is go to a Dodge dealer and learn about the truck and then read my story. Maybe then it will make sense to you.

Love,
Todd

The fact that Todd addresses this note to the "Egalik editors/Andree" further suggests the confusion of audience in this exchange of writing, and it also shows that Todd picked up from my previous note to Rob that Andree's style of responding was perhaps too blunt; he believed she was responsible for the rejection he felt in the feedback he received about his truck description. In fact, it was Cara who had responded to him. In this note, Todd clearly seeks to reclaim his piece. Note his emphasis on possession ("*my* story," "*I* wrote for *my*self"," *my* truck," "*my* suggestion") and the distinctions he makes between "you" and 'I" in almost every syntactic unit. Note also how his use of the imperative syntax mirrors Cara's use of it: in Todd's note, as in Cara's note, the "you," the reader, must do something for the literature to function as it should; for example, the reader is commanded "to go to a Dodge dealer and learn about the truck." Also, Todd's reply, like Cara's original response, uses the first person in some of the more cutting statements: "*I* really don't care what you think . . . , *I* really don't feel like explaining my truck to you." Once the early models for representing "other" begin to evolve, they become easily available options, especially in the face of challenges to identity.

Some days later, a brief exchange between Rob and me served to further kindle the tension between the two classrooms. Rob expressed frustration that faxes for two of his students contained information in conflict with previous faxes they had received during the development of the same pieces. Rob's closing touched a nerve with me, as I was watching my editors put in hour after hour, giving attention to each piece in the deluge of writing they downloaded from the network.

Document 6

2/23
From: Rob Baroz
To: Tom McKenna

I have told my kids that yours are swamped. I noticed in the faxes yesterday that there was a fax for Merle and one for Joan. The comments were different from the previous fax that they had received. How many kids are editing this issue? They were quite different in their comments. For instance, the previous one for Joan had said "wonderful" and a suggestion to change a word here or there. But the one that came yesterday had lots of suggestions for revisions. What gives?

2/23
From: Tom McKenna
To: Rob Baroz

What gives, I think, is that they're doing their best under the circumstances. Yesterday they were very distraught to find out that Merle had received mixed messages. (Andree has been absent for some time, so that's probably the rub.) But please, Rob, be patient with them. They really are putting in 100 percent. Thanks.

That day in class, I talked about my own frustrations, and read the exchange of notes between Rob and me, as I gave my daily briefing to the students in answer to their incessant question: "Has anything come from Vermont?"

The final document in this series is a note from Sandra, on behalf of the Egalik editors. Addressed to "Mr. Baroz and class," the note discusses the problem of multiple perspectives on a single submission, and it addresses Todd's reply in a manner that—from the first sentence—continued to escalate the tension.

Document 7

2/23/96
Dear Mr. Baroz and class,

We're sorry you are confused about our editing, but we are doing the best we can. We only have three editors assigned for this publication, and one has been gone for the past couple days of class.

Editing is like cutting a mat around a picture. We see an edge that isn't straight and we correct it. Then the straightened edge points out another corner or edge that isn't straight. Editing is a many-step process and we know we maybe could have made more of the corrections in one step. But it's hard when we're trying to make corrections on many pieces and we know that the corrections need to be faxed today in order for you to get them.

We have thought quite a bit about the editing process and have come up with a few changes that might help. We thought that if the editors had an opinion about changes in a piece, they could write it down on a Post-it note and post it to the piece. Then another editor would take a look at it and make their comments instead of just writing it on the piece. Right now, we're writing our comments on the piece and different editors have different opinions. This way, before anything was written on the piece to the author, the contradictions between editors could be worked out and maybe more of the corrections could be made in one step.

Todd—We're sorry if our comments sounded harsh about your piece. We were actually trying to make a joke, but maybe we shouldn't do that in the editing process. (We also figured you needed a little kidding because of your comment about girls that loved guys with mean trucks.) We're just trying to do our jobs to edit the piece

to become the best it can be. One of the things you will realize when
you're editing, is that the piece has to be geared toward the readers.
You've got some good detailed description in here, but you don't yet
bring us, as readers, along. (Sorry, no Dodge Dealer within 800
miles. :))

We really want this exchange to work and for us all to cooperate. Hopefully things will work a little better next publication?

Thanks, UHS editors

P.S. Can you let us know when we can expect the last versions of the
accepted pieces? Thanks again.

P.P.S. Cara and Marla would love a response to their personal correspondence if anyone has time.

The first sentence of this letter bears both sides of the truth. I have
no doubt the editors were sincere in their feelings of apology for the
tension that was escalating despite their long hours and painstaking
efforts. Yet, the syntax leads in the other direction. "We're sorry you
are confused about our editing" allows for the possibility that the
responsibility for the confusion is being assigned to the CVU students.

Paragraphs two and three of this note testify to the serious thinking the Egalik students were doing about the confusion. I happened to
visit the group while they were working out the mat metaphor, but I
learned about the Post-it note strategy for avoiding contradictions
only when I approved the draft of the note for uploading.

Still, they seem destined to offend. Although the fourth paragraph
was designed to ease the tension with Todd, it continues to assign the
responsibility for the misunderstanding to him. The pronoun selection
in "We're sorry if our comments sounded harsh" protects the authors
of the comments from responsibility, and places at least some emphasis on the reader's responsibility. And after admitting that maybe they
shouldn't have made a joke in this process of editing, the editors go
on to sneak a couple of additional jokes between parentheses. Like
most jokes, they reveal substantive underlying issues, in this case
involving gender dynamics and aspects of culture.

Responding to an obvious need for levity, the Egalikans seem
inclined to offend because of the complexities of the context and the
constraints of the medium rather than a sheer lack of tact. Jokes cannot be depended on to be heard as friendly in the singular dimension
of email text any more than they might in a foreign language. Todd's
unfamiliarity with his audience made the original gender issue touchy,
and the editors' response posed a danger of ridicule to Todd, since it
appeared in such a public forum as an online note to the teacher and
the students. Sandra's typed-in smiley face indicated a conscious
acknowledgment that the textual resources were perhaps inadequate

to convey the reconciliatory tone that was needed at this point in the exchange.

The Dodge Ram incident contained many important opportunities for student learning. Egalik students needed to do significant problem solving to trace the sources of the bad feelings that were developing, and this, in turn, required extensive dialogue with me and with one another. The conversations that ensued from these "failures" contained the kind of serious reflection, metacognition, and involvement that I have always desired in my classroom. Just yesterday, Rob reminded me of the day our first publication came out. Martha, a student writer from his class, had literally jumped up in the air and spun around when she saw her piece as the lead story in the publication. In Rob's words, "Come on, how often does that happen in your classroom?"

But I suspect that for every Martha there is at least one Todd, and perhaps there are other students who simply choose not to be involved in writing because they sense the risks that real writing contexts involve. I would contend that these risks are often worth taking, but that they are not often understood in the simple terms of "mastery of tasks" or even "engagement." Despite the students' honest desire to make things work, their own language often worked to distance them from one another and their goals, until they began to represent themselves as righteous, and their collaborators as hostile.

Although there may have been much Rob and I could have done to mitigate these tensions, I have come to see this type of representation of "other" as a troubling syndrome in many telecommunications exchanges. Though we may continually attempt to infuse into our teaching a sensitivity to remote and different cultures, we need to rethink our "easy" notions of authentic audiences and telecommunications communities, and remain mindful of the opportunities these exchanges provide for taking a close look at what's going on right at home.

Certainly, I still believe that transgeographical and cross-cultural telecommunications exchanges contain enormous potential for promoting reflection, teaching tolerance, and refining our understanding of different cultures. Yet, I find that the context of exchanges — with their odd mixes of our classroom cultures and depersonalized encounters with others — can create the opposite effect. When we link classrooms with distinct cultural identities, we as teachers are usually cognizant of the tensions those distinct differences create. Yet, I wonder if we are as aware of the *subtle* differences that exist between classrooms that seem, on the surface, to have much in common. Ignoring subtle differences of classroom cultures (i.e., how work is valued; how work gets done; how work gets talked about) may often lead to the kinds of tensions I have described in this chapter. If our differing classroom norms can lead to this kind of miscommunication and mis-representation across a relatively mild gradient of cultural difference, the implications resonate for more ambitious efforts at cross-cultural telecommunications collaboration.

Afterword
Robert Baroz
Champlain Valley Union High School
Hinesburg, VT

In the conclusion to his account of our project, Tom points out the implications of the experience: When relatively similar classrooms use telecommunications to collaborate, the potential for misunder-standing and miscommunication is indeed real. When we use telecommunications to link classrooms representing *distinctly differ-ent* cultures, the potential is magnified. As teachers, we need to be aware of subtle differences among classroom cultures — as well as the obvious ones — when we connect using telecommunications. Furthermore, we should help our students to understand these differ-ences. One way to facilitate this understanding would be for teachers to talk openly with their students and with other teachers about the work in the curriculum, especially the variety of ways teachers might go about cultivating the learning through the classroom norms that they establish over time.

I do not mean to imply that teachers who participate in networked communication activities need to standardize their class activities. Not by any means. Rather, what is important is talk about what hap-pens in the classroom, i.e., complex shared-inquiry with components of reflection and analysis. I envision such dialogue with students as exemplifying what Dixie Goswami refers to as "a new form of pro-fessional development," one that transcends the boundary of our classroom and supports new learning made possible by cross-cultural exchanges with telecommunications.

In my experience, this kind of reflective dialogue about learning is rare among students. And it's not that common among teachers, either, so I am not surprised that little of it happens online. With regard to Tom's and my experience in our project, I would argue that this sort of dialogue is precisely what is needed as a starting point to address the tensions that can potentially arise in online communica-tion when students and teachers hold different assumptions about learning. Students ought to be involved, sharing with each other their observations about learning.

Since the exchange with Tom's students, I've adapted Ken Macrorie's approach to writing with its roots in regular freewriting and frequent feedback. But at the time of our exchange, Tom's class had been working together in this way for several months, whereas my students had been together for only a week. When Tom's students provided specific recommendations regarding freewriting and their expectations for how the exchange would be an extension of what they did in class, my students said, "What makes them such experts on what good writing is?" A timely discussion between our students, on the writing process and the expectations of the project, would have helped our students to avoid the "insider/outsider" or "us-and-them" tensions that Tom observed.

We didn't, however, avail ourselves of the benefit of participating in such a discussion; we simply held to our differing assumptions about what constitutes shared inquiry online. Perhaps my students felt that they were being asked to subordinate themselves to the Alaskan students; some students, like Todd, who wrote the Dodge Ram piece, I suspect were unwilling to submit to this process, especially since they had no part in determining how writing got selected, responded to, or rejected.

I do not want to create a picture that all students were unhappy. A majority enjoyed seeing their writing published. In fact, one student returned a year later asking for more copies to share with her older brother, about whom she had written. How often do students display such enthusiasm over their work? As Tom recounted, my student Martha was so overjoyed when her writing was chosen as the lead story that she jumped and twirled in the air. I hope the writing projects my students do in my classes, such as this project with students in Alaska, are ones they will value a year or even years later. Is there any better standard by which to value a writing curriculum or writing project?

I believe, had there been a greater extent of discussion of activities, both within our classes and online, Tom, our students, and I would have developed a shared set of expectations about the ways telecommunications could support the goal of producing a publication. Indeed, the collaboration and shared inquiry would mean that the students would work together as a research team and become authorities about the learning process in their own classroom. Who else would have better firsthand experience of the activities? At the same time, through collaboration across boundaries with others involved in a telecommunication project, students and their teacher can become familiar with the ideas and practices in classrooms where the culture of learning varies from their own.

8

Reflective Voices
Constructing Meaning in the USjApanLINK Project

Kurt Caswell
Douglas E. Wood

When the devastating earthquake hit Kobe, Japan, in the winter of 1995, a number of frantic messages passed through cyberspace. Some American students in Columbia, South Carolina, wanted to know if their new friends in Hokkaido were all right. They knew from their studies in geography that Hokkaido was in the far north of Japan, but they also knew that big earthquakes were preceded and followed by smaller quakes that could also be life threatening. Among the many questions that the Americans asked about the quake was one that stands witness to how close the American students had become to a group of Japanese students. Did the Japanese students have family in the south, they wanted to know, and were they all right? Such questions suggest the emotions not of mere acquaintances, but of friends. As it turned out, some of the Japanese students did have family near Kobe, but much to everyone's relief, none of them was injured.

The story of the USjApanLINK Internet Project has simple beginnings. We (Doug and Kurt) met during the summer of 1994 at the Bread Loaf School of English at Middlebury College in Middlebury, Vermont. We were both teaching in different corners of the world, Doug at Summit Parkway, in Columbia, South Carolina, and Kurt at Academy of Clark's Spirit (ACS) Gakuin, in Chitose, Hokkaido, Japan. We decided to design a project that would engage our two classes in correspondence throughout the coming academic year. But this was to be no pen pal exchange. We outlined a year-long, week-by-week curriculum of focused writing and reading projects, and funded our online costs with a grant entitled "Advocacy and Action for Cross-Cultural Understanding." Then, as a second thought, we began to imagine a trip to Japan by the American students as the culmination of our project. The Japanese students would host the American students for eight days in Chitose.

On both sides of the exchange, there was a genuine need for improvement on the existing curricula. In Chitose, classes were made up of students who, after regular school hours, desired more practical English study. They wanted to learn how to speak the language. To learn to speak, they would need an authentic audience. They would need to correspond with real people. When we wrote the research proposal, we assumed that the project would help the Japanese students to improve both their spoken and written English.

In Columbia, the project was implemented in one of three thematic units making up the geography curriculum: "World War II: A Severing of Connections." We hoped that the project would provide students with a new lens through which to see Japan. Instead of focusing completely on books, articles, and newsreels, the students would have the opportunity to move beyond the limited collection of classroom materials and engage in personal connections with Japanese students. On the American side, we proposed that the project would change students' attitudes about Japan.

In order for a telecommunications project to move beyond the pen pal stage, it must be driven by the existing curriculum and have a clear focus. The curriculum must drive the technology, not the other way around. Grounded in meaningful, authentic activities, the curriculum transforms itself throughout the exchange and ultimately provides students with a legitimate reason for using technology as a tool for learning. Furthermore, it provides teachers with a rich compilation of student writing for subsequent reflections about their own teaching practices.

At Summit Parkway Middle School, we created a student-centered exploratory class with the teacher as facilitator. The seventh graders in the exploratory class were chosen randomly. The eighth graders were chosen to join the project as an extracurricular course based on their previous academic merit. They met twice a week after school.

The Summit Parkway classroom was equipped with eight computers, two of which were linked to the students in Japan via modem. Three of the computers were portable and could be taken home by the students to work on assignments. Throughout the project, students completed their assignments in their journals and on computer disk. We noted with interest that some students preferred to compose their writing on the computer first and then later transfer the information to their journals. When the students completed their assignments, they edited one another's work and then revised. One student in the class was designated to upload the writing to the Internet. By uploading all the student's work at one time, we avoided excessive long-distance telephone costs that would have resulted from so many students individually uploading their work and being online for long periods. This method of uploading text is efficient and cost-saving not only for the sender, but also for the receiver. In Japan, we were able to save all the writing in one or two files, thus avoiding the tedious task of downloading numerous individual files, and long periods of time online. The whole process could often be completed in under one minute. Although one student was charged with this task, each student was trained to upload and download text.

ACS Gakuin in Chitose is a private English academy where students of all ages come to study spoken English. Because the school is private rather than public, it was perhaps easier to implement changes in the curriculum right away. Four classes of high school students worked on the project, each meeting once a week. In Japan, we chose high school students to correspond with the middle school students at Summit Parkway because we assumed that Japanese high schoolers would be better able to read and write in English than younger Japanese students, encouraging greater communication between the two groups despite the difference in ages. The students at Summit Parkway didn't mind having older partners, and the Japanese students were eager to learn about American culture through practicing the English language. In the public schools in Japan, students study mostly grammar in English class. They came to ACS to *use* the English language. In retrospect, the correlation of language ability between the American middle school students and the older Japanese students proved to be a successful part of the design.

In contrast to the technology access in the classroom at Summit Parkway, ACS did not have access to a single computer other than Kurt's personal notebook computer. With only one computer, Kurt had to collect student writing at school and upload it at home. Correspondence from Summit Parkway had to be formatted for each individual, then printed and copied. Uploading and downloading at Summit Parkway were easy compared to this often mundane task. It was not unusual for Kurt to spend upwards of three hours formatting and printing documents from one download. This was one of the great disadvantages of not having computers in the classroom, but the quality of the students' work and their enthusiasm for the project was well worth the hours at the terminal.

Without a computer in the classroom, students at ACS Gakuin did not have much opportunity to learn how to use email. Surprisingly, Japanese public schools are years behind American schools in educational technology. In-class demonstrations helped, but with such little hands-on training, the students did not experience the real power of electronic mail and computer networking.

The planned activities in our curriculum included the exchange of autobiographical narratives, a chronicle of eight days in each student's life, favorite poems and songs, gift boxes, and the reading of John Elder's book about Japan, *Following the Brush*. The autobiographical narratives described families, schools, and communities. Through these introductory narratives each student found a partner with whom they would correspond for the rest of the year. In "Eight Days," which proved to be very popular, the students recorded and exchanged written accounts of events from eight consecutive days. The students were able to observe and reflect on the layers of detail in the daily lives of their partners, and the activity generated a spontaneous interchange of questions and answers. At this point the students became engaged in meaningful discussions about their lives, and the exchange took on a life of its own. In conjunction with "Eight Days," we exchanged care packages by mail to deepen each other's understanding of our respective communities. These packages included cultural artifacts such as foods, maps, brochures, photographs, and local magazines and newspapers. During the Christmas holidays, project partners exchanged individual gifts. The students at Summit Parkway received gifts such as lacquered chopsticks, green tea, origami paper with an instructional book, and a calligraphy brush with ink. The students at ACS received illustrated books, American music and magazines, a Native American dreamcatcher, and personal home videos. Following this gift exchange, the students grew increasingly comfortable with each other. They exchanged favorite poems and songs, and many wrote personally about their own lives. During the last weeks of the project, we focused on reading and responding to *Following the Brush*. The book chronicles the author's experiences with his family while living in Japan. John Elder joined the exchange online, answering questions and engaging students in discussions about life in Japan.

In addition to the planned online writing activities, we studied the culture, history, and contemporary issues of the United States and Japan through books, articles, and guest speakers. At Summit Parkway, professors from the University of South Carolina and other knowledgeable people from the greater Columbia community presented their insights on Japan. Mrs. Lin, a Japanese American and the mother of two of the American students involved in the project, taught the delicate art of calligraphy and some of the basics of the

Japanese language. Since true community is founded on a give-and-take relationship, we felt that if the Japanese students could communicate in English, the American students should try to communicate in Japanese. A rudimentary understanding of basic Japanese was enough to demonstrate to the students in Chitose the American students' appreciation for the Japanese language.

After the project, we examined the transcripts, looking for emerging themes and patterns. One of the most obvious patterns was "interaction between students," which we coded as weak, moderate, and strong. We identified Braden Core and his partner Chihiro Tosaka, and Alexandra Powell and her partner Kanako Nomoto as having strong interactions. We asked each of these students to reflect upon their experiences with the USjApanLINK project. Their stories are compelling and we hope inspirational for teachers who wish to use technology to facilitate cultural understanding.

An Epic Experience

When I moved to Columbia, South Carolina in 1993, I wasn't expecting anything special. But when I entered Mr. Wood's social studies classroom, the door to technology opened for me. Inside that classroom were all of the computers you could ever ask for. I was excited because I could develop the computer skills I had learned at my old school. With Mr. Wood, we tackled many technological projects, and it became my favorite class.

Corresponding with my partner Chihiro Tosaka was fun and interesting. The visit to Japan was an absolutely wonderful experience and made a great end to the project. I will always remember the wonderful atmosphere, the almost overcourteous people of Japan, the unbelievable first day in Chitose, and the exciting last day in Sapporo. The trip to Japan was so much more than just a trip. It was an epic experience. The people and their ways and culture have left a lasting impression on me. This experience has fueled my interest so much I want to learn, study, and hopefully visit many different countries and cultures.

But just because the project has ended, does not mean that my learning and cultural growth has to end. I'm still receiving letters from the students in Japan. Chihiro, despite having difficulty speaking in English, writes very well in English. In one of her letters she wrote, "I can talk so much in the letter, and yet I couldn't talk with you when in Japan. It is strange."

After the project, I worked with a group of students to create a World Wide Web site about our trip. The site includes pictures and other multimedia examples of our experiences in Japan. It was a long process, but it was great fun and turned out wonderfully. All of this goes to show that the end of a project does not at all have to mean the end of the experience.

Braden Core, Columbia, South Carolina

Something Fresh

For a long time, I have wanted to improve my English and learn more about the United States. Through the USjApanLINK Project, my English skills got stronger, and I learned a lot about the way people live and think in the U.S.A.

Before this project, I had no experience writing letters in English. I discovered right away that real American English is very different from my school textbook. I know my English letters were clumsy and sometimes hard to understand for my partner Braden, but I got a lot of writing practice, and when I received a letter from Braden, I learned a lot of practical English too.

My strongest memory of the project is when we exchanged gifts. The gift box contained music tapes of current popular songs in the U.S., and magazines young Americans read. But what made me most happy was the Christmas card from Braden. In Japan, we normally don't exchange Christmas cards. I found it something fresh.

I was embarrassed when I first met Braden at the Kenshu Center youth hostel at Lake Shikotsu. He looked much older than me. Even though Braden talked to me a lot, I was so nervous that I couldn't talk to him well. In our letters, I could write and express myself. But I could not talk with him face to face. I regret my hesitation. I should have talked with Braden more, and not worried about my poor English.

One of the things I noticed about the students from Summit Parkway is that they are very friendly with everyone, even students of different grades. They all played games and danced together. It isn't like this in Japan. We have such a gap between the social life of junior and senior classes in school. I hope that Japanese students can learn to be more like Americans in this respect.

When we began the project, I was not a very good English student, and I didn't have much interest in computers. Through the year, the project gave me a stronger and stronger motivation to learn the English language. I also enjoyed learning about the power of computers. Now I want to learn more about computers, and meet people from all over the world using email. Perhaps this motivation for study is how the project has changed me most.

Chihiro Tosaka, Chitose, Hokkaido, Japan

Yesterday and Tomorrow

When I was in the seventh grade, I was clueless about computers. That is, until I walked into Mr. Wood's social studies class. I was bombarded with computer language, computer programs, computer everything. It was overwhelming. After only a week, I moved beyond the basics of word processing, and discovered so many possibilities!

Still, I didn't realize how useful this new knowledge was until Mr. Wood got me involved in the USjApanLINK Project during my eighth-grade year. As part of the project, he asked us to keep a journal throughout the year. The following is an excerpt from my journal the night before we departed for Japan:

June 5, 1995

ANTICIPATION! That's my word of the day. Why? Well, maybe its because a whole school year of preparation is finally coming to a climax. Tomorrow I leave for Japan. And it's funny, up until now I've kept so calm and collected. On Friday, Mom asked, "How can you stay so calm and not be bursting with excitement?" Well, I told her that soon enough, the reality of this whole thing would set in. And today I got a BIG reality check. When I think back on when all of this started, I really didn't see myself actually going, and to be honest, the whole thing has gone by so fast I haven't had time to swallow up the situation. Today, I looked back through my journal and read my very first entry, and the author of that entry was so unaware of the future and the magnitude of it all. Tomorrow, I am going into another country, while my family lives in "yesterday." I am walking into a totally different culture, where people have preserved their heritage for thousands of years. I have gone from knowing zilch about the country and its people, to learning some of its language and getting a personal look at the people. For the last nine months I've been preparing and waiting for this day. I've been trying to evaluate the situation and ask myself if I am truly ready for what lies ahead. So am I ready? Am I? Yes!!!!

My trip was absolutely wonderful. I saw many sights, took a million pictures, and had many unique experiences with Japanese food. But unlike a tourist, I returned home with much more. New friends. My partner Kanako and I have so much in common with each other. During our visit, we learned about each other's interests, families, and beliefs. I must admit that at first I was terrified of technology. But through the project, technology became secondary to me. It was the people I was communicating with that were important.

Alexandra Powell, Columbia, South Carolina

Face to Face

Everything that happened during the project was new and exciting for me. Until this time, I had no experience to correspond with foreigners. I had heard about email but had no idea what it was, or how to use it.

Before the project, I worried that my partner would not understand my English letters, and wondered if I could understand the letters from my partner. But Ali's letters were easy to understand. They contained a lot of new information about her everyday school life. I tried to write about things in Japan as they really were. Ali and

I exchanged email letters almost once a week. For me, it was like exchanging personal diaries, and I began to feel that Ali was my very close friend in the U.S.A. As the project continued, I wanted to meet her in person, and talk with her face to face. I was surprised to hear that the students at Summit Parkway raised enough money to come to Japan by selling goods and doing part-time jobs. I don't think it would be possible in Japan. Thanks to the hard work of so many people, my wish came true.

I was a little nervous as the arrival day approached. But when I met Ali for the first time, my fears were gone at once. It was not only Ali's cheerful personality that made me so comfortable, but we felt like friends already through our email correspondence. During Ali's stay, we made a lot of joyful memories. We talked about things we had said in our correspondence, and enjoyed time together on the day trips, at the welcome party, and going to a sushi house with my family. For me, meeting Ali face to face was better than writing to her using email. But I realize now that meeting her was so enjoyable because we had already become friends through our email exchange.

I am thankful to Mr. Caswell and this program for broadening my horizons of life. And I want to thank Ali Powell, my irreplaceable partner.

Kanako Nomoto, Chitose, Hokkaido, Japan

Teachers, administrators, and policy makers can learn a great deal from Kanako, Chihiro, Ali, and Braden. Chihiro identified a fundamental point about learning language skills when she wrote, "In our letters, I could write and express myself." The exchange offered Chihiro an avenue for self-expression, that of writing for an authentic audience. Knowing that real people are going to read and respond to writing gives student writers a sense of purpose. For Chihiro, and all of the students involved, the exchange was an opportunity to write freely about their hopes, dreams, aspirations, and to reflect, not only through their own writing, but on the writing of others.

In addition to writing with purpose, the exchange offered teachers and students the opportunity to meet and engage in the kind of personal contact that can greatly improve a budding relationship. Kanako wrote, "For me, meeting Ali face to face was better than writing to her using email." We would caution, however, that it is important to verify the personal integrity of all parties concerned before planning any face to face meeting.

Braden Core reminds us of another important aspect of electronic mail exchanges. He wrote, "This experience has fueled my interest so much I want to learn, study, and hopefully visit many different countries and cultures. . . . Just because I have returned home from Japan does not mean that my learning and cultural growth has to end." Braden's discovery about lifelong learning and motivation speaks to the value of technology in education. Engaging, meaningful discourse in academic settings provides students with experiences that motivate them to probe deeper, question further, and pursue ongoing learning opportunities.

Finally, as teachers, we must be aware that however valuable technology is, it can also be abused. Therefore, it is important to plan the use of technology around a curriculum with the student at its center. Remember what Ali wrote in her journal: "technology eventually became secondary to me. It was the people I was communicating with that were important." When we put the students first, we ensure that technology remains a tool in the classroom and never interferes with the development of valuable human relationships.

But as teachers, we should not be too rigid in determining the curriculum. It was the students' personal relationships with each other that drove the correspondence, sometimes sending discussions in new and worthwhile directions that we could not have anticipated. Our job was to strike a balance between adhering to already established framework and letting the students direct their own academic pursuits. Our decision to support the students' inquiry gave them ownership. We have learned that success in a project like this requires a flexible curriculum so that there is a balance between structure and freedom.

Further examination of the transcripts from the students' correspondence helped us learn a great deal more. We found that students on both sides of the exchange better understood the language, culture, history, and contemporary issues of not only their counterparts, but their own country as well. We noticed improvement in the Japanese students' writing, and greater confidence in their spoken English. Although Chihiro laments her lack of confidence, she greatly improved her personal skills as a communicator through the course of the project. The American students began to develop an understanding of Japan as a complex culture of customs and rituals. They not only learned about Japanese culture in the classroom, they lived it. In our minds, the USjApanLINK Project's greatest success is the consistent pattern of increased trust and friendship among the students, a trust we think is rare in academic environments. This kind of trust, which develops between good friends and family members, has positive effects on student learning. In many ways, the exchange opened the students' minds more than we could have imagined. Chihiro articulates how this technology helps students become lifelong learners when she says, "Now I want to learn more about computers, and meet people from all over the world using email. Perhaps this motivation is how the project has changed me most."

9

Using Computer Conferencing to Extend the Bounds of the Writing Curriculum
Or, How I Quit the Symphony and Joined a Jazz Band

Claire Bateman
Fine Art Center, Greenville, SC

Chris Benson
Clemson University

Boundary. What does that mean?
A place where something ends
Or the refrain we hear constantly.
This is a boundary; stop here.
Don't touch that, him, her.
Don't step there; danger awaits.
Beware of the dog,
The infectious disease,
The broken sidewalk,
Where our family ends
And yours begins.
　　　　　　—Clint, ninth grader, South Carolina

I receive mail from around the world on a variety of topics.
After I read it, I write maybe a dozen thoughtful replies. I store
copies of the correspondence in an archive. No I'm not a
masochist. I'm just another digital slave, hunched over an
ever-expanding file of unanswered electronic mail, tap-tapping
at the computer keyboard, in the grip of an absurd passion
that's hard to explain to those not yet similarly afflicted.
　　　　　　—Richard Starr

An Electronic Landscape

The setting is South Carolina, an irregular triangular state, a little puzzle piece extending from the Atlantic Coast to the foothills of the Appalachians, a state whose economic and educational ranking is relatively low compared to those of others, a state where people tend to focus on what is practical and right in front of them, their families, their towns, their daily concerns. The setting is six South Carolina schools—one university, one technical college, and four high schools—each of them rural, isolated, and remote from the others. The setting is a few brutal weeks of winter in a state poorly equipped for winter, a time when pipes freeze and burst, the flu rampages through the population, and the only desire people feel is to hunker down in blankets in front of the TV flickering like a hearth, a time for hibernation, not intellectual ventures and collaboration with strangers. The setting is the hearts and minds of young people of varied racial and economic derivations and differing ambitions. The setting includes a dozen poems they've agreed to explore together over a period of five weeks. The setting is cyberspace, an unfamiliar landscape that is everywhere and nowhere at once, an invisible web of electronic communication that all of them—students, teachers, and an "online poet in residence"—will spin together from the tentative strands of their individual thoughts.

Such was the anticipation of the participants who undertook the Online Poetry Project, a telecommunications venture sponsored by the Bread Loaf School of English, Middlebury College, in the early weeks of 1994. While use of the Internet by students and teachers is not nearly as uncommon as it used to be, rural schools still have trouble finding money for equipment and service access, and this project would not have been possible without the technical support of Bread Loaf and access to its computer conferencing system, BreadNet, which connects hundreds of English teachers, who are students or alumni of Bread Loaf, and their students across the country and the world.

In our experience, the Internet is a web of information superhighways where thirty million people on the planet, most of them strangers to each other, commute daily. And some researchers have noted that communication on the Internet, on the other hand, is characteristically impersonal; emotions, when they are expressed, tend to be negative (Hiltz, Johnson, and Turoff 1986, 228). But the cold climate of the Internet contrasts with the friendliness of the people traversing BreadNet, which is like a small town where most people know each other. There are no visible police on BreadNet. Most of the conference work is public space, and the same manners that are expected in public classrooms are exhibited on BreadNet. There is very little swearing; "hell" and "damn" are not uncommon, but the use of other four-letter words is very rare. When there is disagreement, it is between ideas, not people. To our knowledge, there has never been an instance of "flaming" on BreadNet, the Internet equivalent of flipping someone the finger in traffic.

One reason that BreadNet tends toward greater friendliness is that most of the teachers using it share the experience of having studied at Bread Loaf; many become close colleagues through that experience, and project ideas that connect classrooms via BreadNet are often spawned during the summers of study at Bread Loaf.

Thus began the Online Poetry Project. The participants began this collaborative study of poetry, in part, to test the claims that others have made about computer conferencing's ability to transform classrooms, curricula, methods of classroom interaction, and ways of looking at knowledge. In fact, they found that their study of poetry led them further from traditional ways of reading poetry in school. The conference experience led the "conferees" to find ways of integrating poetry into their lives in what can only be described as a nonscholastic experience. Before we tell the story of this project, we'd like to offer a few reflections on classroom discourse, oral and written, which we feel will shed some light on our story.

Talking and Writing in the Classroom

Most teachers and students are at least subconsciously aware of the traditional hierarchy of power at work in the public schools. Though public education likes to pretend it is fully democratic, it exhibits a tower of hierarchy as sturdy as that of corporate America. State department officials dictate to local superintendents; local supers dictate to principals, principals to teachers and professional staff, and staff to building custodians and students. Students remain at the bottom. Students may not express it this way, but they are aware of it since it is, after all, a culture they've been trained in. In fact, students may be more aware of the rigid hierarchy than their teachers are. For instance, let's take the term "class discussion." To the teacher, it may mean a chance for students to have a break from "hearing my voice," to express their own reactions and interpretations, to engage in a lively dialogue generally focusing on, but not necessarily limited to, the given subject, probably a reading assignment, in the context of other similar discussions that have preceded this one. To the student, however, "class discussion" may be a temporary relief from taking notes *or* a confusing time when it is unclear whether one should in fact be taking notes. Class discussion may seem to students like a landscape that hides hundreds of land mines just under the surface—occasions to be *wrong* about the interpretation of the text, to blurt out something that proves one has not read or retained the material, to betray an insufficient understanding of previous material, even if this is not the case. But then, a strictly self-maintained silence may give an *identical* impression!

Such is the complexity of student/teacher relationships in the tower of power that is the public educational system. But peer relationships among students further complicate discussion of subject matter, and we intend to focus on this as well. Imagine the myriad ways an adolescent might see himself or herself in relation to peers: There is the studious one, the dweeb, the one with the squeaky voice, the bullshitter, the one who displays pseudo-intelligence by dissing the views of the teacher or another student, the smartass who gets by on wit, the obfuscater who diverts the conversation long enough for the bell to ring so no homework can be assigned.

Indeed, a class discussion may be thought of not so much as an open arena, a forum for the development of ideas, but rather as a dense jungle where the inhabitants, insecure in their territory, survive by various strategies of camouflage, mimicry, subterfuge, and predation. Students realize the law of the jungle prevails, that they are not equal in insight, reading and articulation, and social fluency. Discussion periods in classrooms can be a test of academic and social survival as much as they are opportunities to learn.

Likewise, writing, even freewriting, may seem to the student a process that is anything but "free." Everything a student writes has implications in terms of evaluation by one's teacher or peers; students and teachers hold many unspoken but powerful assumptions about the nature of "correct" writing in the traditional academic culture. Kenneth Bruffee (1983), among others with similar observations, has succinctly described the relationship of writer to reader in academia: "The tradition sees the writer as an individual who prepares a product designed to have a specific effect on another individual. That person in turn is obliged to read defensively, with conscious awareness of the writer's design. The relationship between writer and reader tends to be adversarial" (159). While in this passage Bruffee is not specifically speaking about writing for a grade, the description certainly applies to graded writing, for the relationship between student as writer and the teacher as evaluator is certainly adversarial. The burden is on the student to convince the teacher that he or she has mastered the material and can formulate it in an acceptable, often prescribed, fashion.

When students and teachers perceive grades as the primary reason for school writing, communication is skewed, we think. Moffett notes this in *Teaching the Universe of Discourse* (1987) when he says that student writers "almost always find the teacher entirely *too* significant. He is at once parental substitute, civic authority, and the wielder of marks. Any one of these roles would be potent enough to destroy the writer-audience relationship" (193). Writing for a grade undermines the rhetorical context where communication is supposed to take place and creates a different task: proving that the student has mastered the required content and the prescribed form of presenting it. Nowhere outside of academia do we know of a person who writes for such a reason. In the workplace, such a practice would be absurd. Since school writing is intended to give practice in writing for life, we believe school assignments should more closely mimic the dynamic that is observed between writers and real audiences. What is a real audience? One that has need of the information or insights a writer possesses; one that responds to the content of the writing.

Planning an Online Poetry Project

The teachers participating in the Online Poetry Project used their BreadNet connection in the fall of the school year to plan a computer conference that would bring students online in the winter. From the start, it was agreed that while the teachers would create a basic outline for the discussion, they would also leave room for students to create and manipulate the curriculum as it evolved. Since none of the participating teachers had ever done an online collaborative study, the conversation in the early online planning focused on the question "What does an online collaborative study of poetry look like?" All participants voiced opinions: One said, "Let's get a poet to join us!" Another asked, "Who will pick the poems?" Another teacher wrote a poem that seemed to imply no planning was necessary; all they needed to do was to get started writing poems: "We celebrate what we know/We celebrate what we will learn/We celebrate our likeness and we celebrate our diversities/ . . . because our tapestry is too beautiful . . . for us to unravel/into anger, violence, chaos, and confusion." After much discussion, a minimalist open-ended structure was chosen to allow the conferees to explore a variety of ideas. This structure consisted of:

1. allowing students at the beginning of the project to post personal notes introducing themselves to the rest of the conferees

2. limiting the length of the study to five weeks, with each of the five participating classrooms leading one week's discussion

3. asking students to choose two or three poems to present online to the conferees and to lead the discussion for that week

4. requiring all the conferees to engage in the discussion online

5. finding a recognized poet to present and discuss some of her
   poems with the students

Aside from these few parameters, the project was left open-ended. No
formal objective or goal beyond having students discuss poetry
online, in writing, was posited, although Janet, a high school teacher
in a small mill town, said she hoped students would eventually write
poems as part of the project. Firmly, Janet described for the rest of us
one important purpose of the collaborative project:

> I am still sure that what I want to do is to lead my students to use
> poetry to talk about their real life experience. I want them to be able
> to see that poetry is not something for the erudite, upper class, but
> that it can be for all people. I want them to hear the speakers and
> then to become speakers. I want them to learn to use imagery and
> language and self-expression, and I want them to see it modeled in
> published poets and in their own classmates' work.

Such were the general goals of the project beginnings: to encourage
intelligent discussion about poetry relevant to students' lives.

Afraid that a wide-open selection of poems would create a sense
of chaos or confusion of ideas, all the teachers agreed early on that the
study should have a theme, which would help the students to explore
ideas in depth. Two themes that students helped to choose were "family" and "boundaries." Obviously, the theme "family" was relevant to
students. The theme "boundaries," being less concrete and perhaps
more unfamiliar to teenagers, was encouraged by Claire Bateman,
the project's "online poet in residence":

> The theme of boundaries might be an interesting one that would
> leave a lot of room for variety. For example, boundaries [exist]
> between the human and the natural worlds, as in James Wright's
> poem 'A Blessing' in which the speaker encounters two Indian
> ponies. Or boundaries [exist] between the human and the divine, as
> in James Dickey's poem 'Falling,' about a flight attendant falling out
> of an airplane—he imagines her as undergoing a sort of transforma-
> tion as she descends, entering into myth. And of course, boundaries
> between people—family, race, etc., as in Phil Levine's poem 'What
> Work Is,' in which the speaker confesses that though he knows all
> about hard physical labor, he is unable to do the emotional work of
> telling his brother that he loves him.

No one at the beginning of the project realized how intertwined our
dual focuses on boundaries and family would become.

Chuck, English department head and teacher at the two-year technical college, agreed with Claire about the potential of boundaries to
enhance the project: "I prefer 'boundaries' as the topic. I feel that we
are establishing new boundaries through telecommunications, and

that seems like a logical place to go." Chuck also added some advice on choosing poems:

> A good poem is like any good story, it lets the reader in bit by bit, it builds, and it rewards the reader with meaning. Further, I want to see us all start "remembering the story" of a poem, and get away from the artificial measurements of sound and sense, which is crafting, and not meaning. For that reason, I suggest we choose poems that have a clearly implied story.

Erasing the Boundaries of Knowledge

Obviously, an open-ended project like this would be exciting, like a voyage to uncharted places. In such an enterprise, each decision is based not necessarily on where one is going but on where one has been and what's happening at the moment. Though traditional curricula typically lead students through a course designed to increase their knowledge and skills in a certain area, the participants of the Online Poetry Project recognized from the beginning that this project was, in that sense, untraditional. In fact, the subject under study would turn out to be the lives of participants in the project as much as it was the poems themselves. This open-endedness and flexibility in the curricular design is based on the idea that knowledge is socially constructed, and that knowledge and experience are continually reevaluated in relation to new knowledge and experience. It's a way of learning in the moment. Computer conferences provide the perfect forum for learning in the moment.

By their collaborative and discursive nature, computer conferences accrete information that is open-ended, always under consideration. The participants in a computer conference are actively engaged in *generating* knowledge as well as mastering existing knowledge. This kind of learning experience is radically different from the way textbooks have traditionally presented information, as discrete, concrete building blocks that are fixed just as real bricks are fixed in mortar. Although most textbooks make a pretense of asking students to speculate by posing open-ended questions at the end of a chapter, such a linear, lockstep approach doesn't easily lead to new questions, new ideas, or new knowledge, and students must continually be prompted to speculate. Students in an online discussion, however, have a greater opportunity to speculate, and the discursive and collaborative nature of online conferencing often leads to greater and more elaborate insights.

In their book *The Quantum Society: Mind, Physics, and a New Social Vision* (1994), Danah Zohar and Ian Marshall reiterate scientific concepts that illustrate how knowledge is constructed in nonlinear fashion. Visiting the ideas of physicist Von Foerster, they discover his theorem has remarkable application to the manner in which individuals generate knowledge:

> Von Foerster's Theorem itself was originally formulated to describe the behavior of cybernetic systems, systems that achieve a kind of internal, homeostatic control through the free exchange of information between the parts (e.g., our central heating systems, most information technology systems, and many of our own biological functions). To our mechanistically conditioned imaginations, the theorem seems to go against common sense. It argues that if one element of a system is rigidly determined, rigidly fixed in place, that element loses its relationship to the whole. It becomes isolated, or "alienated." Conversely, the theorem says the less fixed or the more uncertain the behavior of any element of a system, the greater will be its influence on the system as a whole. Our mechanistic intuitions run counter to this. . . . Our impulse is that the wholeness of a system is best determined by "nailing" its pieces in place. Too often we see the elements of a situation as being related like the cogs and wheels in a machine. Each cog, we think, plays its most efficient role in the machine if it is securely fitted in place. (117)

Von Foerster's Theorem seems to describe the nature of online conferencing. Responses to the poems that were nailed in place, that lacked speculation, that left no room for further inquiry tended to have little effect on the general flow of ideas. Responses to the poems that invited others to expand on them tended to shape the discourse to a great extent. Using language in this way, to form ideas collaboratively, is by nature an unbridled and complex process. Italo Calvino echoes this view in *Six Memos for the Next Millennium* (1988), in which he speculates that we are in the midst of a second industrial revolution, the information revolution, which is changing the way we view knowledge and the "natural" order of things. He says,

> The second industrial revolution, unlike the first, does not present us with such crushing images as rolling mills and molten steel, but with "bits" in a flow of information traveling along circuits in the form of electronic impulses. . . . [And] the least thing [can be] the center of a network of relationships that the writer cannot restrain himself from following, multiplying the details so that his descriptions and digressions become infinite. Whatever the starting point, the matter in hand spreads out and out, encompassing ever vaster horizons, and if it were permitted to go on further and further in every direction, it would end by embracing the entire universe. (107)

Online discussion, in the way it appears to a conferee and in the effect is has on thinking, we believe, challenges the notion that rigidity equals stability and it creates a generative power in the thinking and writing of students. If this claim has merit, we need to think about creating space, or cyberspace, in classrooms where collaborative writing can operate in its natural generative manner.

Speculating, Collaborating, and Telling Their Stories

The conferees worked in two significant ways to generate new forms of knowledge:

1. Through stories they told about themselves, they articulated a value system based on the merit of exercising personal courage in times of adversity and loss.

2. They collaborated on the interpretation of certain poems leading to a consensus of sorts.

We were amazed at the number of stories being told, and awed by the content of them. Having peers as a primary audience certainly was a factor in the students' and teachers' willingness to talk about themselves. The storytelling mode in evidence at the beginning of the project—some of it true, some of it suspiciously fanciful—remained constant throughout. Here are some conferees introducing themselves:

> I'm a senior at Edisto High, I've got this distinct southern accent. I love to write . . . In fact, I'm the editor of my school newspaper and I am planning a career in journalism. I know this is wild and dreamy, but I am determined to write for the Wall Street Journal. . . . I'm engaged to a wonderful guy who's studying to be an architect. Next year I'm planning on going to Appalachian State. After a few years I'm going off to NEW YORK!!!! I'm a highlife kind of girl.

> I am Karen . . . I am a professional alligator wrestler who at last count has lost a total of thirteen limbs (you figure it out). I am sixteen, have blonde hair, green eyes, and an extra finger on my right hand. I have webbed toes too. I get made fun of alot, but I'm really a good swimmer. . . .

> I am Sharon, an eighteen-year-old senior at John Calhoun High School. I have an eight-month-old daughter. My plans for the future are to attend Columbia Jr. College majoring in Business Admin. After I complete college, I plan to open my own business, in Atlanta. . . .

> I'm Terrance. . . . I'm not a very active person. When it comes down to having fun, I'm there. Mostly I stay home and hang around the house. . . . Believe me, I do have a really bad temper. Some people say I want things to go my way. I don't see it that way. I just don't want people to get over on me. . . . I do plan to go into the Air Force after graduation.

> My name is Tonika. I think of myself as being a kind and generous
> person. . . . My father is deceased. Since my father's death, my fam-
> ily has become very dependent on each others' love. Also, since my
> father's death, my family has become very close to God and most
> importantly, we learned that we are nothing without him. . . . My
> nephew turned a month old on the day my father died and my niece
> was born the day before his funeral. God took my father, but he
> blessed us with two special little people.

Taking their cue from the subject of conference, two ninth graders
chose to introduce themselves in verse:

> Thom is a very intelligent guy.
> He is courageous as a lion.
> He is dashing as Santa Claus.
> He is stunning in all his glory.
> He is lying all through this poem.

And from Bob:

> Bob is as tall as a skyscraper
> And as fast as a supersonic jet.
> He has brownish blonde hair,
> That will never work with him.
> His legs are so long
> He can step over a building.
> His arms are so strong
> He could hug the world.

From the start the voices began to converge, some serious, even med-
itative, others playful, as they crisscross the state from classroom to
classroom. You can sense the enjoyment the students took in introducing themselves. Certainly their writing was effervescent (even if at
times full of so much breeziness). Classroom writing has often been a
lonely experience; students are accustomed to sitting in their cubicles
writing to their teacher who sits in his cubicle reading. It's not sur-
prising that the opportunity to write to peers was exhilarating, as evi-
denced by the playfulness in the language above. While we wouldn't
try to claim that any of the above introductory student stories are
classic pieces of writing, as teachers of writing we can't help but
admire certain turns of phrase that the students created in this forum.
The conference was a jangle of voices in a way competing with each
other for a chance to tell a story.

Though the students obviously enjoyed writing in the narrative
mode, they equally enjoyed the speculative mode, and it cropped up
spontaneously throughout the conference discussion. None of the discussion of "Cross," a Langston Hughes poem, was prescribed or planned
by any of the participants. Instead, the discourse, naturally following

the generative pattern that Italo Calvino describes above. In "Cross," a poem from the point of view of a person of mixed race, the speaker presents his conflicted and complex emotions toward his parents, at once angry toward the "legacy" they've left him and resigned to his particular lot in life. Although perhaps the conferees raise more questions about this poem than they answer, we believe the raising of the questions is as important as answering them since it enables the student writing to go beyond patented interpretations of the poem. In the following series of responses, we've reproduced the student writing with actual errors. Some names of students have been changed to conceal their identity.

> I think that the person in the poem "Cross" used to feel angry or ashamed of having racially mixed [parents], but now seems to be lightening up a bit and becoming more accepting towards the idea. The person doesn't really know who to identify with, either—his mother or father, black or white. I don't like how the speaker uses the terms old "man" and old "mother." It should be *father* and mother, or man and *woman*. Does this make sense.
>
> Karen, eleventh grade

> Dear Karen: I agree with your interpretation of the poem "Cross." I feel the writer may have been confused about his racial background. He might have had some hostility towards his parents over his race, but eventually came to terms with it and accepted it as what makes him who he is.
>
> Drew, ninth grade

> Dear Karen: I agree with your response to Langston Hughes "Cross." The speaker was ashamed of his parents. Both, because one was white and the other was black. When he was younger, he resented his parents. He had racial boundaries put on him by black and white people. He probably never really fitted in anywhere. And now that he is older and wiser, he is more forgiving. He still has a little confusion about things, and that is why he asks where he will die. I don't think that it really makes sense for him to use "old man" or "old woman" because that has connotations of disrespect. He indicates that he regrets cursing them and he still doesn't fully agree with his situation.
>
> unsigned, ninth grade

> The man wonders where he will die because of the boundaries of color. Since his white father died in a fine house and his black mother died in a shack, he wonders where the in-between will die. Will it be in a middle class home since he is neither rich and white nor poor and black?
>
> Amber, ninth grade

And from a teacher in the conference:

> To Karen: I'm glad you noticed that Hughes used the terms old man and old mother. I too wondered what Hughes was getting at. Good

question. Maybe Hughes was pointing out that though the rich white man loved the poor black woman, he obviously didn't love her enough to love the child of that union or he would've been a father instead of "old man." The poem gets at gender boundaries too. If the black woman had been rich and white man poor, would the kid live with the mother or the father? It's this unknown information, the stuff that is left out of the poem, that makes it so interesting.

                                                                            Chris

This series of notes indicates how the discursive nature of online writing enables students to question what they are learning. Note eleventh grader Karen's initial invitation for others to help her read and understand the poem. Her collaborative disposition toward the endeavor was typical of the conference activity: Interpretations were tentative, inquisitive, and open at all times to further revision. Although the text from the discussion contains its share of mere summary of the poems, it's instructive to note that pure summary tended not to engender a response from anyone. As Zohar and Marshall (1994) would say, pure summary appeared to be "rigidly determined, rigidly fixed in place" and therefore "[lost] its relationship to the whole" and became "isolated, or 'alienated'" from the rest of the discourse (117). The most interesting discussions developed from notes like Karen's that invited others to participate. This mode of collaborative inquiry by students was especially refreshing in a study and appreciation of poetry, which, we observe, is often served up neatly for students by their English teachers.

The final response in the above series of notes, from Chris to Karen, illustrates a kind of teacher to student writing that we believe is lamentably rare in school environments. In his response to Karen, Chris, an English teacher, represses the "teacherly" tendency to respond to the correctness of Karen's writing. He does not criticize the vagueness of the first sentence, the mistaken use of nominative case in the second sentence, or the misuse of the plural pronoun reference to refer to the solitary speaker of the poem. Had this exchange in writing between student and teacher been a test of Karen's ability to present her interpretation of the poem, as most school writing is a test of students' understanding of some thing or other, then Chris may have responded very differently. For example,

> Karen: It's obvious you've read the poem but your understanding of it seems uncertain or confused. You raise a good question regarding Hughes's use of the terms *mother* and *man,* but you fail to provide a coherent explanation. Your last sentence indicates you need to reread the poem.

This kind of teacherly response, which we believe to be typical of how many teachers at all levels of the educational system respond to students' writing, effectively shuts down the student as a thinker. When speculative student writing is acknowledged with criticism of style and grammar, and worse yet, belittlement of the student's attempts at inquiry, as the above response illustrates, student thinking shifts into neutral, and the ideas generated by the writing, though they may adhere to rules of grammar and style, will not be very thoughtful or interesting.

The following words were written by Chuck, a teacher, as a response to Robert Hayden's bittersweet poem "Those Winter Sundays." Note that Chuck's response is pure narrative:

> Growing up, with three brothers and a sister, on the Northern Plains, we lived in a huge, two story house in Hyde County, South Dakota. The children slept upstairs, and our parents down. The ceiling had heat vents, since heat rises, but the entire house was heated by a potbelly, coal-burning stove in the living room downstairs. I shared a room with my brother Randy. Each cold winter morning, as we lay huddled underneath our quilts, in our stocking caps and stockinged feet, we would hear my father below, cursing and coughing, as he stirred the dying embers of what was left of the roaring fire from bedtime and heaped new coals on to build a new fire. Later, the aroma of bacon would seep through the vent, letting us know Mother was also up. Then it would be a game, each of us waiting for the moment we thought it would be safely warm enough to jump out of the bed, and then running to stand, in stocking feet, above the vent, feeling the heat rise up to meet us. First one there got the treat.
>
> Chuck

Though this is Chuck's response to Hayden's poem, there is no mention of the poem; the response is purely narrative. Chuck has internalized the meaning of the Hayden poem and is using it to uncover a story about himself. And this is typical of much of the online responding by students as well. Often the students' reading of a poem functioned solely to allow them to tell a story about themselves. The discussion was not just discursive but digressive as well, but since the goal of the project is "to lead . . . students to use poetry to talk about their real life experience . . . to hear the speakers and then to become speakers," as teacher Janet described at the onset, then such purely narrative writing is evidence of learning.

Students' stories aren't always as idyllic as their teachers would hope. Trying to understand the inherent paradox of a bittersweet memory, eleventh grader Belinda compares the anger in her home to that described by the speaker in Hayden's poem, and she comes to some conclusions about her own experience:

> My childhood memories seem to parallel the memories of Robert Hayden's "Those Winter Sundays." I can remember vividly . . . the awful anger in our home that was always present. My early memo-

ries were confusing. I was too young to understand then that alcoholism was a disease that affected the entire family. I don't know what caused the anger in the author's home, but I am still grateful for the memories of my father's love for us on those precious Sunday mornings.

And Terrance imagines the future by glancing back at the past:

My childhood memories aren't like those of the speaker's. I didn't have the opportunity to stay with my father. By reading the poem, I realize I would have liked having those memories. My Sunday morning is everyone for himself. I hope we will have unity in my household. When I have children, I want them to admire me like the speaker admires his father—even if it is with hindsight.

For these online writers, the stories are not just static memories of discrete events in their lives; with continued readings of poems, the students find their stories approaching the mythic, informing them of the meaning of their past, present, and future. Each act of reading and writing has the capacity to recreate memory. Below, online poet-in-residence Claire articulates this propensity of narrative writing:

It's interesting that some of you have memories of what you experienced, and others of you, sensing a gap between what happened and what you would like to have happened, are more concerned with creating memories for your own future children. Others of you are reevaluating your memories of early family life in the light of your own growing understanding of the dynamics and costs of living in a family. . . . So memory isn't a fixed thing, is it? It's always being created and recreated.

Affirming Values Through Poetry

Throughout the conference the students responded freely to other conferees about the poems. A disappointment to us was the high incidence of summary in the responses. Without specific instruction to do otherwise, students seemed quite accustomed to summarize the action or events in the poem. Less frequently, conferees would interpret a poem's meaning and then relate that point to their own lives. Placing a poem in the context of their own lives often manifested as a value statement or an affirmation of personal values. For example, in the following series of notes, the students responded to Jenny Joser's poem "I Shall Wear Purple," whose speaker is a middle aged person who lists all the outrageous things she will do in her golden years to make up for the sobriety of her youth. The response of ninth grader Trey generalized negatively about old people, saying

When people get old, they go around acting like they have no money
when they really do. They never can match clothes. Old people are
always looking for free samples and other folks trash. These people
sit where they want and get in other people's way. Then they try to
be a good example for children and grandchildren. When they eat
they get fat because they don't have as much energy as when they
were younger.

Trey, ninth grade

Several conferees called attention to Trey's overgeneralizing, using
the poem as a means to state personal values.

Trey : We feel that the response about elderly people showed stereo-
typing. We disagree with what was said about old people. All elderly people don't look for a hand out; yet, they deserve one for trying
to teach us about life. All elderly people are not fat nor do they get in
the way. We think the poem should be read again to see what is
really being said about old people.

Tonika, Darlene, Willamena, and Sherryl, twelfth grade

Trey : It doesn't matter if they can't match clothes, or if they act like
they don't have money, or even if they get in the way once in a
while, you should give them a chance to see what they know and I
just bet you'll be surprised.

Allee, ninth grade

The main idea of the poem is that the speaker will do anything she
wants when she is old. . . . I want to be able to do things the way I
want them done. I think that the older men and women have served
their purposes on earth. I think they should have time off to enjoy
life. I also think the younger generation should respect them for their
work and for making our lives easier.

Candy, ninth grade

What's going on in these responses? The students are more or less
unanimously affirming the value of elderly people to society in general and specifically to themselves. Trey's rather flippant attitude
toward the elderly sent a ripple effect through the conference, and
while the conferees restrained themselves from attacking Trey personally, they did question his unreasonable statement as well as state
reasons why they value elderly people as workers, teachers, and
providers.

Other conferees recognized the Joser poem as an example of
carpe diem and used the poem as a way to affirm the value of living
spontaneously:

. . . To me [the speaker] sounds like she didn't have much fun when
she was younger so she's going to do whatever she didn't do when
she was young. It speaks to my awareness, letting me know that I

need to do what I possibly can now while I am young instead of waiting until I am old.

Jolene, ninth grade

"I Shall Wear Purple" . . . informs people that life is too short and that you should enjoy it when you are young. . . . The woman needs to broaden her horizons and lengthen her boundaries and enjoy life now and not wait until she is old to enjoy herself, because you never know when your life might be taken away.

Ritchie, ninth grade

. . . The woman talks about doing all the things she never did, but really she is also talking about renewing the youthful spirit that makes people do such spur of the moment things. I think if a person forgets to try to be young in spirit, he or she will get old and maybe turn out like the old people that Trey described: people who "sit where they want and get in other people's way."

Chris (teacher)

After reading Alice Walker's poem "Women," Janet Atkins asked her students to write briefly to other conferees about significant women in their lives. Perhaps because Walker's poem describes women in military terms as warriors, many of the students chose to write about strong women in their lives who had also faced adversity:

My grandmother, in my opinion, is the one who went through the roughest times. She had thirteen kids all before she turned forty-five. Her oldest son was burned up when he was only ten. Another one of her sons was pushed off a five-story building when he was thirty-five. The same year another son was shot and killed. She always tells me how easy it was in her days, but she's just hiding it all. She's now at the age of seventy-three and still running the road and going strong.

Arlene, twelfth grade

My mother is a strong woman. She is a superwoman. She has been through so many pains. Being thirty-nine and having lupus, my mother has overcome all the obstacles that have approached her. Her troubles come to her and stick her like a needle, and though it hurts, she has toughed them out.

Sherryl, twelfth grade

Tonika, I couldn't agree with you more. I agree with you because my grandmother is the same way. She is a very strong person. She also keeps our family going even though we have had hard times. Many women today do not think being a housewife is hard but my grandmother lives alone. Her husband is deceased and she has to pay her own bills, her car payment and everything. Her kids do help though. She is a strong, healthy sixty-year-old woman who cares about everyone and she loves to help out other people no

matter what type trouble they are in. You can depend on my grandmother.

Mary Jane, ninth grade

In this exchange of notes, the students collaboratively affirm the value
of individual courage and strength in the face of difficulty. Typical of
these messages were introductory sentences that established primarily an emotional connection between the students rather than the
shared intellectual pursuit of the meaning of the poem. Many of the
notes begin with a sense of empathy as Mary Jane's note to Tonika
does. Other examples of such introductory comments included "I am
somewhat like you. I also feel . . ." "I like your response. Here's what
I got from the poem . . . " "I agree with your response. . . . Everything
you said is true to me . . ." The text of the conference indicates that
students found it was more important to hear other students' stories of
struggle and to share their own stories. Each student, it seemed, had a
tragic story to share with the electronic community.

In "Socialising in Cyberspace," Dan Charles (1992) goes so far as
to claim that we are beginning to need virtual communities in cyberspace because "traditional neighborhoods, churches, and extended
families," the kind of groups that used to offer emotional support to
individuals, have disappeared. Certainly, we observed students using
the network for this reason, and in such instances the discussion of the
poems was secondary to the socializing and empathizing that
occurred. Computer conferencing may encourage this kind of emoting
for another reason though: The lack of social cues, such as race, gender, age, and other aspects of physical appearance, ensures that every
participant is more or less equal at the start of things. This equalizing
factor had the effect, we believe, of allowing some conferees, normally shy in face to face encounters, to be more assertive.

Finally, family values were affirmed in the conference. The following notes are typical of how the students viewed sacrifice for family as a noble struggle:

> My grandmother is a very special person. She raised her children at
> home while her husband lived in Charleston with his job and only
> came home on the weekends. She took care of the garden and the
> children, cleaned the house. . . . My great-grandmother lived across
> the field with my great-uncle. When my great-grandmother got very
> sick, my grandmother had to take care of her, and they became very
> close. When my great-grandmother passed away, my grandmother
> took it very hard because she had lost her best friend. My great-
> grandmother made my grandmother promise that she would take
> care of my great-uncle, and see that he had a place to live and some-
> thing to eat. Now my great-uncle is too old to work, and my grand-
> parents are also too old to work as well. She has to plant the garden

to provide food for them to eat because they don't have a lot of money.

Fernando, twelfth grade

After reading the poems "Those Winter Sundays" and "Women," I stopped to reflect on my parents. It is sad that children usually have to grow up before they realize the love and sacrifices their parents have for them. . . .

Priscilla, college freshman

I am making a connection between the two poems . . . by finding a sense of duty and sacrifice in both of them. Both poems contain the idea that the ones who benefit by the sacrifice aren't even aware of the sacrifice until later. My wife takes great pains to make sure our sons have every care provided; once someone asked her if she thought they appreciated everything she did for them, and like a prophet she said, "They will." There seems to be some truth in this: The older I get the more I realize the sacrifices my own mother made for me.

Chris (teacher)

Does Computer Conferencing Have a Place in Language Arts Curriculum?

The short answer to the above question is an enthusiastic "yes!" All the conferees spoke animatedly about the project, and many of the teachers and students who participated began other online projects that built on the Online Poetry Project. The experience was clearly a fun one for the conferees. But can such online writing projects constitute an incontestable place in a writing curriculum? On the basis of the success of this project and similar projects that we have observed or participated in, we feel computer conferencing has an important place in the language arts curriculum. It's not just fun; it improves student writing. Computer conferencing has a beneficial effect on students' writing because it resonates clearly with the way humans learn naturally to speak. Linguists and psychologists such as Lev Vygotsky have remarked that the human brain must be "wired" to learn language socially through practice and interaction. And linguists and parents alike marvel at how a child of four or five can generate unique and complex sentences without ever having had a formal lesson in the rules of speech. All the basic conventions of language are learned by most very young children seemingly without effort through practice accompanied by feedback from nurturing family and friends. Likewise, writing, a visual symbol system as words are an aural symbol system, is more naturally learned through practice accompanied by nurturing feedback. Just as a mother would neither chastise her four-year-old for using *bringed* for *brought*, nor drill him in the irregular conjugation of the verb *to bring*, conferees don't dwell over-much on grammar or style, but improvement of grammar and style are made implicitly through the interactive nature of computer confer-encing. For example, we noted that students who wrote in a direct, readable style were more likely to draw responses than students who wrote in a stilted or formal style. Moreover, it is clear that computer conferencing allows for much more practice and feedback than tradi-tional textbook methods of learning to write.

When students write in a computer conference, the emphasis is on making meaning for others. Such communication is rare in acade-mia, where students are usually required merely to *demonstrate* their knowledge. Rarely are they called upon as writers to make meaning for an audience that has a need and a reason for the information that the students are communicating.

How different the online writing is from traditional themes we've read! Though at the beginning of the conference, the students were writing to virtual strangers, almost immediately those initial hesitan-cies that one feels toward speaking to strangers evaporated. In tradi-tional classroom writing, students immediately look to the teacher to discover what "he likes." This is even discussed among students: "He likes 'flowery' language," or "He likes a lot of examples," or "He likes a lot of big words." But in the Online Poetry conference the students did not look to their teacher to discover what they should write. They had to look to strangers online to find out what they liked. Because most readers like and respond to writing to the extent that it engages them, students in the conference quickly had to find out how to write and engage a broad audience. This task called for more than a basic strategy that had perhaps served them in their classroom writing in the past. Using "flowery" language was not enough; using multi-syllabic words from the thesaurus was not enough; humor was not enough. In fact, students found themselves using many rhetorical strategies to engage each other. Isn't that what writing is all about, according to Aristotle, to find the best available means to persuade or engage an audience? So we believe that computer conference writing approximates a market of ideas, where solid, substantive, polished ideas are superior to cheap, cracked, and gilded ones. Most school writing rarely approaches this kind of intensive communication.

This doesn't mean that computer conference writing is flawless. In fact, the conference text contains numerous errors in grammar, lapses in reason and slips in style, but the primary function of the students' writing—*to communicate meaning*—was attended to with skill. Though one would assume that the language ability of the con-ferees would vary widely due to the age differences, we noted that the writing of the students was more of one piece. The range of language abilities of these students was compressed by the social dynamic of the online experience. We believe that the peer audience and the freedom to write in the narrative mode encouraged formal stilted writers to write in more natural sounding voices, and we believe "poor" writers were encouraged to write with greater clarity and adherence to basic grammar.

If practice makes perfect when it comes to writing, then conferencing has the potential to perfect student writing since it can generate greater volumes of discourse than one teacher can possibly keep track of. Some of the conferees in the Online Poetry Project were limited in the amount of time they had to use the computers; however, with unlimited access to a lively conference discussion, even a timid student could easily generate twenty pages of single-spaced text over the course of a semester. In our experience in the classroom the most thoughtful student insights are sometimes not made public, and the minority viewpoints are suppressed by the traditional dynamic of the classroom discussion. Computer conferencing, because it is written, slows down the thought process and gives students greater opportunities to consider the complexity of ideas. Students find themselves more carefully crafting their views, and though there may not be a "right" answer, students discover that some answers are definitely better than others, and for good reasons.

Finally, computer conferencing makes sense in a writing curriculum because the collaborative nature of online writing functions the way real fields of discourse do. In professional discourse—academic, business, journalistic, legal, medical, and so on—writers may compose alone, but they are in constant communication with peers in their field, reading and building on the ideas of others. Criticizing, applauding, and borrowing from other writers are all part of the composing process of professional writers. And online writing resembles professional discourse more than the limited writing tasks often found in the traditional classroom forums. In fact these traditional writing tasks may impede the development of language skills:

> The traditional forums comprising . . . classrooms—group discussions, lectures, teacher-student conferences, written assignments—generally support a traditional hegemony in which teachers determine appropriate and inappropriate discourse [and] . . . this political arrangement encourages intellectual accommodation in students, discourages intellectual resistance, and hence may seriously limit students' understanding of, and effective use of, language. (Cooper and Selfe 1990, 847)

At their best, traditional classroom forums are like a prescribed, yet static, symphony; students play the same part in class after class. They know what to expect from each other, and they often have their teachers figured out and know how to succeed. Good teachers can and do make such a traditional class harmonize well, encouraging each student to play his or her part to the best of his or her ability. But the online classroom is more like a jazz ensemble than a carefully charted symphonic affair, and it encourages the harmony and occasional discord necessary to professional discourse. There is the element of spontaneity. Students don't look to the teacher to figure out the charts for them. They look to each other and build an exciting, often fast-paced, creation of their own.

Works Cited

Bruffee, K. 1983. "Writing and Reading as Collaborative or Social Acts." *The Writer's Mind*. Urbana, IL: National Council of Teachers of English.

Calvino, I. 1988. *Six Memos for the Next Millennium*. Cambridge, MA: Harvard University Press.

Charles, D. 1992. "Socialising in Cyberspace." *New Scientist* 134 (1821): 12.

Cooper, M. M., and C. L. Selfe. 1990. "Computer Conferences and Learning: Authority, Resistance, and Internally Persuasive Discourse." *College English* 52 (8): 847.

Hiltz, S., K. Johnson, and M. Turoff. 1986. "Experiments in Group Decision Making: Communication Process and Outcome in Face to Face Versus Computerized Conferences." *Human Communication Research* 13: 225–52.

Kuhn, T. 1970. *The Structure of Scientific Revolutions*. Chicago: University of Chicago Press.

Moffett, J. 1987. *Teaching the Universe of Discourse*. Portsmouth, NH: Boynton/Cook.

Starr, R. 1993. "Information Superhighway May Be Road Back to Literacy." *Insight* (November): 22.

Zohar, D., and I. Marshall. 1994. *The Quantum Society: Mind, Physics, and a New Social Vision*. New York: William Morrow.

10

Walking in Many Worlds

Lucy Maddox
Georgetown University

Recently, a group of teachers who were spending the summer studying at the Vermont campus of the Bread Loaf School of English came
together to discuss their common interest in teaching Native
American literature to their students. The group brought a variety of
needs and concerns to those initial meetings. Some teachers were primarily interested in introducing Native American materials into their
existing courses, some were interested in creating new courses with
Native American components, and some were simply concerned with
doing a more effective job of teaching the materials that were already
in their curricula.

One result of those summer meetings was the establishment of a
new conference on BreadNet, the telecommunications network of the
Bread Loaf School of English. The Education NA Conference,
designed as an electronic extension of the face-to-face meetings on
the Bread Loaf campus, has continued to reflect and build on the energy of the initial conversations. By providing an electronic forum
where teachers can confer with each other and solicit many kinds of
advice, the conference is meeting a genuine need of teachers (K–12
and above) who want to bring more Native American materials into
their classrooms but are unsure about the best way to go about it.

Since many of us who are now teaching—perhaps most of us, at
all levels—have had little or no formal training in Native American
literature and history and may have gotten much of our information
from various forms of pop culture, including Hollywood movies, we
approach the teaching of those materials with great insecurity, no
matter how good our intentions. We don't always know what texts are
available and which texts are sufficiently "authentic"; we don't

always know if what we have learned about one group of people, such as the Lakota Sioux, also applies to other groups, such as the Navajo; in introducing Native American materials to our students, we often worry that we might be just plain getting it wrong and even perpetuating damaging stereotypes. One of the organizers of the Education NA Conference spoke for many of her colleagues in the conference when she wrote, "There is nothing sadder than a white girl teaching Native American literature to a group of white students when no one in the room, including the teacher, has any real knowledge of the culture." Education NA has offered a safe place to raise questions, to try out teaching plans, to ask for advice about texts and approaches to them, to share both insecurities and areas of expertise. It has also been a place where everyone has been made aware that when we speak of the "culture" of Native Americans, we are in fact speaking of many widely varied practices, beliefs, and ways of living.

One of the many advantages of Education NA is that several of the regular participants have been teachers of Native Alaskan and Native American students; teachers of Yup'ik, Athabascan, Tlingit, Navajo, and Laguna Pueblo students have contributed to the conversations. Some of these teachers have also arranged exchanges between their students and other students, both Indian and non-Indian. The conference thus expands the monolithically white classroom of many teachers and allows them and their students to listen to people who have "real knowledge" of cultural situations other than their own. The contributions of the Native students and their teachers are especially useful as a way of reminding everyone that there are often fundamental differences among Indian tribal groups and communities; their contributions help to make it clear just how vast and how truly multicultural a place "Indian country" really is — and always has been.

One of the most energetic student exchanges arranged by Education NA teachers has been the "Walking in Two Worlds" exchange, which included Native Alaskan and Navajo students. In reading the students' writing about what it means to them to walk in two worlds — a Native one and one that is predominantly white — one quickly comes to realize that those two worlds multiply into many; the two worlds in which Yup'ik students walk, for example, are not identical with the two worlds in which Navajo or Tlingit students walk. The dividing line between Native and non-Native may be drawn all over the map of the country, but what falls on either side of that dividing line varies significantly as one moves around the map — even the map of a single state.

The teachers who participated in this exchange assigned literary readings for their students that would both introduce them to the worlds in which others walk and provide models for the students' own writing about the ways in which cultural influences sometimes converge and sometimes conflict in their lives. Students in the participating classrooms read a common set of poems and posted their responses to the conference; the students then wrote their own poems and shared these online. One of the Alaska teachers noted that this process of responding to poetry and then writing poems, which they share with an audience of people different from themselves, "can help students understand their ethnicity in new ways."

Some remarkably frank, thoughtful, and even accomplished writing emerged in the course of the exchange, as students attempted to communicate through their poems what it meant to them to walk in two worlds. The following example, written by Ernestine Chaco, a Navajo eighth grader, is worth quoting in full.

Memory

I get up in the morning
And get ready for school.
I go to my Grandma's house;
She fixes my hair.
My Mom works hard
So there is food on the table,
And she has little time.

I ask her one day,
"Mom, why don't you fix my hair anymore?"
She says to me,
"It is hard in the real world,
But you're too little to know what I'm saying."

I walk to my Grandma's house.
She is lonely.
This is the first time I have seen her so lonely.
She has three daughters and four sons,
But one of her sons is dead.
"Where are your boys?" I ask.
"They're at a baseball game," she replies.
I pull a cushion towards where she is sitting.
"What kind of style do you want?" she asks.
"The usual."

We sit quietly
I hardly know
How to speak
Navajo
Except for a few words.

This morning my Grandpa is herding sheep.
I can't believe he can walk
Down the canyon

And back up again.
I say good-bye to him in Navajo.
He replies, *"Ha goh nee."*

Finally, her hands are done
Braiding my hair.
I sit with her a little longer;
I can hear the clock
And the loud silence.
During this moment
I wish I could speak Navajo.

At the same time that the conference drew the attention of all the students and teachers to their differences from each other, the contributions of the students are also reminders that American students everywhere, no matter where they live or what their home language may be, do share some of the same interests and concerns. It has been my sense, as the result of my participation in Education NA and other teacher-student electronic forums, that we teachers are often inclined to head as quickly as possible for this common ground, to look for the similarities among the differences, to encourage students to locate themselves in a larger world by finding the places where they can connect with others who are in most ways not like themselves. And while I sometimes become nervous about the rush to find "universals," fearing that in our haste we will elide the differences that make us who we are, I have also come to recognize that if we are to talk with each other across our differences, it is important to find a ground that will allow us to have genuine conversation.

This need for a common ground was brought home to me in a telecommunications exchange that Lauren Sittnick and I arranged—through Education NA—between her Native students at Laguna Middle School in Laguna, New Mexico, and my graduate students (most of them white, and none of them Indian) who were taking a course in Native American literature at Georgetown University. Lauren and I agreed that her students would first write about superstitions they were familiar with at Laguna, and my students would respond; in the second phase of the exchange, the Laguna students would write imitations of the mixture of myth, history, and autobiography in Scott Momaday's *The Way to Rainy Mountain*, which my students had also read, and my students would again respond.

When I first proposed this electronic exchange to my students, they were hesitant; they weren't sure how they should respond to students who were so much younger, and they were especially insecure about how they should correspond with "real" Indians, when they were still making their way tentatively through the "foreignness" of Native American literature. When the Laguna students' superstition stories arrived, however, my students were immediately fascinated. The Laguna students wrote about many things: the prohibition against looking out the window after dark; the mysterious "pajama boy" who walks the reservation after dark; the greedy man who turned into a devil figure after winning too much money at the casino. My students responded by writing about their own superstitions, about stories they had heard, about things that they feared. Their stories said much about the places they came from, their childhood experiences, the folk wisdom they had acquired orally—sometimes from immigrant grandparents, sometimes from suburban parents or older siblings, and in one case from a karate teacher.

By exchanging stories about fearsome things, the Laguna students and my Georgetown graduate students were simultaneously underscoring their differences and locating a common ground in their stories about superstitions they were not willing to discard. Once this connection was made, my students were eager to hear more from the Laguna students. Beginning a correspondence about Momaday's incorporation of traditional Kiowa myths into his personal memoir then made more sense to my students, since they had, perhaps unconsciously, already been conversing with the Laguna students about the conflation of myth and autobiography in all lives. They felt connected.

If my students became more comfortable writing across the age and culture gap by exchanging superstition stories, and if they learned some things about what it means to live in Laguna, Lauren Sittnick had other, perhaps more important, reasons for finding the exchange useful. As Lauren noted, one of her goals was to help her students "carry what they have in Laguna and in other modern settings without feeling one place puts an 'X' through the other and vice versa." Her students were able to tell stories to an audience that would take them seriously, and then to connect those stories to their lives, and to hear from others very different from themselves about the stories they carry with them. Her students, Lauren observed, "noticed patterns in superstition stories from different regions. . . . It is amazing how quickly they pick up on how language is used for various purposes. . . ." My own students were, I think, surprised to discover that they too could use their stories, and their language, to communicate with people they had thought they could only read about in books.

The kind of electronic communities that Education NA encourages, among teachers and students, can help to educate all of us to our differences, at the same time that they can encourage us to value what we carry with us and to realize that we have important stories to share.

11

Rural Teachers and Students
Connecting and Communicating

Rocky Gooch
Bread Loaf School of English
Middlebury College, Middlebury, VT

The Bread Loaf Rural Teacher Network, founded in 1993 at
Middlebury College's Bread Loaf School of English with
funding from the DeWitt Wallace Reader's Digest Fund, is
not a network of a hundred thousand people, whose messages on line are faceless. What we are is a very small network of like-minded individuals who share common beliefs,
who read common texts, who share a love of literature and
writing. We have a unique bond. We focus not primarily on
technology but on content and curriculum . . . on students
and their learning. That's what drives the Rural Network—
not the technology, although we could not function as we do
without BreadNet to keep us together and to bring our students into this learning community.

—Doug Wood

Doug Wood, who taught at a middle school in South Carolina before he
began doctoral studies at Harvard in 1995, is a Bread Loaf graduate
(1997) who has been a technical consultant to the Bread Loaf Rural

Teacher Network (BLRTN) since 1994. Doug is right when he says that the focus of BLRTN is content and curriculum; he's also right when he says that BreadNet, our conferencing system, is a necessary tool that we use to connect and communicate, which we do with great intensity and regularity. BreadNet may be accessed by virtually any type of computer, either over the Internet or via a modem. It is very user-friendly, and even the most stubborn technophobe can learn to surf conferences with a minimum of time, trouble, and anxiety. Accounts are given out, free of charge, to any student, graduate, or faculty member of the Bread Loaf School of English who makes the request.

The avid use of BreadNet by teachers in our relatively small network (less than five hundred people) demonstrates the resourcefulness and flexibility of the system, and I continue to receive inquiries about the network from others who are interested in creating small-scale electronic communities of teachers. Since our network provides rural teachers with the kinds of professional development and opportunities to collaborate that can be lacking in many rural places, I'd like to answer some of the common questions I receive about how teachers use the BreadNet conferencing system and participate in the network.

What do teachers who integrate computer conferencing into their teaching require, in terms of training and support?

Teachers let us know very quickly that integrating computer conferencing into their teaching and their professional and social lives is a demanding and time-consuming task. They require a user-friendly system with plenty of technical support in the form of phone calls, troubleshooting, visits to their classrooms and, in some cases, their homes. And they ask for fairly intensive training in computer conferencing during the summers when they are studying at the Bread Loaf campuses, preferably reinforced by networked Bread Loaf courses in literature and writing.

Using BreadNet as a teaching and learning tool has been described as a developmental process, which is not to say that every teacher follows the same pattern in the same sequence. Generally speaking, it works this way. Teachers who are enrolled in their first Bread Loaf summer session in Vermont come to the Computer Center regularly for six weeks for individual or small-group sessions, depending on their level of expertise. Some of these teachers are in networked classes during the summer, which reinforce and deepen their understanding of how computer conferencing promotes conversations about literature, writing, and theater. During the summer, teachers begin planning BreadNet "exchanges" that will take place during the academic

Figure 11-1
Icons for BreadNet "Conferences" as They
Appear to Teachers on BreadNet

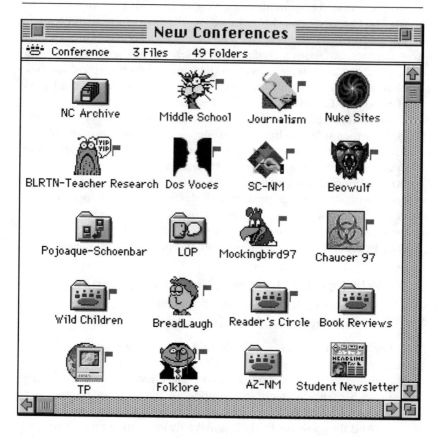

year. An exchange is a writing-intensive online collaboration focused on a particular interest and limited usually to two or three teachers and their students. Exchanges take place online in BreadNet conferences. Since Bread Loaf is a graduate school of English, the collaborations are often related to literature or other interests specific to teaching English. Teachers spend some time online planning, adjusting schedules, talking about what's happening among their students, and figuring out exactly what works best for them and their students, given constraints such as equipment, time, and support. Some teachers ask for transcripts of their online exchanges, and—with their students' help—analyze what they find in the transcripts as a prelude to planning the next exchange, which may be with a different set of teachers and students on a different topic entirely.

Gradually, over a period of two or three years, teachers experiment with different approaches and techniques in the exchanges, including students in planning and decision making. They become aware of issues of privacy, censorship, inappropriate student access, and technology costs: they become critical users of technology.

Some rural teachers become recognized as experts in their schools and districts: they lead technology planning and become advocates for using technology in thoughtful and productive ways; they offer workshops and invite colleagues to join in BreadNet exchanges. They become aware of culturally sensitive issues and of ways that pedagogies and assumptions can clash online. The teachers on BreadNet form a group of reflective teachers who have much to offer policy makers, planners, and practitioners: they are capable of evaluating software and commercial programs—and their own exchanges. A number of these teachers are in the process of creating online literature and writing courses for middle and high school students.

Does the reading and writing going on in classrooms decrease as students participate actively in BreadNet exchanges?

So far as we can determine, students read and write more frequently when they are part of active exchanges. The actual BreadNet exchanges are the tip of the iceberg. Most of the learning activity related to an online exchange takes place in the individual classrooms: reading, discussing, writing, interpreting, analyzing, and presenting. The distillation of these activities and further refinement of the ideas are what actually take place online. Quite often the culminating event in an online exchange is a hardcopy publication of student writing that is generated and revised through the collaborative experience.

Aside from BreadNet exchanges and projects involving students, how do teachers in the Rural Teacher Network use BreadNet?

Random checks indicate that at least 70 percent of BLRTN members, network leaders, and staff log in at least once a week; about 25 percent log in every day. A rough description of major activities on BreadNet includes: social interaction; conversations about practice, theory, and research; collaborative inquiries; drafting, writing, and publishing; planning exchanges; sharing resources; and exploring ideas, texts, and issues. BreadNet activity is shaped by participation in the six-week summer sessions at the Bread Loaf campuses; technical training; state meetings; audio conferences; phone calls; letters; manuscripts and student writing exchanges by mail; videotapes; the *BLRTN Magazine*; and classroom visits. A few members of the network use BreadNet infrequently, for one reason or another, but remain important members of the Rural Teacher Network.

BLRTN is a flexible, generative model for professional development, with experienced members passing along their expertise to fellow teachers and administrators, students, and college faculty.

How about equipment and access?
Do BLRTN teachers have comparable equipment and BreadNet access in their classrooms?

Although the situation is changing slowly, many BLRTN teachers are struggling with inadequate equipment, technical support, and access to the Internet. In school after school, we hear about plans to change all this; and in school after school, we learn of other needs: books, teachers, repairs, special programs. At its best, BreadNet presents an alternative to commercial programs that deplete time and resources and ignore good practice.

Every rural teacher's situation is different. A few teachers have five or six networked computers in their classrooms; others have limited access to networked equipment in their school libraries. Many teachers must use their home computers, with students typing messages and saving them to disks that are taken home and sent out on BreadNet at night. We estimate that about a third of BLRTN teachers have Internet access and enough networked computers in their classrooms for students to participate actively and directly in collaborative work online. One thing is clear: exemplary (and busy) rural teachers will not spend time, money, and energy on technology that does not provide them with personal satisfaction and their students with opportunities for connecting and communicating that pay off in improved skills and understandings.

How is BreadNet different from most K–12 networks?

BreadNet is a conferencing-based network. We use FirstClass Intranet Server (FCIS) because it supports a great variety of online activities. Rather than using personal email only, BreadNet teachers are able to join or open a conference, which they do with minimal assistance from network administrators.

A teacher's personal mail is found in her BreadNet desktop in the "Mailbox" folder.

Figure 11-2

Each Fellow in the Bread Loaf Rural Teacher Network can receive mail in his or her personal mailbox (see upper left) and has access to numerous conferencing areas where collaboration can take place.

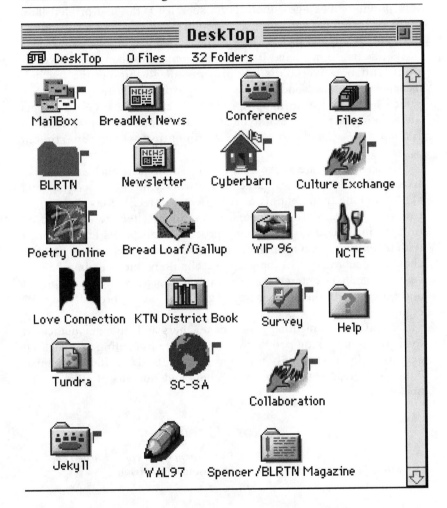

Instead of logging into the network and using an email client like Eudora to open a list of mail which has to be sorted, saved, filed, and deleted, a BreadNet teacher logs in, goes directly to her mailbox for personal mail from other Bread Loafers or from folks on the Internet, then quickly goes to conferences where current work is taking place. All messages that have been sent, for example, to the Culture Exchange Conference are there waiting; older messages haven't been deleted; the new ones are identified with red flags; and topics of discussion within the conference can be threaded (grouped together). The teacher simply reads and replies to new messages, sends her students' new work to the conference, and then moves on to the next conference area that she's participating in. It's very easy to refer back to a previous message—there is no search for the lost printed hard copy, or search for a file with a forgotten label—just open the conference area again and the message is there.

Students do not have BreadNet accounts: exchanges, conversations, collaborative publishing projects all go through the teacher. Teachers, students, and parents are comfortable with this process, which helps us avoid inappropriate or hurtful exchanges. Students are working on a document to be entitled "Golden Rules for BreadNet Exchanges," and we are now experimenting with a few student accounts.

Teachers who are active members of small-scale teacher networks like the Bread Loaf Rural Teacher Network gain the experience and skills to guide their schools as they invest in technology and design training programs for teachers and students; teachers should be brought into the decision-making process at all levels and provided with incentives to act as mentors and innovators. Technology budgets should reflect realities of integrating technology into teaching: 35 percent for teacher-centered teacher training; 65 percent for equipment and access, with the teacher training always taking precedence over equipment.

BreadNet is a meeting place for teachers and students, dedicated to encouraging young people to take pleasure in reading and writing, and users find it extremely useful to promote and facilitate nonracist, culturally engaged teaching for teachers and students of all ages and backgrounds.

Work Cited

Wood, D. 1998. *The Bread Loaf Rural Teacher Network: Rural Teachers, Rural Schools*. South Carolina Educational Television.

12

A School at the Crossroads of the Ancient and the Contemporary

Philip Sittnick
Laguna Middle School, Laguna, NM

Students at Laguna Middle School, located on the Laguna Pueblo Indian Reservation, don't think twice about using modern technology to explore and explain their ancient culture and traditions. This juxtaposition of ancient and modern, which to outsiders might seem unusual, is as natural to them as sunrise. At Laguna Middle School, students use technology to learn about their own culture, and also to connect with different people and cultures beyond the reservation, both near and far. For them, technology is a bridge between worlds—between the traditional and modern worlds that coexist on the reservation, and from their world into other spheres beyond the reservation. Technology is the bridge that helps them to feel increasingly more comfortable on either side of those multiple worlds.

The Laguna Pueblo Indian Tribe is a sovereign nation, with a viable culture and traditions which date back many hundreds of years. Ancestors of the Laguna people lived in the high desert country of western New Mexico for centuries before the first European settlers arrived in the area almost five hundred years ago. Today, the tribe endures, despite the powerful forces of colonization and assimilation they have faced. They still occupy their ancestral homeland, and vestiges of their ancient ways persist in daily life. Few cultures or people in America can claim a heritage as old or as tenacious as the Laguna Indians.

Many of the old ways are still in evidence at Laguna. Families still live in homes made of stone and adobe, built using techniques which date back to pre-Colombian times. Artisans continue to make fine pottery, using virtually the same methods as their great-, great-grandmothers. On special feast days, traditional foods like chile stew and roasted corn are served, and in the plaza the people practice ancient ceremonial dances, performing rituals handed down for countless generations.

While the Laguna people have managed to maintain much of their ancient heritage in their present-day life, their culture is neither static nor anachronistic. The Lagunas have a reputation as one of the most progressive tribes in the area. Long accustomed to the influence of other cultures, particularly because of their geographical location, over the years Lagunas have deliberately chosen to incorporate the ways of others into their own. Especially in the areas of business and education, the Lagunas have kept abreast of the larger society, in terms of their acceptance and incorporation of technology.

For centuries, Laguna has been the first stop for travelers heading west out of the Rio Grande corridor from Albuquerque. Early in this century, it was the railroad that brought people and goods to and through Laguna. Later, Route 66, the first east-west transcontinental highway, and finally the four-lane interstate, I-40, connected Laguna to the world beyond the Pueblo. Today, Laguna is connecting to the world via an electronic highway as well—the so-called information superhighway.

Economically, the Lagunas were one of the first tribes to succeed in establishing a wage-earning economy on the reservation. For a few decades, from the late 1950s to the early 1980s, the world's largest open-pit uranium mine, on Laguna land, provided a wealth of jobs and income for the tribe. Eventually, the mine shut down, and hard times befell the reservation. Yet, the tribe has worked aggressively to establish new businesses and jobs for its people. One such enterprise is Laguna Industries, the first on-reservation business owned and operated by a Native American tribe to receive and fill contracts from the federal government. There, as well as at other workplaces around the reservation, modern technology like computers are very much a part of the scene.

The Laguna Pueblo tribe has also taken a dynamic approach to education. Tribal leaders have envisioned and pursued educational self-determination for many years, and the Laguna Pueblo was one of the first tribes to establish their own Department of Education. When Laguna Middle School opened its doors in 1992, the tribe reached a major milestone in its struggle to direct the educational future of its people.

Laguna Middle School is the first tribally planned, designed, built, and operated school in New Mexico. It is special not simply for that reason, but because it provides Lagunas with the opportunity to create and implement educational programs specifically designed to meet the community's needs and desires.

The Lagunas, like other Native American tribes, are not an ideologically homogeneous people. Not everyone agrees about what exactly those needs and desires are. However, there is one especially significant message that consistently emerges from the whole community with a clear and strong voice: They want their children prepared for life in "two worlds"—the world of the pueblo and the world of mainstream society.

For most Lagunas, the challenge of living in modern society is not about choosing between the reservation and the "outside" world, but about learning to be comfortable, knowledgeable, and successful in both. Laguna people acknowledge the value in their own culture and in the many cultures that exist beyond the reservation. Most Lagunas seek to find a balance with their participation in multiple societies. They work to preserve their traditional culture, while simultaneously adopting and incorporating ways from other cultures.

Consequently, Laguna Middle School has been charged by the community to help fulfill this goal. Our mission statement is the distillation of the community's sentiments regarding the education of their children:

> It is the responsibility of all school staff, parents, and the community, working cooperatively, to ensure: all Laguna Middle School students will emerge as successful learners, who are responsible and participating members of Laguna and other worlds.

Technology plays a vital role in helping us to accomplish this mission.

Technology was built into Laguna Middle School (LMS) from its inception. The educators and tribal leaders that planned the school knew they wanted to incorporate computer technology into it but were unsure exactly how to best accomplish that goal. While the school was still under construction, the newly hired principal, Nick Cheromiah, did extensive research to find out how other schools were incorporating and using computer technology. During his own teaching years, he had seen how a single computer in his classroom could enhance and extend his students' learning. Early on, he had developed his own knowledge of computer programming to incorporate computing in his math curriculum. The Laguna community was fortunate to have a knowledgeable computer veteran establishing the foundation for LMS's technology integration.

In the early 1990s, very few middle schools were providing examples of how to integrate computer technology, especially in New Mexico, so Cheromiah went beyond the educational arena to find ideas and answers. At that time, the business world had more fully developed and integrated computer technology and offered a good model of how a network of connected workstations might be used in schools. Our principal could see how such a network, with greater information-sharing capabilities, would be of value to teachers and administrators who needed to exchange lots of data.

Despite limited financial resources, Cheromiah decided to include in the school's construction the infrastructure necessary to support a schoolwide local-area network, or LAN, which connects computers in every classroom and office to a central server. This system allows students and staff at each workstation to access a wide array of software applications, from games to word processors to grading programs, from a central server. It allows information to be easily shared from station to station. Security systems are built in so that students do not have access to confidential or sensitive files, such as grades. A private contractor was hired to supply the equipment, set it up, and maintain the network.

Initially, several staff members were chosen who had at least a basic knowledge of computing, and in our introductory in-service, the whole staff was made aware of the community's desire that their children learn to access and use the latest technologies. During our first year, the administration encouraged teachers to use the computer network but didn't require it, preferring that staff find their own comfort level with the technology.

At first, using the network *was* frustrating. Lots of glitches and bugs needed to be worked out of the system. While some of us were computer literate, there was little if any knowledge on staff about how to run a network. It was unreliable, and getting service out on the reservation was a challenge. Those of us who jumped into using the network, mostly for word processing, were often thwarted by technical problems, and we couldn't count on the technology to perform consistently. Consequently, we were reluctant to plan lessons that incorporated the computers, afraid that they wouldn't work when we most needed them. That first year, if students used the computers, it was primarily to play games during snatches of free time before or after school, or as a reward for completing their class work early.

We learned much from the problems we encountered during that first year. The administration realized that we needed a more reliable system in order for reluctant staff to even begin to consider using the computers. Technical difficulties only make technophobes more averse to trying new things. And for those of us who were champing at the bit, anxious to include technology in our curricula, dependability was also a major issue. Still, the students enthusiastically requested to use the computers at every chance they got, so the promise of a technology that would motivate and excite learning was very evident. We appealed to the administration for a specialist on staff who could provide us with consistent service, keep our network running, and provide staff with training to develop their computing skills.

By our second year of operation, enough teachers had committed to using the computer network to convince the administration to expand our capabilities. We decided to go beyond a single computer in each classroom and to create a computer lab with multiple work-stations that would permit large groups of students access to the network at one time. We invested in more computers, and one teacher was chosen to coordinate activities in the lab.

For the most part, students still use the classroom computers and the computer lab for word processing and playing computer games. However, word processing developed into desktop publishing. Many students have become adept at creating professional-looking posters, cards, stationary, and other print media. Spreadsheet programs have also been used to make graphs to augment reports. As we've added several CD-ROM machines in the lab, students have started to use the computers as research tools, too.

Our students' keyboarding skills were weak. They needed considerable amounts of time to complete even short assignments on a word processor. We initiated a program to give our sixth graders an in-depth introduction to computer use and keyboarding right at the start of the school year, so they would have a basic comfort and ability level with the technology as they entered the school, one that they could build on as they progressed in grade level.

Besides beginning with a principal who understood and supported technology, our librarian also played an instrumental role in getting us to the "on-ramp" of the information superhighway. She was familiar with computing applications on wide-area networks, or WANs, from her work in helping to create an electronic interlibrary system for New Mexico. She planted the seed of the idea that we could have an electronic library, one in which actual books would become somewhat obsolete, and library users, both students and staff, would access information electronically through computer networks via the Internet. She made sure that a dedicated phone line was installed in the library and set out to connect us, via a modem, with "other worlds." Because our students live in a remote, rural setting, their access to information and cultural opportunities offered by urban society is limited; she understood how technology could help equalize those opportunities for our students.

Telecommunications really began to enter our technology picture in our second year. Various members of our staff, including myself, were attending national education conferences and began to hear and

read about educational opportunities on the information superhighway. In fact, news seemed to be everywhere about the Internet.
Everyone from business people to politicians were touting its possibilities. Several of us became intrigued by these prospects. We began
asking ourselves, "Could this be a way to link our school with worlds
beyond the pueblo? How might we employ this technology to form
bridges between ourselves and others?" Soon, a few of us teachers
obtained accounts with a local Internet service provider, attended
their free training sessions, and began exploring the new frontier of
telecommunications.

   With students, only one telecommunications project was tried
that year. After much difficulty getting the equipment to cooperate,
our science teacher managed to involve some of his students in an
online chat. Chatting proved frustrating for the students, mostly
because of the technical problems and their slow keyboarding skills.
Yet, the exchange did reveal possibilities for future telecommunications projects to both students and staff.

   That spring, a fortuitous opportunity presented itself to me and
my school, especially regarding our future with telecommunications
initiatives. I received a fellowship to attend the Bread Loaf School of
English of Middlebury College, to work on my master's degree, and
to join the Bread Loaf Rural Teacher Network. Participation in the
fellowship program required that I commit to incorporating the use of
BreadNet, the graduate program's telecommunications network, into
my curriculum and teaching life. So while attending graduate school,
I spent much of that summer learning to use BreadNet. Already interested and involved in telecommunications, I tried to pick up as much
as I could from veteran teachers and Bread Loaf staff, some of whom
had been involved in online educational networks and projects for
over ten years already. Their guidance, instruction, and support
proved to be the key for me and my school in moving forward with
integrating telecommunications into the curriculum.

   During that summer, I began to learn how I could make telecommunications a part of my teaching. At first (like most everyone I know
of who's considered the idea), I thought of pen pals. But interaction
with other teachers in the Bread Loaf Rural Teacher Network taught
me to raise my sights and expand my vision. BreadNet offered a way
for students to extend their various inquiries beyond their classroom
and to create learning communities that included multiple classrooms
in diverse locations. Telecommunications technology that connects
classrooms encourages an exchange of ideas through online writing
that includes many perspectives, opinions, and voices. I returned to
Laguna Middle School in the fall committed to getting my students
and school online and communicating with others. In my work at

Bread Loaf during that summer, I had sensed that a real audience was waiting out there to communicate and collaborate with my students.

I also discovered that working on a closed private network, like BreadNet, was more understandable, more manageable, and less intimidating than trying to arrange student communication out in the wide world of the Internet. Through BreadNet I could work with teachers I had met face to face, and we could plan projects cooperatively through both our own online communication, and more ordinary channels, like the telephone. I also had the advantage of being in touch with numerous telecommunications veterans who had successfully planned and carried out online activities with their classrooms already. I started spending more and more time online, on BreadNet, excited to find such a supportive cadre of educators to communicate with. School personnel learned to look for me in the library, at our school's one computer with a modem, when I couldn't be found in my classroom. In fact, I was spending so much time there that it piqued the curiosity of many of my colleagues, who in turn got more interested in getting online themselves.

From my BreadNet cohorts (and later, confirmed by my own experience), I learned that the most successful online communication between students occurs when they get past the pen pal stage and into speculative dialogues about topics of mutual interest. Planning online student conferences on BreadNet requires finding a topic that several classrooms in remote areas could study simultaneously. Then, teachers encourage their students to exchange information about their questions and concerns which arise from their study. For many of us English and language arts teachers (the majority of BreadNet users), those topics in common are frequently works of literature, but increasingly, interdisciplinary studies are being attempted, too. BreadNet conferences have been organized around such diverse topics as birds of prey, wetlands, music, sense of place, community celebrations, and hunting and fishing.

At first, I naively believed that interesting others in communicating with us would be easy. Nationwide, curiosity about Native Americans and their cultures is high, and I thought many teachers would relish the opportunity for their students to find out about life on the "rez" first hand. I chose for our first foray into BreadNet and telecommunications a topic that I felt the students would be comfortable writing and sharing about: the Laguna Feast. This annual feast is the biggest celebration in their community—one that blends ancient elements such as traditional dances and foods with more modern elements, like carnival rides and country western dances. Virtually every student participates in the feast to some extent. I hoped that they would be able to write about it with some interest and clarity.

I was wrong. They were willing to write about their experiences at the feast, but reluctant to tell about any of the traditional activities in any detail. And that's exactly what I thought others would be most interested in hearing about. "We have traditional Laguna dances in the plaza," was a typical student description. They wouldn't believe that other people in far-flung places who might read their accounts of the feast wouldn't have a clue about what a "traditional Laguna dance" was, or even a "plaza," for that matter. To my students, these things were commonplace, and they all had an understanding of them. I couldn't convince them that most Americans really had no idea of what their culture was like and that they'd have to use more detail to describe it if they wanted others to understand. They resisted. They didn't have a sense of their audience, and I couldn't seem to convey it to them.

Nonetheless, I uploaded their stories on BreadNet using what's come to be called the "post and hope" method—post some writing online and hope for some response. I hadn't arranged to engage a specific audience for their feast stories; I was simply counting on some teacher to find them interesting and share them with their students, who would in turn want to respond. Although I didn't know it at the time, this method is very risky. If you encourage students' writing by holding out the promise of the response of a real audience, and then that audience never materializes, the students' disappointment can become a barrier to their future cooperation and enthusiasm to participate in the future. Still, I was innocent and anxious to get them online. I took a chance.

We got lucky. A teacher in Vermont downloaded the Laguna Feast stories and shared them with her ninth graders. They wrote back to us and asked questions about the feast that bore out my predictions—in ways that were much more meaningful to my students than any teacherly response I could have offered them. The respondents also told us about some of their favorite celebrations (like the Vermont State Fair) and even wrote back about some traditional New England activities such as Christmas tree cutting and skiing. My students were astounded. I don't think they really expected any response, but when we got one, they got turned on. As the responses came trickling in over the course of several days, students pestered me from the minute I walked into the building each morning, begging me to check the computer and see if they'd received any word from Vermont. We wrote back to them with answers to their questions, and asked some questions of our own, to which they responded. The correspondence continued from October through December. Eventually, because we didn't provide them with more grist for their dialogue mill, the students ran out of things to say to each other.

Later in the year, we participated in another online conference, this time with more structure. Several teachers in the Southwest chose the topic "raptors" (birds of prey) as a focus for a BreadNet conference. I felt this would be an ideal topic for my students, as there are many raptors in our area, and because eagles and hawks have a special significance in traditional Laguna culture. In fact, our school mascot is the eagle, and the Lagunas are well known among the Pueblo tribes for their Eagle Dance.

We spent several weeks in class learning the natural history of raptors, as well as reading literature about raptors, mostly Native American myths and legends, in which raptors were characters. Then the students wrote to other students about what they had learned, described raptors in their area, and even wrote some of their own literature about raptors. This time, my students enjoyed the opportunity to share their ideas and other information about their traditions, and they took pride in mentioning to other students their cultural connection with eagles.

We had one other significant online event during the year. We were very fortunate to have the opportunity to participate in an online exchange with author Leslie Marmon Silko, perhaps Laguna's most famous daughter. After reading several of her short stories, and discussing her local notoriety in class, the students wrote to her with questions and expressed what they felt about her stories. She honored us with a personal reply to each student, and she addressed all their often personal and sometimes difficult questions. This exchange again provided students with another opportunity to examine and reflect on their culture.

Through these exchanges, LMS earned a place on the educational telecommunications map. While other teachers at the school had not yet integrated telecommunications into their curricula, there was plenty of interest and action underway to expand our capabilities. Many teachers as well as the administration saw how excited my students and I were about our online exchanges. I was clamoring for my own phone line in my classroom because I wanted my students to be able to actually participate in the telecommunications technology. Up to this point, they had been creating their messages using a word processor, saving them to disk, and I was the only one doing the actual transfer of the electronic missives online, the up- and downloading.

Earlier in the year, we had obtained a large grant from the U.S. Department of Education to incorporate Native culture into our curriculum using technology. Through this grant we were able to hire the technology specialist that many of us had been anxious to have on staff. She joined us with her own progressive vision of how LMS could become an important site of learning with technology, and she had the expertise to actually make it happen. With her leading the way, several interested staff members and I moved us toward a major decision: We decided to invest in becoming a node on the Internet—in other words, instead of just having an "on-ramp" to the information superhighway, we were going to become a stopover, an actual site, on that road.

As a site on the information superhighway, our school is becoming increasingly more involved in telecommunications. Our technology "bridge" is always under construction as we upgrade from a simple one-lane route to a multilane superstructure, and we are beginning to interface electronically and culturally with the world. Soon, we will be creating our own World Wide Web site, which will involve our students in hypertext publishing. We will be developing multimedia materials about the school, and our lives, which will include information about the local culture, to publish on the Internet. LMS students will research and develop the virtual electronic "face" that Laguna shows to the world, as well as field the questions and comments that are received in reply.

Undoubtedly, creating such a powerful link with the world beyond the borders of the reservation will have profound effects on Laguna society, just as the railroad and the Interstate did. Only this "highway" will link Laguna to a global network, permitting instantaneous communication worldwide. Many Lagunas are apprehensive about sharing their traditional culture with the greater society. They feel that if they openly share their traditions with others, they risk being misunderstood, or worse, exploited. At LMS, we are proceeding with sensitivity to the community's cautious feelings about sharing their culture. Some areas of culture, such as the traditional religion, are simply off-limits. However, we're working to expand the community's definition of *culture* to include more than just the language and traditional religion of the people. For us at LMS, who have been charged with helping to teach and perpetuate Laguna culture, it includes everything that makes up Laguna society, both the ancient and the modern, the "full blood" ways as well as the "mixed blood" ones.

Laguna Middle School is set to become the telecommunications hub for the entire community. Eventually, others will be able to access the Internet through our connection locally with a modem and computer in their remote home or business. We are already training students to be technology trainers—of their peers, of course, but also, and perhaps more significantly, of their parents and other adults in the community. One of the platitudes of education is that children represent the future of the country. But a singular, Native American pueblo culture like that of the Lagunas does indeed rely heavily on its children for its continuity—these children are responsible for the perpetuation and development of the one-thousand-year-old Laguna culture. At LMS, we're working to ensure that they have the tools they need to keep Laguna viable and to fully participate in the global arena.

As we've escalated our venture into technology, we've proceeded very carefully with investing our resources. Decisions about technology acquisitions, as well as training opportunities for staff, are made most often by groups of concerned participants, with input from all the major stakeholders in the school: teachers, students, parents, and community members. The administration has been very willing to share in decision making regarding technology. In this way, we have not wasted resources for equipment or training that go unused. Before investments are made, they must be justified. We only purchase equipment and training when they can be shown they'll fill a need. In fact, for the most part, the administration has allowed the staff and community to extend a hand and pull the school forward into technology, rather than to push from behind.

Actually, the students are the ones who have really pulled us forward with technology. They are the ones who are most excited and enthusiastic about integrating technology into the curriculum. Every survey we've ever given them has consistently shown they want more access to technology. In fact, it doesn't take a survey to see how much they want it. Many otherwise reluctant teachers have been prodded into developing computer applications for their classes by students who are constantly urging them on by asking, "Why don't we ever get to go to the computer lab?"

Technology is one of the most powerful motivators we have yet discovered to encourage learning. Our students, like middle school students everywhere, are sometimes notoriously apathetic about academics. However, given the opportunity to use a computer to complete an assignment, students' motivation is sparked and kindled. We've also found that telecommunications and literacy education work hand in hand: Giving students real audiences with whom they can share authentic communication produces genuine growth in language skills, and all the while students are enjoying the process. In fact, our students are overwhelmingly the most enthusiastic group in the community about using computers and other technology. They insist on access to these new technologies; they sense how important they are to their future, and when we give them entry to that technological world, they respond with excitement and a desire to learn and share.

Students at Laguna Middle School face the challenge of learning to succeed in multiple cultures. The greater society faces an equal challenge in accepting and valuing diversity. Technology has become the key for LMS students to more fully explore and understand their own culture, while also providing them with a bridge to other cultures. To a great degree, Laguna culture has evolved to where it is today because it has never been isolated from the rest of the world. Now, with the advent of instantaneous electronic global connectivity at their doorstep, many peoples can work and learn together in harmony, creating bridges of understanding that benefit us all.

13

Reflections on Cross-Age Collaboration
Networking College and High School Students

Wayne M. Butler

The notion of cross-age educational collaboration—older and younger students working together—is certainly not new. During the nineteenth century, for example, the rural one-room schoolhouse fostered cross-age collaboration, if not by design then out of necessity, when older children worked with younger children so that the teacher could attend to other issues. The contemporary idea of learning communities, given various sobriquets including cooperative and collaborative learning and popularized over the last thirty years by educational researchers like Robert Slavin (1983) and David and Roger Johnson (1985), language arts researchers like James Moffett (1968), and writing pedagogy theorists like Kenneth Bruffee (1983) and Anne Ruggles Gere (1987), also has its roots in late-nineteenth and early-twentieth-century educational theories, particularly those of John Dewey and Colin Scott of the Social Education Association. According to Joel Spring (1986), "Dewey's methods emphasized student interests, student activity, group work, and cooperation" (172), and Scott believed that "the classroom should initiate group projects as preparation for entering a society of cooperative groups" (175).

Cross-institutional collaborations have existed for a number of years in a number of forms as well. For years classroom teachers have been arranging collaborations among students working in different schools across the country and the world through pen pal exchanges, and colleges of education have worked with local schools through student-teaching arrangements and joint research projects. In addition, colleges and universities, in attempts to bolster recruitment, improve retention, and otherwise serve as good citizens in their local communities, have sponsored outreach efforts to build stronger bonds between the higher education institutions and the high schools that feed into them. The new wrinkle, then, in cross-age, cross-institutional educational collaborations is the infusion of computer technology, particularly networked computers, to link students of different ages and different institutions together into electronically mediated learning communities.

In the early 1990s, several members of the University of Michigan's English Composition Board (ECB) embarked on such a collaboration with Ann Arbor's Pioneer High School, and the project came to be known as the Pioneer–University of Michigan Connection (PUM). Our project was not only cross-age and cross-institutional; it was also cross-curricular, as the writing specialists of the ECB worked with an American history teacher to implement a writing-to-learn history curriculum. As has been reported elsewhere (Butler 1995; Butler and Wax 1993; Wax 1993, 1994), the project was successful in many ways, but what we achieved was not without discovering and addressing a number of logistical problems. When developing and implementing projects that involve cross-age and cross-institutional collaborations, writing across the disciplines, and computer technology, much can go wrong. On a day-to-day basis, participants must struggle with technological failures such as network servers going down moments before class begins, with the difficulties of scheduling meetings among the university and high school teachers, or with struggles over how much time should be devoted to disciplinary content and how much should be devoted to writing.

From close up, such obstacles, although numerous and serious, seem unrelated and isolated. In retrospect, however, I have come to interpret the obstacles not as mere logistical problems but issues that arise out of a clash of educational cultures. I do not use the term *culture* with a capital C or in a way that refers to the differences within our national culture, although it might be argued that those too come into play. What I am referring to here are the differences—material, ideological, and in working conditions—between universities and high schools. During the Pioneer–University of Michigan Connection we learned much about the very real professional, technological, financial, and logistical gulfs separating the educational cultures of the high school and higher education. More importantly, we learned many valuable lessons about and techniques for spanning such gulfs. In this chapter, I offer a background on PUM and identify clashes between the curricular and pedagogical assumptions, technological contexts, and financial realities of the university and high school. I then offer an analysis of how we addressed the gaps and fissures that grew out of those clashes and offer suggestions for those who wish to engage in similar projects.

Background on the Pioneer–University of Michigan Connection

Beginning in September 1991, two faculty members, Director Deborah Keller-Cohen and Margaret Marshall, and several peer tutors of the University of Michigan's English Composition Board (ECB) joined forces with an American History teacher, Robin Wax, and her at-risk "basic skills" juniors at Ann Arbor's Pioneer High School to collaborate on a cross-age computer-supported literacy project. In September 1992, I joined the project when Marshall left the ECB to teach at the University of Pittsburgh. In the beginning, the project's goals, though ambitious, were simple enough: to use computer-mediated communication (CMC) as a way to link university writing tutors with at-risk students to improve the academic achievement of the latter. The original project designers presumed that since CMC is a text-rich environment through which university tutors and high school students could write to one another, the principles of writing-to-learn theory and research would help the latter group improve their writing by allowing them to get frequent and pragmatic opportunities to write to actual audiences for real purposes. We hoped, also, to improve the high school students' knowledge of American history by inviting them to engage more actively with the course content.

From the very beginning, those who planned the project recognized that the Pioneer-University of Michigan Connection was an exercise in educational reform employing experimental technology. Knowing that the project would disrupt business as usual, they addressed from the outset what they perceived to be major time and financial issues. During that first year, Keller-Cohen brokered a number of key transactions. First, knowing the public school's financial constraints, Keller-Cohen arranged for the university to donate user accounts for Wax and her students so they could have dial-in access to the university's mainframe online services, including email and the university's electronic conferencing program called Confer. Without these accounts, the students would have no way to engage in CMC with the university peer tutors. Second, she arranged with the Daedalus Group, developer and publisher of the Daedalus Integrated Writing Environment (DIWE), a local area network application that facilitates both synchronous and asynchronous computer-mediated communication, to donate a site license of DIWE to Pioneer. Keller-Cohen also arranged for Marshall to have up to a quarter release time from her teaching duties to work with Wax and conduct on-site visits to Pioneer. Keller-Cohen also secured university funds to compensate Wax for the extra time (Wax continued teaching a full load of five classes during the 1991–1992 school year) she would have to dedicate to the project. And finally, but not incidentally, Keller-Cohen wrote letters to public school administrators to declare and explain the ECB's and the university's support for the project. The preparatory phase in which Keller-Cohen built a coalition among the university, the public school, and a software vendor, and in which she compensated Wax for her contributions to the project, was crucial to the success of the project.

In many ways and for many reasons, we considered the project successful. Robin Wax, a twenty-five-year classroom veteran, reported observing academic, behavioral, and attitudinal improvements among her at-risk students, the type with whom she had been working for much of her career (Butler and Wax 1993, 21). The students also reported—during interviews, on exit surveys, and during group discussions—satisfaction with the project. They reported that on the whole they enjoyed the computer-mediated course more than those in more traditional settings, that their attitudes improved toward learning history, and that they believed by the end of year that they had improved as writers and history students. Much of the data we collected demonstrated that students participated more in online discussions than they normally did in face-to-face conversations or during teacher-led class discussions, and their on-task behavior improved. These students generated more CMC text and electronically produced school text than similar students in more traditional settings had. Students wrote more for two reasons. First, students used writing to communicate with peers within the classes and the university tutors; and second, Wax incorporated more writing activities into her curriculum once writing-to-learn became a pedagogical focus (Butler 1995, 19). Eventually the project would receive building- and district-level attention and coverage in the local newspaper, and Wax would win both statewide and nationwide awards for innovative uses of instructional technology.

Our successes, however, did not come easily. Although we had numerous meetings and wrote lengthy and detailed plans, and as a group we had vast experiences with collaborative learning, writing across the curriculum, and the use of networked computers in the writing classroom, the implementation of the goals, objectives, and activities proved more challenging than we might have expected, because we often had different assumptions about pedagogical and curricular issues, different experiences with and expectations for the technology, and our students lived in vastly different technological worlds.

Clashing Curricular and Pedagogical Assumptions

Robin Wax is an institution at Pioneer High School. Because for the last twenty-two years she has taught effectively and with distinction both college prep advanced-placement history courses and basic-skills American history courses, she is greatly admired by her colleagues, students, and the community. She is the chair of the History Department. She takes well-deserved pride in her deep knowledge of American history and her success with all types of students. When reflecting on her teaching style, Wax (1993) reported, "My classroom is definitely 'teacher-centered.' I lecture, lead discussions, and take responsibility for making sure learning takes place."

After several classroom visits, it became clear to me that Wax believes in attending to students' individual needs as learners. Her individual interactions with students—interactions that occurred during seat work, during pre- and postlesson social banter, and in the hallways between classes—are warm and genuine. For the most part, her students sat in rows as she stood at a lectern at the front of the room. Wax is a charismatic presence. A good storyteller and an organized lecturer, she alternates between writing notes on the chalkboard for her students to copy into their notebooks, drawing students' attention to passages in a textbook, and using a Socratic method to encourage class discussion. During our early conversations, Wax admitted that her teaching style was more successful with her college prep students, and she was actively looking for other ways to engage her basic-skills students. She reported that she sought to make an impact on all her students, but particularly the at-risk students, by nurturing and "mothering" them as a way to attending to their individual needs.

Over the years Wax had studied and explored various alternative pedagogies like cooperative learning and writing-to-learn, but she was often disappointed with the outcomes for one major reason: As a history teacher, she was often left with the feeling that the slower pace of collaborative learning, and what she considered the potentially valuable but often frivolous writing-to-learn activities, robbed her and her students of valuable time that could be spent covering content. She had built a highly successful career around the basic premise that as a history teacher her primary goal was to develop in her students a deep knowledge of history. "I was really nervous about changing teaching techniques which had provided twenty-five years of comfort and relative success," reports Wax. "Writing-to-learn, collaborative learning, and student-centered classrooms all sounded fine, but could I construct the course content and assignments to fit these new models, hold the interest of this particular student population, and maintain the academic integrity of the history and the skills the students learned?" (1994). While alternative pedagogies and curricular approaches appealed to her on numerous grounds, she found that direct teaching methods were most efficient.

On the surface, Wax and I had little in common. Yes, I had been a high school teacher earlier in my career, but I was an English teacher. Had I grown up in Ann Arbor, I might have been one of Wax's students early in her career. As I developed into a college writing instructor, I had come to embrace collaborative learning. I had long abandoned a teacher-centered pedagogy and had developed the habit of rearranging the classroom furniture from rows to circles or pods to better facilitate student-to-student interaction. Of course, I had the luxury of working with fewer and smaller classes of college-age students who were not considered at risk nor were they enrolled in my classes due to compensatory education laws. While a graduate student, I enjoyed the benefit of teaching in a technology-rich university where the English department had its own networked computer classroom, and my good fortune continued when I was hired by a university where access to instructional technology was at least equal if not superior to that at my graduate school.

Even though I had gone through public education and had spent the first six years of my career as a high school teacher, I had forgotten much of the day-to-day realities of working in a high school. I was startled by the constant reminders that high school educational culture was vastly different from university educational culture. Looking back, I suspect that for the first several weeks of our collaboration, Wax and I had talked but not really communicated, because her sense of what it meant *to teach*, one validated by years of measurable success, was vastly different from mine, which was based on experiments with student-centered writing pedagogy in a comparatively low-stake and low-stress setting of a networked computer-based university classroom.

When Wax and I came together, then, she considered herself a history teacher; I was a writing teacher. She was successful and comfortable in the more traditional teacherly role; I was skeptical of any style of teaching that evoked Freire's banking mode of education. I was a firm believer in writing-to-learn's demonstrated ability to help students actively engage in the learning process (Gere 1985; Glaze 1987; Farrell-Childers, Gere, and Young 1994). Wax (1994) "was skeptical that writing-to-learn could work with this population. All of the literature I reviewed sounded great but the examples given of

writing in the social studies curriculum were rarely content-based."
Although Wax had been introduced to technology, she was uncomfortable with it; I had come to embrace it. In sum, I represented an
educational culture that privileged theory and research over practice.
I came from the world of higher education that is often perceived by
classroom teachers as being aloof and critical of what teachers do, a
world whose representatives swoop upon the public schools to dictate
in top-down fashion what should be done and drop in long enough to
observe, collect data for research, and pass judgment. Wax (1993)
wrote, while reflecting on her concerns about the project: "How
would my interaction with the UM staff proceed? How would I be
treated? Would I be able to maintain the integrity of my curriculum or
would their agenda be imposed on my course?" Wax's anxiety was
warranted, since I came from a learning environment that had comparatively small classes of students who were admitted based on academic achievement. As a teacher in the university environment, I did
not experience the great external pressures of state-mandated curricula, local boards of education, and close supervision by administrators. I had the luxury to turn my classroom into a pedagogical proving
ground to explore the latest theories. By contrast, the realities of
Wax's world included compulsory education laws and state-mandated
achievement standards. She worked with twenty-five or so students—
whose abilities might touch both ends of attitudinal, ability, and
achievement scales—in five sections per day, five days per week, one
hundred and eighty days a year.

Clashing Technological Contexts

As noted above, our goal was to use network technology as a vehicle
for implementing collaborative, writing-to-learn activities. After
experimenting with a number of configurations during the project's
first year, we ultimately connected the high school students to one
another on Pioneer's local area network using the Daedalus Integrated
Writing Environment, linked the university students together on the
university's network, and then linked the high school students with
the university students through a 2400-baud modem and a shareware
remote bulletin board system (RBBS). While this model appeared
sound on paper, the differences between how the two institutions
allotted technological resources and in students' access to the technology sometimes undermined efforts for smooth CMC interaction
among the students.

When PUM began, Pioneer High School had relatively sophisticated computer technology. The building had three computer classrooms. Two of them were equipped with fifteen IBM PC 386s, color

monitors, and one printer per five workstations. More importantly, these machines were linked into a local area network. Several of the library computers had modems which allowed users to link up with the University of Michigan's email system, online library catalog, and other online services. The networked computer classroom Wax's students used, however, had only one machine with a modem — a 2400-baud model at that.

Even though Pioneer High School was considered at the time to be technologically rich, access to the computers was limited. While there were only fifteen computers, Wax's class rosters hovered around twenty five students. There also existed a number of territorial issues concerning access to the computers. The networked computer classroom was built with a private donation, with the stipulation that the room be used for general education purposes. Control of the facility, however, was conferred upon the science department. During the project's first year, Wax found gaining access to the computer classroom problematic. She encountered resistance because of her students' reputations. Those who controlled the room wondered if her at-risk students, many of whom had records of disciplinary problems, might not vandalize the equipment. Through haggling and wrangling, Wax was eventually able to get occasional use of the room, but could do so only by going through a labyrinth of permissions and sign-up sheets.

Wax also had to overcome the stigma that computers were best suited for math and science applications — it was difficult in the beginning for her administrators to imagine how a humanities class would make viable educational use of the computers beyond word processing. Only after the project gained some momentum was Wax able to get equitable access to the computers. Even after access became easier, the computer classroom remained a general-purpose facility. Because Wax had to share the classroom with colleagues in other departments, she could only bring her classes to the room twice a week.

At the university end of the connection, the technological context was much different. Like most major research institutions, the University of Michigan had at the time hundreds, perhaps thousands, of Macintosh and IBM computers, many of which were upgraded regularly. The workstations all had access to the university's mainframe for email functions, and the bulk of them were located in public computing sites spread out across campus in dormitories, libraries, and in computing classrooms. Most of these sites were open twenty-four hours a day, three hundred and sixty days a year. All university students were, and still are, given computing accounts with email addresses and access to a plethora of applications for which the university holds institutional site licenses. The university peer tutors, most of whom lived on or near campus, had access to the computer platform of their choosing virtually any time of the day or any day they wanted. Those who owned computers and modems were even able to engage in CMC from the comfort of their rooms.

Our goal of creating email exchanges between university and high school students was regularly undermined by communication bottle-necks. Initial first attempts to create a CMC connection between the high school and university students resulted in the high school students standing in line at the one machine with a modem waiting to upload the messages that they had composed on diskette using a word processor. By the time the messages were all uploaded then read and responded to by the university tutors, the feedback the tutors might have offered was moot because the feedback would arrive well after the high school students had revised their drafts. The technological transfer of messages, drafts, and feedback became so difficult that during one point Wax resorted to bringing hard copies of drafts and messages to the university so she could hand them to the university tutors.

During the second year, we ended up creating communication cycles where on a Monday, for instance, the high school students would compose their essays and email messages in the computer classroom and post them on the classroom electronic bulletin board. Over the next several days, I would serve as a netweaver by sending each individual message to the university tutors, who then had several days to read and reply to the high school students' messages via a shareware remote bulletin board software package. I would then manually redirect those messages to the high school students by the next time they were scheduled to use the computer classroom. During that next session, the high school students would then have forty-five minutes (which after tardies, log-on problems, and negotiating share-time on the workstations would quickly wither to twenty minutes or so of actual on-task time) to read messages they received. While such a cycle lent more organization to the communication and better used the limited technological and time resources, the cycle became corrupted if one of the high school students happened to be absent on email days. And, since absent students had no access to the technology other than during those two or three forty-five-minute sessions a week, Wax and I constantly juggled, tweaked, and otherwise dedicated additional time to keeping the cycle rolling.

Truthfully, had Wax and I understood the clash of technological contexts at the outset, we might have not been so bold as to push through the university–high school connection. What I and my university colleagues assumed could be done with the technology was largely a result of our experiences working with college students in a technology-rich setting that offered almost limitless technological resources. The relative transparency of technology at the university level allowed us to develop pedagogies and form assumptions about CMC that just would not transfer smoothly or even that successfully to the high school setting.

Clashing Financial Realities

As noted above, Pioneer was fairly well outfitted. At the time, their machines were leading edge, and the powers that be had the foresight to use Ethernet as the building backbone. In addition, they had in place a robust suite of software including spreadsheet and graphics programs, word processors and programming languages, and science and communications programs. But, they only had what they had. No significant funds existed for upgrades, new software, or infrastructure renovations. Even worse, no funds existed for technical support. So, when our pedagogical and curricular goals called for a new piece of software or hardware or some special technical expertise, we had to make do.

When we discovered, for example, that having students wait to upload email messages through one modem connection resulted in a communication bottleneck, we started thinking of other solutions. One solution involved providing the high school students more access to the university network and the other involved giving the university students more access to the high school's network. We surmised that the best way to implement the first solution would be to have access to more phone lines. When we inquired about more phone lines, we were told that the phone system installed in the 1960s had reached its limit, and to get more phone lines for the classroom would require a comprehensive upgrade to the school's phone system. That was not going to happen any time soon. We were left, then, with the second solution—to give the university students more access to the high school network. We expected we could provide such access with better email software, net modems, or gateway servers. We quickly discovered that there existed no budget for new software or hardware. Instead, we scanned the Ann Arbor's local electronic bulletin boards, found a shareware RBBS, downloaded it, and installed it on the one machine with a modem. By doing so, we permitted the university students—who could get to a computer and a modem any time of the day—to call into the high school network and leave their electronic messages there. By simply reversing the locus of the communication hub from the university network to the high school network we effectively broke up one of the major logjams in the communication bottleneck. Even this solution, one jury-rigged because we had no budget for more technologically sophisticated solutions, created problems. We first installed the RBBS because we had learned we could build a "door" between the RBBS and the local area network, but we lacked the technological knowledge to make it work. And, of course, we had no budget to hire a technical consultant. As noted above, I then served as a netweaver to transfer manually the RBBS messages to the local area network email system. This solution would have been impossible if I had not been just a few miles away from the high school and able to show up several times a week on an as needed basis.

As a result of the limited financial resources, we found it difficult to get the kind of technical support we needed. Before PUM, Pioneer had given partial release time to a math teacher to serve as building technology coordinator, and he had one half-time assistant. To be fair, I must emphasize that the technical assistance that they did provide us with far outweighed what they were required to provide us. Although their responsibilities were buildingwide and they were not granted any extra time to help me and Wax, their support was of Herculean proportions, considering they assisted us on their own time. Nevertheless, tasks like installing an electronic bulletin board, repairing broken printers, and resplicing frayed network cables took several days to several weeks, which meant that on some days there might be only ten of our fifteen computers working or that the network wasn't running at the start of a new communication cycle. These obstacles meant that our carefully crafted computer-mediated pedagogy would be undermined, class time would be wasted, and the pace of the curriculum slowed. Once again, my experiences in university computer-based educational settings did not prepare me adequately for this aspect of the project.

While financial constraints hampered our ability to solve hardware and software problems, the more significant effect was that because the financial realities of our two settings were so different, Wax and I brought different attitudes and expectations to the project. Because she fully understood the financial constraints of her setting, her pedagogical, technical, and curricular view of what was possible was often limited. Because Wax had not had the professional development opportunities to become fully computer-literate herself and to explore various uses of CMC from a user's perspective, she was not always aware of the possibilities. When the CMC bottleneck hampered our efforts to connect the high school and university students, her response was to hand deliver hard copies of messages. At this point, Wax began to doubt if the collaboration between the high school and university students was worth the effort.

Even when Wax became more comfortable with the technology and more aware of the possibilities, she knew much better than I what funds existed and how much competition existed for those limited funds. Her twenty-plus years of experience taught her that most public school allocations were in the teens or hundreds rather than the thousands of dollars we could have used. There exists, furthermore, a great premium in terms of expectations placed on those dollars. Had we been able to get school funds for more hardware, software, or technological support, opportunities for experimentation and risk taking might have been reduced in the name of investing the dollars into what worked rather than into what *might* work. Had the school district dedicated more money toward professional development and funded more technical support, Wax might have been better prepared to imagine possibilities. (I should note that recently the Ann Arbor Public Schools took major steps in articulating a districtwide technology plan, hired a director of instructional technology, and raised millions of dollars through a school bond for new hardware and human resources.)

I, on the other hand, accustomed to easy access to hardware, software, and technical support, had been lulled into thinking that such issues were insignificant. I worked in places where I rarely had to ask for more hardware or software because there was already enough. In fact, my experiences are shaped by my attempts to fulfill the potential of the technological contexts provided for me. When we first planned the curriculum and pedagogy, I would make suggestions based on assumptions that students would meet in the computer classroom every day, and that they could and would access the network in the library during their lunch periods, during study halls, and after school. Of course, none of those conditions were true. When we were confronted with a problem during PUM, my first reaction would be, "Well, let's buy X," or "Who could we call to fix X?" Expecting answers that ranged from "OK, we'll cut a purchase order" or "We can call our technical consultant," I felt constrained by "We can't do that." In short, my own attitudes toward and practices with instructional technology were based on a utopian perspective, while the attitudes and practices of Pioneer High School were shaped by a reality-based perspective.

Spanning the Gaps and Fissures

Had we not found solutions to the differences and challenges described above, the project would have undoubtedly become an utter failure in that it most likely would have lost momentum and not have reaped enough professional and educational benefits to deem it successful. The fact of the matter is, however, that much did go right during the Pioneer–UM Connection. What follows is an explanation of how we spanned the various gaps and fissures. Some of the following solutions we put in place during the initial planning phases, and others we devised on an "as needed" basis as we encountered problems. Others resulted from sheer serendipity, but we came to understand that such solutions were in fact crucial elements that led to our successes.

Separating the types of problems into categories, or course, is deceptively artificial. None of the problems were mutually exclusive; in fact, they interacted and contributed to one another. Certain issues, like the technological/financial constraints, were often beyond our control. But recognizing those problems that were in our control and those that were beyond our control helped us understand how we could find effective compromises between what we wanted to do and what we could do. Furthermore, the technological issues will prove, we hope, to be transient, since Pioneer High School, like most schools, is continuing to purchase more personal computers and obtain direct access to the Internet, which will allow its students more transparent computer-mediated communication. As it turned out, addressing the time issue—finding time for professional development and creating time for collaborative work between me and Wax— turned out to be the linchpin allowing us to address the differences between our curricular and pedagogical assumptions.

Making Time

During the first year of the project, frustrations arose from complications associated with providing Wax's students adequate access to the high school's technology, finding a reliable way of exchanging digital text between the high school students and the university tutors, and providing Wax time to learn the technology. Indeed, her stipend compensated Wax for the extra time she would dedicate to the project, but it could not buy her time during her school day. Marshall's release time, however, proved crucial in that it allowed her to visit Pioneer regularly to observe Wax's students, to work with Wax on technical and curricular issues, and to develop formative evaluation, planning documents, and reports that both summarized progress and made recommendations for future improvements.

The greatest triumph of that first year, however, was that Wax wrote an application for a sabbatical. By the end of the year, she learned that she had indeed been granted a full-year, half-time sabbatical for the 1992–1993 school year. The sabbatical would allow her to teach just her two basic-skills sections, with the explicit goal of transforming PUM's goals from objectives into a workable pedagogy. As I was to learn when I joined the project in 1992, Wax's sabbatical was to make all the difference. As Wax notes, "I had the luxury of time. My half-time sabbatical allowed time for reflection, time to read the research literature, time to plan a lesson, teach it and then re-do it

for the next day" (Butler and Wax 1993, 21). I too was granted
approximately one-quarter release time from my teaching duties.

Using Time

How Wax and I used our time together became a crucial element in
finding a common ground for our own collaboration, and as our professional relationship grew, we found it easier to address our different
curricular and pedagogical assumptions which paved the way for us to
address the technical and financial obstacles. During our first meetings, Wax explained to me how the project went during its first year,
and although she was enthusiastic about the successes and energized
by the realization her sabbatical would allow her the time to address
the first year's shortcomings, she openly shared with me her concerns. She had already established a relationship with my predecessor,
and now she would have to begin again. She also admitted she had
not learned the technology as well as she would have liked, and even
though the first year gave her a better understanding and more faith in
collaborative learning and writing-to-learn, she knew she was not
about to throw out what worked for her in the last two decades. Wax
also attributed many of the problems to too much happening too fast.
Her first attempts in the classroom with using cranky technology,
writing-to-learn techniques, collaborative learning methods, and
cross-age collaboration were overwhelming.

During these early meetings, I began to define the roles I should
play. There was much ground to cover. I feared that if all of Wax's
previous experiences with writing-to-learn, collaborative learning, and
computer technology had not made her a true believer, I would have
no chance at all. My immediate impulse, I must admit, was to run
back to my office library and pull together as many articles I could
about writing-to-learn, collaborative learning, and computers and writing. But as I listened to Wax closely and thought about it more, I realized she was already familiar with the theoretical aspects, and it would
be inappropriate for me to hand her yet another article which did not
speak to her particular situation. While talking with colleagues who
had previously worked on university-high school projects (Morris et
al. 1994), I came to recognize that I would have little effect if I were to
adopt the stance of a visiting "expert" who was going to "fix" what
was not working at the high school.

Doing so would have been inappropriate for a number of reasons.
First, as stated elsewhere, Wax was a highly successful and respected
teacher who willingly and enthusiastically volunteered to participate
in the project—it would have been arrogant of me to tell such a
teacher how she should conduct her business. Such arrogance would

have discouraged a trusting relationship between us. More importantly, I had much to learn from Wax. I knew next to nothing about the
goals of a high school American History curriculum, especially one
geared for at-risk students. Wax taught me that the facts of history
were not an end in themselves but rather created a context so that
students could understand enough about their cultural heritage to
become active participants in the democratic process—a role that
requires citizens to make present and future decisions based on their
knowledge of how our culture articulated and addressed previous economic, political, and social issues. Wax taught me about the social
fabric of the school, one she knew intimately from having taught the
older siblings, and sometimes even the parents, of her current students. Wax taught me about the political structure of the high school
and the district. Her two decades of working with several generations
of administrators and riding the ebb and flow of educational reform
provided her with the instincts for who would serve as allies and who
would put up roadblocks. Having experienced numerous educational
reform movements over the last two decades, Wax had a highly
attuned sense of what might be a fad and what might constitute a
significant improvement. She reminded me that students were complex individuals who deserved and responded to individual attention,
and not "types" a "system" could accommodate. Perhaps most importantly, Wax reminded me that caring, reflective, and dedicated teachers provide the cornerstone of quality education. Curricular, pedagogical, and technological reforms that lack support and input by
those whom they will most affect—the teachers—are doomed to fail.

I recognized that I would have to adopt a participatory role and
began to think of myself not as a consultant but as a collaborator. I had
to overcome my initial impulse to employ what Morris et al. (1994) call
a "transmission" model of collaboration and adopt a "dialogic" model
in which Wax would "have time to explore and adjust what can work"
(167). My goal, then, was to learn as much as I could about the site
before becoming a partner. First, I spent at least two days a week at
Pioneer High School, and as the project progressed, I spent even more
time on site. Some of that time was spent sitting in Wax's classroom,
observing her students, participating in their discussion groups, and
otherwise learning all I could about the day-to-day realities of their
lives in school. On other days I would meet with the technology coordinator to learn about how the computers were set up, what applications
were available to us, and what support he could offer. But mostly Wax
and I spent a good deal of time together.

Because of her newly found time provided by her sabbatical, I
was able to offer Wax intensive training in the technology. She was
able to teach me about her students and her course goals. We spent

time in the teacher's lounge drinking coffee and eating lunch, and Wax introduced me to her colleagues. After a short while, I was on a first-name basis with most of the history teachers. On the day I was not asked to show a security pass, I realized that I had become a recognized member of the school community. Wax also visited my university classroom and learned how I used collaborative learning and technology in my own teaching of writing.

As our time together progressed, I served less as a consulting expert and became a partner, an aide, helping Wax accomplish what *she* wanted to. Our planning meetings then worked as collaborative sessions in which she would discuss with me her unit and lesson objectives and activities, and I would discuss with her how those goals and activities could be accomplished in a computer-mediated, collaborative writing-to-learn environment. Eventually, we wrote lesson plans, activity sheets, and handouts collaboratively. I spent time in the computer classroom with Wax, serving as her technical assistant and eventually as her aide as she invited me to work not just with the technology but with the students and their writing.

There was yet another way Wax and I spent time together, a way that could never have been written into a plan or a grant. At the time, I could not provide my own transportation to Pioneer High School, and public transportation could not have gotten me to the school in time for Wax's 7:30 A.M. classes. Wax generously volunteered to pick me up at my home and take me to work with her. During these twenty-minute commutes (Wax provided the vehicle and I provided the coffee) we had time to talk about our families, our lives, and other issues that didn't always relate to the project. As a result of this serendipitous time together, we were able to build personal ties, and we came to understand much about one another's personal, professional, and educational beliefs. I am convinced that this social context—one leavened by laughter and mutual admiration—provided us knowledge and trust of one another, allowing us to frankly articulate and address differences of opinion. In short, we became a team.

Reflections on Lessons Learned

Indeed, it is dangerous to draw generalizations about how to plan, implement, and otherwise facilitate cross-age, cross-institutional computer-mediated collaborations from one case. But given another opportunity to work on such a project, there exist a number of principles to which I would adhere.

Build Coalitions and Partnerships

University facilitators must abandon the sense of authority that comes from being perceived as experts because they work in higher education. Unless they have spent significant time in public schools as teachers themselves, they will learn, though perhaps not quickly enough, that what they understand about students, teaching, and educational bureaucracies and processes based on their university experiences will not transfer to secondary schools. Secondary school teachers must be assertive and open with their university partners and not be suspicious or intimidated by the status markers such as "Ph.D." and "professor." In such collaborations, the power to implement educational reform resides with the public school teacher and not the university representative because such reforms will have a greater effect on the daily professional lives of the former rather than the latter. As project principals set the stage for such cross-age, cross-institutional collaborations, they must foster relationships beyond the teachers and the university faculty members. School and university administrators must be brought on board, kept informed of progress, and otherwise become invested in the project. Without the support of the infrastructure beyond the classroom level, the principals will have a more difficult time reaching their goals.

Plan for Adequate Funding

In an ideal world, all projects like PUM would receive multimillion-dollar grants from foundations, the federal and state government, and local school districts. While funding is available, the grant writing process can be so cumbersome that it discourages busy teachers from seeking such funds. For educational reform to move forward, it is often not possible to wait to see if one can find major sources of funding, and thus, in most cases, teachers must work with what they have. Nevertheless, it seems that no matter how much money such projects start with, you will find yourself muttering, like one of the characters in D. H. Lawrence's short story "The Rocking Horse Winner," "There must be more money. There must be more money" ([1933] 1989, 852). A relatively small project, PUM began with a solid plan that included release time for the university facilitators, free computer guest accounts for the students, and a stipend for the teacher. And while these were adequate for getting us going, it became clear that we needed even more funds to get the technical support we eventually needed, to buy appropriate software and hardware, and to secure necessary release time for project principals. In addition, to keep the project from withering on the vine, it is crucial to cultivate the interest of other colleagues. Budgeting should include, therefore, funds for involving others in demonstrations and training workshops.

Make Time

During PUM, the university facilitators had some release time from their teaching duties, and Wax's sabbatical during her second year gave her time to dedicate to the project. This variable was perhaps the most crucial. All the principals ended up dedicating much more time than they were allotted, so if we had tried to run PUM in addition to our other full-time responsibilities, it would have been doomed to fail. Allocated time allowed me to transform my role as "expert consultant" into "collaborator"; it allowed Wax to reflect on her practice, and it allowed both of us time to find common ground between our sometimes diverse views of education.

Phase in Changes over the Long Term

All educators find themselves under tremendous pressure to embrace technology and implement it *yesterday*. But one does not just plug in the machines and go. The technology better matches some pedagogies than others. Also, teachers' and students' attitudes toward technology, attitudes that range from overly skeptical to overly optimistic, need time to change. Another successful feature of PUM was that we identified transformations that might have to occur and then addressed those transformations individually. For example, with PUM we were introducing at least four major changes:

- from a teacher-centered classroom to a collaborative learning classroom
- from a content-oriented pedagogy to a writing-intensive pedagogy
- from a nontechnological curriculum to a computer-mediated one
- from a model that views public and higher education as mutually exclusive entities to a model that celebrates collaboration between the two

Attempting these many significant changes simultaneously without properly addressing each one could have led to disaster.

Publicize and Disseminate Information

At various points during the project, we invited key people, including Wax's principal, district-level administrators, and the school and local press to visit and observe. Furthermore, we sponsored demonstrations and computer training for other building faculty. We also sent formative evaluation reports to these people, and the project was reported in a district newsletter, the school newspaper, a university publication, and the local newspaper. As a result, we garnered communitywide support that proved helpful when writing district grants for additional funding. We also applied for a number of state and national educational award programs, two of which Wax won.

A successful university/high school collaboration project using technology involves much more than linking a group of high school students with a group of college students via networked computers. Such projects require more, also, than planning for the apparent and tangible logistical issues such as hardware and software needs, holding meetings, and writing goals and lesson plans. Because high school students and their teachers and college students and their teachers often learn in quite different educational cultures, the technical aspects of collaborating online are far less significant than are the challenges of bridging "cultural" differences. If such differences are identified, articulated, and addressed, then the appropriate groundwork has been prepared for all entities—university faculty, high school faculty, and most importantly, the university and high school students—to enjoy meaningful professional, educational, and intellectual stimulation and growth.

Works Cited

Bruffee, K. 1983. "Writing and Reading as Collaborative or Social Acts: The Argument from Kuhn and Vygotsky." In *The Writer's Mind: Writing as a Mode of Thinking*, eds. J. N. Hays et al., 159–69. Urbana: National Council of Teachers of English.

Butler, W. 1995. "Writing to Learn History Online." *The Clearing House* 69 (1): 17–20.

Butler, W., and R. Wax. 1993. "The Pioneer High School–University of Michigan Connection: Writing to Learn History on Computer Networks." English Composition Board, University of Michigan, Ann Arbor. Internal Report.

Farrell-Childers, R., A. R. Gere, and A. Young, eds. 1994. *Programs and Practices: Writing Across the Secondary School Curriculum*. Portsmouth, NH: Boynton/Cook.

Gere, A. R., ed. 1985. *Roots in the Sawdust: Writing to Learn Across the Disciplines*. Urbana, IL: National Council of Teachers of English.

———. 1987. *Writing Groups: History, Theory, and Implications*. Carbondale: Southern Illinois University Press.

Glaze, B. 1987. "A Teacher Speaks Out About Research." In *Plain Talk About Learning and Writing Across the Curriculum*. Richmond: Virginia Department of Education.

Johnson, D., and R. Johnson. 1985. "Internal Dynamics of Cooperative Learning Groups." In *Learning to Cooperate, Cooperating to Learn*, eds. R. Slavin et al., 103–24. New York: Plenum Press.

Lawrence, D. H. [1933] 1989. "The Rocking-Horse Winner." Reprint in *Annotated Teacher's Edition: Adventures in English Literature (Pegasus Edition)*, 852–62. Orlando, FL: Harcourt Brace Jovanovich.

Moffett, J. 1968. *A Student-Centered Language Arts Curriculum, Grade K–13: A Handbook for Teachers*. Boston: Houghton Mifflin.

Morris, B., G. Cooper, C. Childress, M. Cox, and P. Williams. 1994. "Collaboration as Sharing Experiences: A Detroit Public Schools/University of Michigan Course." In *Programs and Practices: Writing Across the Secondary School Curriculum*, eds. P. Farrell-Childers, A. Ruggles Gere, and A. Young, 154–70. Portsmouth, NH: Boynton/Cook.

Slavin, R. 1983. *Cooperative Learning*. New York: Longman.

Spring, J. 1986. *The American School: 1642–1985*. New York: Longman.

Wax, R. 1993. "University–High School Collaboration, 'Writing to Learn,' Student-Centered Learning, and Computer Technology: Can You Teach an Old Dog New Tricks?" Paper presented at the Ninth Conference on Computers and Writing, University of Michigan, Ann Arbor, MI.

— — —. 1994. "University-High School Collaboration: Writing to Learn, Student-Centered Learning, and Computer Technology." *Wings* 2 (1): http://daedalus.com/wings/wax.2.1.html.

14

Making Technology Count
Incentives, Rewards, and Evaluations

Rebecca J. Rickly
Texas Tech University

Educators, particularly those in the humanities, have traditionally not been known or rewarded for their work with technology; in fact, work with technology has been seen as contradictory to the goal of the writing teacher in the past. Lisa Gerrard suggests several causes for this resistance: Computer enthusiasts are aligned with "foreign forces"; humanists distrust or resent technology; computers are mere "fads" or nuisances; computers invite collaboration and cooperation, which traditionally has been "suspect" in English; and there is ultimately no proof that computers make students write better (1991, 3–7). In addition, computers pose other problems for teachers. Joseph Janangelo (1991) cites potential abuses of technology, calling it "technoppression." Computers allow students to harass other students, teachers to monitor their students from a position of omnipotent anonymity, and they even allow teachers to monitor one another. These fears are echoed by Susan Romano (1993), who described a situation in which students actually lost their singular voices by engaging in collaborative online discussion. At all levels of the educational system, there are some teachers who fear they will lose control of pedagogical goals by investing in technology. Yet, those of us who teach writing and work with technology on a daily basis are continually growing in number. Learning the technology can be a time-consuming process, and one which some teachers are simply not interested in or capable of engaging in. The chances that they will be compensated for their efforts through release time, merit raises, better working conditions, promotion, tenure, or even simple retention are far from guaranteed. The postsecondary curriculum, including the teaching, learning, and reward structures, tend to influence how K–12 structures are organized, and those conditions that may be problematic about learning, teaching, integrating, and maintaining technology at the university level will likely concern high school, junior high, and elementary instructors. Unless clear and positive reward systems are put into place to compensate teachers for the professional risks they must undertake when they work with technology, those who work with computers will continue to meet with resistance in their departments and school systems. This chapter examines this problem, existing models of evaluation of academic work, and how professional organizations are rising to meet the challenge of evaluating work done with technology.

As technology becomes increasingly prevalent in homes and workplaces, schools are expected to prepare students to use the technological tools of our culture: computers, faxes, videos, computer networks, and so forth. Today, more than 50 percent of workers use computers on the job, and two-thirds of college graduates use computers in their work (NSTAS Reports! 1995). Many schools are rising to meet the challenge: In 1995, 75 percent of school systems had at least one computer lab, and over 35 percent of schools had Internet access (NSTAS Reports! 1995). Almost all of today's colleges and universities are "wired" to integrate mainframe and personal computers, indicating at least a grudging acceptance if not an enthusiastic embrace of technology in education, even in the language arts and composition curriculum.

Advances in computer technology since 1990 have allowed for radical changes in the composition classroom in both secondary and postsecondary schools. Local-area networks, or LANs, link computers together and, in effect, link people together. Students using LAN communication software are able to conduct online conversations, share ideas, view each other's work, and even work collaboratively on a project in real time (i.e., the same time) as well as asynchronously (at different times). Similarly, students hooked up to the Internet via a wide-area network (WAN) can communicate in writing with others outside the physical boundaries of the classroom walls through email, hypernews, the World Wide Web, chat programs, ftp, and a host of other Internet applications. In essence, LAN and WAN technology have changed the computer from a tool used in school for individualization, in which the student works by him or herself and interacts with no one except the teacher, who normally grades a final product (as seen in simple word processing and "drill and kill" exercises) to one used for socialization, whereby students can, both physically and intellectually, form a community of writers who learn from instructors, each other, and themselves as they enter and begin to navigate and participate in larger, interconnected academic communities. Granted, in the latter example students still produce a final product to be evaluated, but the process used in creating the product parallels more closely how real-world intellectual products are created. This type of recursive, interactive group instruction resembles George Hillocks's 1986 description of the environmental mode of instruction, which, according to his meta-analytical study, has proven to be far more effective than traditional lecture classes for teaching writing. Paulo Freire, in his *Pedagogy of the Oppressed*, puts it this way: "Education must begin with the solution of the teacher-student contradiction, by reconciling the poles of the contradiction so that both are simultaneously teachers *and* students" (59).

In LAN- and WAN-based discussions, teachers and students tend to interact with each other more frequently (see, for instance, Rickly 1995), and since networked computers tend to level the playing ground by effacing gender, age, and physical appearance, etc., students and teachers are more likely to work together with greater collegiality to create knowledge in this kind of environment.

However, mastering and using this kind of technology in a process-oriented, socially based writing class requires substantial effort on the part of the teacher. Yet, this effort, over and above what the instructor must do, anyway, is not always sanctioned by the traditional administrative power structures. As a result, many teachers are reluctant to commit themselves to teaching with technology, no matter how great the potential pedagogical benefits might be. For those who have already established their careers and settled on pedagogical methods, there is little incentive to encourage the amount of time it takes to learn to use the new technology. As a result, tenured professors and public school teachers are less likely to make the effort to incorporate technology into their existing course structures. Too, those who teach with technology are often those with less power: new hires, fresh from colleges or universities that offered computer access to students; part-time or adjunct faculty, trying to infuse something new into their pedagogy; or graduate teaching assistants and student teachers, eager to explore the most recent advances in technology. When work with technology is done by those whom school administrations view as marginal, the activity itself is seen as nonessential and subsequently is not rewarded. This situation is particularly observable in departments of English in universities where, traditionally, those who teach writing are the disenfranchised: new hires, graduate students, part-timers, adjuncts. More often than not, it is these teachers of writing who experiment with new pedagogical applications such as technology. This association has placed the "computerist" on the same ladder rung as the compositionist, near the bottom. Unless technology is embraced by those with decision-making power in the postsecondary level and in the K–12 levels, it's less likely to be accepted by American educational institutions in general.

Parlaying Existing Values: A Proven Model

The question of how teachers with less power in the traditional institutional structures graduate teaching assistants, part-time faculty, public school teachers, writing center administrators and employees, to name a few—can be treated more equitably in secondary and post-secondary education has been the source of much frustrated debate in the last decade. Probably the most notable response to this debate for postsecondary teachers has been the Wyoming Resolution, which is one of the most powerful models to date for how institutional change can be initiated. An examination of this model of change may be useful in determining how to change institutional educational policy regarding the use of technology and learning. At the Wyoming Conference on English in June of 1987, several teachers gathered under auspices of the National Council of Teachers of English (NCTE) to draft collaboratively a document to be adopted by NCTE. The resulting statement aimed to give writing teachers, especially those experimenting with new forms of technology, and "who are not satisfied with their conditions of employment clear and forceful principles and a policy from which to negotiate for changes at their institutions if they choose to do so" (Crowley 1991, 332). It contained three provisions: "it asked for a definition of the minimum standards under which post-secondary writing teachers should be employed; it asked for the creation of some mechanism that would help teachers implement the standards on their campuses; and it asked that some means be found to enforce institutional compliance with the standards" (Crowley 1991, 330). According to the statement, in the teaching of writing, quality is dependent upon the positive working conditions of teachers. Because teachers of writing devote more time and effort to their students than anywhere else in the academy, they should be given the academic freedom to design and implement curricula; an adequate, relatively private working space; access to telephones and other communication media; eligibility for research support; a fair salary commensurate with workload, rank, and teaching experience; eligibility for promotion and tenure according to "prevailing standards of the institution"; and job security (Crowley 1991, 333). Since the statement from the Wyoming Resolution has been, at least in part, embraced by College Composition and Communication (CCC), the National Council on the Teaching of English (NCTE), the Associated Departments of English (ADE), the American Association of University Professors (AAUP), and the National English Association (NEA), organizations sanctioned by writing departments in both secondary and postsecondary schools, it's a good model to examine as we attempt to instigate institutional changes and sanction our efforts to incorporate technology at various levels of education.

The Wyoming Resolution, and the resulting dialogue that ensued from the publication of the "Statement of Principles and Standards for the Post-Secondary Teaching of Writing," attempted to set forth activities that should be valued in the current reward structures and working conditions of the academy. For instance, the statement argued that the publication of composition textbooks should be seen as a "primary form of original research"; collaborative research that draws on "diverse scholarly backgrounds and research orientations" should be valued; professional activities, such as seminars and workshops for faculty, should be rewarded, as should be administrative service (Crowley 1991). Teachers of writing should "demonstrate superior writing ability, professional involvement with composition theory and pedagogy, and present successful experience in the teaching of writing" (Crowley 1991, 333). Expectations for teaching, service, and research should be made clear from the start, and instructors should be evaluated according to those written expectations (Crowley 1991).

Secondary school teachers are normally held to a slightly different standard, and while their reward structure seems less complicated, it is often no less ambiguous. Teachers in the public school systems start out with an initial "evaluation" when they're hired, and as technology becomes integrated into the management and pedagogy of public schools, those with computer experience are more likely to be evaluated positively. Once hired, public school teachers normally receive raises and other rewards (priority in course assignments, etc.) based on seniority rather than merit, as long as their teaching continues to be "satisfactory." The rating of teaching effectiveness is often done solely according to their students' performance. So while they are rewarded first and foremost for "good teaching," good teaching is determined primarily by how well their students do on standardized testing. Rarely are K–12 teachers given release time, raises, or other rewards for what the postsecondary administration would deem "service" or "scholarship." However, whether a teacher receives tenure or rises in rank (e.g., to a senior or administrative level) in her school system might depend on criteria such as professional development, which can include working with technology. Similarly, most teachers now are expected to continue their schooling after they've been hired, and more and more this type of education includes (and even requires) work with technology.

As we resituate ourselves within our institutions, we also begin to reconstruct the institutions themselves. But change can occur only if individuals are willing to take responsibility for themselves and speak out on their own behalf. In "Shooting Hoops," Mick Doherty recounts how three junior faculty members at different institutions completed what might be seen as the same type of work, building a home page for the department on the World Wide Web; yet, the work of each person was valued quite differently: "One of these faculty was granted a course release in return for the work; another was told it was 'department service'; the third was told to include it in the tenure dossier as 'non-refereed, invited publication'" (1996). Doherty suggests that if we want to get recognition for what we do, we need to learn the language of our discourse communities (our schools, departments, administrations, etc.), and we need to "explain what we are doing on the terms of those already in the discourse community" (1996). The Wyoming Statement broke ground in this respect; for instance, it deemed writing textbooks equivalent to research and, using the terminology of the field of teaching composition, explained how collaborative writing was valuable. Similarly, advocates of integrating technology and teaching might begin to argue for the following equivalencies in our review processes, keeping in mind how these activities might be presented in the language of our particular professional discourse communities. As with the examples above, these equivalencies may be used for promotion, tenure, release time, or other department- or school-sanctioned rewards:

- Writing software is equivalent to writing an article, chapter, or book, depending on complexity and critical reception. Just as authors must do a significant amount of research, critical thinking, and careful writing when they compose an article or book-length manuscript, so authors must do all of the above when composing software: They must familiarize themselves with the technology; they must learn the language used to program, and they must carefully research their audience, taking into consideration its background and needs. The program or, as is most often the case, series of programs must be carefully edited, revised, and tested on target audiences before it is ready for "public consumption." Too, depending on the medium used, the development process can be quite different: a series of Web pages or hypermedia stacks will be quite different from creating a CD or interactive software program, yet the demand for excellence, for rigor, for critical thinking, and awareness of the rhetorical situation is similar.

- Belonging to or participating in a listserv is equivalent to belonging to or participating in a professional organization. Most listservs present the opportunity for professional growth and collaboration, and these may be springboards from which other professional work evolves.

- Attending an electronic conference is equivalent to attending a professional conference. Once again, conferences provide a time and space for professional growth through interaction and discussion. Online conferences offer the same types of opportunity.

- Being the resident "computer counselor," the one everyone comes to for help, answers, and advice, is equivalent to chairing a committee. Here, the main contribution is time and departmental service. In both cases, a significant amount of time is involved and the department is served.

- Leading an electronic symposium such as a MOO discussion is equivalent to conducting a roundtable at a face-to-face conference. Roundtable discussions do not require the rigor of presenting a paper, but they do require a significant amount of research and preparation, as well as the ability to facilitate a group. Likewise, leading an online discussion requires a solid background as well as an ability to facilitate a productive discussion.

- Running a network or computer lab is equivalent to directing a writing program or learning center. Depending on the size of the department, of course, administering a computer lab, particularly a networked computer lab, requires not only an enormous amount of technical expertise, but pedagogical expertise as well.

And so forth. These parallels, of course, will vary from institution to institution. But they can and should be articulated. It's up to us, those of us who work with technology, to help those who don't understand the value of what we do, and we can do this by offering to use existing reward and working condition structures.

Technology Teaching Reconsidered

In our quest to redefine our place within institutional structures, we might consider alternatives to the traditional paradigms of evaluation we hold for teachers: teaching, scholarship, and service for postsecondary institutions, and outcome-based teaching for K–12. One alternative structure we might look to benefit both K–12 and higher education is Earnest Boyer's reconceptualization of scholarship. In *Scholarship Reconsidered*, Boyer (1990) recognizes that "to sustain the vitality of higher education in *our* time, a new vision of scholarship is required, one dedicated not only to the renewal of the academy but, ultimately, to the renewal of society itself" (15–25). Boyer goes so far as to suggest that teaching effectiveness, rather than publication, should be the primary cause for promotion. He urges a more "inclusive view of what it means to be a scholar," enlarging the current narrow definitions of *research* and forgoing publication as the primary criterion for tenure. Boyer suggests a four-part taxonomy, based on the notion of "scholarship":

1. **The scholarship of discovery:** that disciplinary research that provides new knowledge, ideas, art forms, and interpretations. It's what we most frequently mean when we use the word "scholarship."

2. **The scholarship of integration:** activity "making connections across the disciplines, placing the specialties in larger contexts, illuminating data in a revealing way, often educating non-specialists too." It can lead to nonconventional forms of publication such as videos, hypertexts, or cross-disciplinary study.

3. **The scholarship of application:** those service activities performed as an extension of the scholarly life. It blends theory and practice, and goes beyond mere department service to helping to shape public policy, working with public schools, changing the macrostructures we operate within.

4. **The scholarship of teaching:** the creative act of informing students, motivating learners, stimulating others to examine their world, and helping people think more clearly. (57)

This expanded definition of what it means to be a good scholar-teacher can and does include work with technology, and these categories can help us and our colleagues understand what it is we do with technology in our teaching, scholarship, and service. By valuing all aspects of being a professional educator, it encourages us to diversify, to grow, and to continually incorporate new models of scholarship and knowledge into our pedagogy and service not just for institutionally sanctioned rewards, but to become more effective at doing what we do. Educators are encouraged to become three-dimensional, integrating work from other disciplines, other realms into our practice. By allowing for "flexible boundaries," instructors are not situated solely within one department or institution, but within a field, so that we may be held responsible not by the few, but by the many. Those educators in public schools can encourage the local colleges and universities to offer more continuing-education courses involving technology so that they can attend these courses as a means of professional development or renewing certification. Similarly, those educators in the university should be actively engaged in working with technology and with public school teachers to propose such courses. However, it is up to us to persuade the powers that be how our activities and accomplishments fit into existing structures. Boyer recognized that each institution would be somewhat idiosyncratic, and he suggests that each institution should "develop its own system of faculty recognition that relates to what the campus is seeking to accomplish."

Such an institutional dialogue between those who work with technology and those in charge of the reward structures or working conditions is not as unlikely as it may seem. Chris Anson and Greta Gaard (1992) describe how the University of Minnesota reacted to the Wyoming "Statement" essay:

> After the "Statement" was received by most Minnesota composition faculty late in 1989, the composition program on the Minneapolis campus received funding from the University's central administration to hold a retreat for all directors of composition, rhetoric, and speech across the University's five-campus system. Using that document as the focal point of the retreat, participants were asked to describe the quality of writing instruction on their campus in relation to the "Statement." (173)

The article described how the participants used the "Statement" as a point of departure for their discussions. The ensuing dialogue allowed each campus to create a statement they thought possible and necessary. After a period of "norming" to take into consideration inter-campus differences, those involved in the retreat were prepared to make specific recommendations that would apply across campus, "ranging from the employment and training of instructors to the support of computerized instruction" to the function of textbooks and administrative work in tenure and promotion reviews (173).

This type of communal restructuring can help each institution come to a professional consensus on matters of reform and to call for initiatives to enact these recommendations. Those involved with incentives, reward structures, or the establishment of working conditions among those who work with technology must learn about, analyze, and recommend written criteria for future evaluation. These criteria must be site-specific, flexible enough to accommodate new technology, forms of scholarship, and pedagogical application, but most importantly, they must take into consideration existing standards of evaluating excellence within the institution and work productively with them. The Rutgers 1997 "Report on the Committee on Electronic Publishing and Tenure"[1] outlines such a process. Committee members were asked to "provide specific recommendations . . . for a University policy on electronic publishing to guide the practices of departmental,

unit, and University appointment and promotion committees." Over
the course of a year, the committee conducted interviews with academic leaders within Rutgers as well as elsewhere. The resulting report
is currently under consideration within the institution. The committee
recommended that electronic publication be considered an appropriate
means of scholarly, artistic, and professional communication, that the
content of electronic publication be evaluated within the traditions
and habits of each discipline, that electronic technologies be considered appropriate formats for teaching and service, and, perhaps most
importantly, that these recommendations be periodically reviewed
(Committee on Electronic Publishing and Tenure 1997). While such a
dialogue is perhaps not as common in public school settings, where
hierarchy tends to be rigid and teachers have little power, this model
nonetheless presents a positive process of negotiation within institutional confines.

Looking to the Future

We must recognize that, in the current climate, simply working with
technology does not warrant immediate reward. This type of work
can be time-consuming, difficult, frustrating, and, frankly, it can
limit time that could be spent on more sanctioned pursuits. And
those who evaluate the work we do with technology are often ill-
equipped to do so. According to Deborah Holdstein (1994), those
who would assess others who work with technology must be prepared to evaluate their own facility with computer writing, their
own knowledge of the issues surrounding computer use in the teaching and learning of writing, and their own perspectives on nontraditional teaching methods. Moreover, evaluators must focus on the
same criteria they would use in so-called traditional classrooms:
course design; strategies for motivating student learning; complex
problem-solving assignments (177).

Faculty must assume responsibility for explaining their work to
nonexpert reviewers. Appropriate use of technology in the writing
curriculum (not merely how much or how often we use it) should be
the bottom line in evaluation. Holdstein reaffirms that the "effective
teacher of writing with the computer must first and foremost be an
effective teacher of writing and its processes" (178). Those involved
in the development of new media must do so in ways that "reflect
the intellectual assumptions of their disciplines" as well, being careful to clearly articulate to others the worth of these projects
(Committee on Computers and Emerging Technologies in Teaching
and Research 1995).

The following guidelines can serve as a basis for evaluation of work with and about technology:

- What theories or hypotheses inform the work?
- Why is it useful to the discipline?
- What evidence is there of rigor and intellectual content? (Committee on Computers and Emerging Technologies in Teaching and Research 1995)

These guidelines are, of course, only a base; the actual criteria should be made explicit by those doing the assessment for those being evaluated. For example, in public school systems, these guidelines might look like this:

- What evidence is there that this work will improve student performance?
- How does this work enhance the professional development of educators?
- How is this work contributing to work students will do in other classes?
- How will this work contribute to the success of the student?

Currently, organizations such as the National Council of Teachers of English (NCTE) and the Modern Language Association (MLA) are coming together to draft guidelines for the evaluation of computer-related work in writing. The MLA guidelines emphasize that "it is important that existing policies and procedures for reappointment, tenure, and promotion be updated to include references to work dealing with computers and electronic technologies" (Committee on Computers and Emerging Technologies in Teaching and Research 1995). In 1995 the Instructional Technology Committee of NCTE sponsored a roundtable on "The Politics of Technology" at the Wyoming Conference. The participants drafted the following suggestions in response to the question of which work with technology should be valued and how.

Create an accreditation and consulting program, modeled on the WPA Consulting programs.

This program would help departments and schools establish criteria and evaluate programs and the work of technology administrators. A program backed by an organization such as NCTE[2] could bring about leveling and systematic standards by providing a consistency among various institutions while at the same time enabling departments and schools to develop a methodology for accrediting and valuing work with technology.

Focus attention on work with computers and writing as "applied research."

By presenting work with computers and writing as applied research, those working with technology could bring in existing academic standards for evaluating work in other fields. Though applied research is more frequently found in the area of the scientist or social scientist, it provides a relevant comparison for the interplay between research and teaching for those working with technology. Further, by referring to existing institutional methods for valuing and evaluating work, applied research can provide a familiar tool for determining the value of work with technology.

Set standards that are consistent and inclusive.

The energy expended on weighing work for tenure and promotion is tightly tied to the system of weighing and evaluating students; thus, the system must consider how it perceives the work of graduate students as an outgrowth and impetus for valuing the work of adjuncts, instructors, and tenure-track and tenured educators. For example, an institution's acceptance of a dissertation on CD-ROM or hypertext should come to bear on the acceptance of a professor's publication on CD-ROM or hypertext.

Develop links between the economic value of the work and its value for promotion and tenure purposes.

The monetary value of the work should raise the value of that work within the promotion and tenure system, especially in terms of moneys brought to the institution in the form of grants, fellowships, and corporate gifts. Outside economic validation should influence institutional valuing on the same level.

Create evaluative paradigms that explain "foreign" work by analogy to traditional scholarship.

Nontraditional forms of publication and research should be presented as extensions of the traditional system for sharing findings in the academy. For example, listserv participation and MUD discussions should be compared with the intellectual conversation surrounding attendance at a professional conference; but the comparison should also explore the differences, including the fact that listserv and MUD participation are more easily documentable.

Propose and encourage a system to document work with technology for those in the field.

Because much work with technology goes unseen and the effort involved often goes underestimated by those not directly involved, any system of standards should include recommendation that those involved document their work in terms of projects completed and research time committed to the work. For administrative duties as well, a log or other system of documentation allows a way to demonstrate the scholar's contribution to the institution.

Recommend the local establishment of specific job descriptions that include work with technology.

Establishing an institutional expectation for a job description that specifies all tasks and responsibilities for those working with technology, especially in administrative positions, enables a tangible statement of the institutional expectations for those involved. Furthermore, it provides an evaluative rubric that can be instrumental in determining the value of work and provides explanations for more traditional work that might not be included in an educator's promotion and tenure portfolio (Gardner 1995).

All of the above suggest that the teacher must be prepared to expend the incipient period of learning about technology on his or her own time. The initial investment is individual, but with dedication to good teaching and scholarship, a working knowledge of institutional practices, and an awareness of existing evaluation standards embraced by our profession, this investment will pay off. Being visible, both in and out of one's home department, helps focus attention on important work being done. Publications, both traditional and nontraditional, are still an important method of disseminating information within and outside the institution. Finally, looking to and emulating successful models that incorporate technology and education will help promote workable policies regarding release time, grants, proposals, promotion, merit, tenure, and so forth. Online organizations such as the Alliance for Computers and Writing[3] and the NCTE[4] are making World Wide Web resource pages, linking successful models to these pages for others to use at their own institutions. This kind of increased exposure at an institution can promote good will, attract top-notch students, and bring in funding.

Finally, institutions must recognize the message they convey when they neglect to provide a specific, yet flexible, framework for the evaluation of administrative, scholarly, and pedagogical work with technology. Often, these institutions emphasize the use of technology in their classrooms yet fail to provide structures for ease in implementation and evaluation of such work. Technology can help a department or an institution reenvision itself, its students, and its faculty. This light can be both flattering and harsh. In order to view clearly the strengths and weakness of any program, its goals, objectives, and criteria for evaluation must be made clear in an ongoing dialogue between those being evaluated and those doing the evaluation.

Notes

1. The Rutgers report, which recounts the process and presents a clear, usable model can be found at http://aultnis.rutgers.edu/texts/ept.html.

2. The NCTE-sponsored Instructional Technology Committee is at present drafting guidelines for the evaluation of computer-related work for secondary and postsecondary schools. Information about the evolving guidelines can be found at http://www.ncte.org/committees/itc/recognition/.

3. The ACW can be found on the World Wide Web at http://english.ttu.edu/acw/.

4. The NCTE Web page can be found at http://www.ncte.org/.

Works Cited

Anson, C. M., and G. Gaard. 1992. "Acting on the 'Statement': The All-Campus Model of Reform." *College Composition and Communication* 43: 171–75.

Boyer, E. L. 1990. *Scholarship Reconsidered: Priorities of the Professoriate*. Princeton, NJ: The Carnegie Foundation for the Advancement of Teaching.

Committee on Computers and Emerging Technologies in Teaching and Research. 1995. "Draft Guidelines for the Evaluation of Computer-Related Work in the Modern Languages During Hiring, Reappointment, Tenure, and Promotion Decisions." http://jefferson.village.virginia.edu/mla.guidelines.html.

Committee on Electronic Publishing and Tenure. 1997. "Report of the Committee on Electronic Publishing and Tenure." http://aultnis.rutgers.edu/texts/ept.html.

Crowley, S. 1991. "A Progress Report from the CCCC Committee on Professional Standards." *College Composition and Communication* 42: 330–44.

Doherty, M. 1996. "Shooting Hoops: In Response to a Question from Karen LeFevre." *Rhetnet*. http://www.missouri.edu/~rhetnet/hoops/.

Freire, P. 1970. *Pedagogy of the Oppressed*. Trans. Myra Bergman Ramos. New York: The Seabury Press.

Gardner, T. 1995. "Wyoming Session Report." http://kairos.daedalus.com/promo/promo.html.

Gerrard, L. 1991. "Computers and Compositionists: A View from the Floating Bottom." *Computers and Composition* 8: 5–15.

Hillocks, G., Jr. 1986. *Research on Written Compostion: New Directions for Teaching*. Urbana, IL: National Council of Teachers of English.

Holdstein, D. H. 1994. "Evaluating Teachers in the Computerized Classroom." In *Evaluating Teachers of Writing,* ed. C. A. Hult, 167–78. Urbana, IL: National Council of Teachers of English.

Janangelo, J. 1991. "Technopower and Technoppression: Some Abuses of Power and Control in Computer-Assisted Writing Environments." *Computers and Composition* 9: 47–64.

NSTAS Reports! 1994. October–November: 42–48.

———. 1995. April.

Rickly, R. J. 1995. Exploring the Dimensions of Discourse: A Multi-Modal Analysis of Electronic and Oral Discussions in Developmental English. Dissertation, Ball State University, Muncie, IN.

Romano, S. 1993. "The Egalitarianism Narrative: Whose Story? Which Yardstick?" *Computers and Composition* 10: 5–28.

Contributors

Donna Ashmus is an educational technology specialist for the SouthEast and Islands Regional Technology in Education Consortium (SEIRTEC). She works with schools, districts, and state departments to provide technology-related assistance through awareness, policy development and planning, staff development, and evaluation. A former middle school teacher, Donna's special interest is integrating technology into the classroom environment.

John F. Barber is a dynamic figure. He manages time efficiently, pays his bills on time, and is often acclaimed for his ability to prepare extraordinary four-course meals using only yogurt and granola. He has navigated the Mississippi River, been caller number nine, and spoken to Elvis.

Robert Baroz currently teaches English grades 10–12 at Champlain Valley Union High School in Hinesburg, Vermont. Robert is the recipient of several teacher-research awards from the Bread Loaf School of English; Write to Change; the National Council of Teachers of English; and The Spencer Foundation. He graduated with an M.A. from the Bread Loaf School of English, Middlebury, Vermont, and serves as the vice-chair of the Ripton Elementary school board. He lives in Ripton with his wife, Dianne, and son, Timothy.

Claire Bateman is a poet and a teacher. Her first book, *The Bicycle Slow Race,* was published by Wesleyan University Press in 1991. Formerly a Bread Loaf Fellow and an NEA Fellow, she's taught English at Clemson University and worked for the South Carolina Governor's School for the Arts.

Chris Benson has taught literature and writing at Clemson University. He is the editor of the semiannual *Bread Loaf Rural Teacher Network Magazine*, a research associate at the Strom Thurmond Institute of Goverment and Public Affairs at Clemson University, and an associate of Write to Change, a nonprofit organization for literacy and social action.

Wayne M. Butler cofounded the Daedalus Group, Inc., an educational software and consulting firm, and currently serves as chief executive officer and director of training and information services. While a lecturer, associate director, and then acting director of the University of Michigan's English Composition Board, he codirected the Peer Tutoring Program, taught computer-assisted writing courses, and worked on school-university outreach projects. He also coauthored, with William Condon, *Writing the Information Superhighway* (Allyn & Bacon 1997).

Kurt Caswell has taught literature and writing in Hokkaido, Japan, on the Navajo Reservation, and currently on the thirty-thousand-acre Orme Ranch near Mayer, Arizona. In the classroom, his interests are nature writing, the literature of place, and the use of journals to help students develop a personal environmental ethic. He is a graduate of the Bread Loaf School of English, and his writing has appeared in *Orion Notebook*, *English Journal*, *Boise Magazine*, and other journals.

Anna Citrino, a lover of the desert and the wilderness of wide spaces, taught at the American International School in Kuwait from 1993 to 1996, working with grades 7, 8, and 12. Anna currently teaches seventh graders at the Singapore American School. Her permanent home is Santa Cruz, California.

Brian Gentry lives outside Salt Lake City at the base of the Wasatch Mountain Range. In his spare time he loves to fly fish. He also enjoys playing basketball and tennis. He currently teaches grades 10 and 12 at Jordan High School in Sandy, Utah.

Rocky Gooch is the director of telecommunications for the Bread Loaf Rural Teacher Network, a professional development program of the Bread Loaf School of English at Middlebury College. He provides support, guidance, and training to public school teachers who are Fellows in the program.

Dixie Goswami is professor emerita at Clemson University, a longtime faculty member of the Bread Loaf School of English at Middlebury College, coordinator of the Bread Loaf Rural Teacher Network, and the founder and executive director of Write to Change, a nonprofit agency for literacy and social action. She is the coeditor, with Peter Stillman, of *Reclaiming the Classroom* (Boynton/Cook, 1987) and, with Lee Odell, of *Writing in Non-Academic Settings* (Guilford, 1985).

Susan Hilligoss teaches at Clemson University, where she has coordinated the master's program in professional communication. Involved with computers and writing since the early 1980s, she has edited a collection on literacy and technology with Cynthia L. Selfe and also published a study of child psychiatrist Robert Coles. Currently, she teaches visual communication and is designing multimedia support for instruction.

Tharon Howard is associate professor of English at Clemson University, where he directs the Multimedia Authoring Teaching and Research Facility, the Document Design Laboratory, and the Usability Testing Facility. He chaired the NCTE Instructional Technology Committee from 1993–1996, and is the author of *A Rhetoric of Electronic Communities* (Ablex, 1997).

Lucy Maddox is professor of English at Georgetown University, where she teaches courses in American and Native American literature. She has been on the summer faculty of the Bread Loaf School of English since 1980.

Tom McKenna is a language arts and technology teacher. After teaching for five years in rural Alaska, he served as the technology coordinator for a K–12 international school in Barcelona, Spain. He is presently teaching in Juneau, Alaska. In 1996 Tom received his M.A. in English from the Bread Loaf School of English.

Jane Perkins is an assistant professor of English at Clemson University, where she teaches professional communication courses and conducts workplace communication research. Drawing on her three-year ethnographic study of communication in an international software development corporation, she has published and presented papers on the relationship between intercultural communication and technology transfer and between narrative and professional communication. Her articles have appeared in *Studies in Technical Communication*, *IEEE Transactions on Professional Communication*, and *The Bulletin of the Association for Business Communication*.

Rebecca J. Rickly is a visiting assistant professor at Texas Tech University. Previously, she coordinated the University of Michigan's Online Writing and Learning (OWL). She has served on the CCCC Committee on Computers and Composition, NCTE's Assembly on Computers in English, and currently chairs NCTE's Instructional Technology Committee. Rickly has participated in numerous panels at national conferences, and her publications include the coedited book *The Online Writing Classroom* (with Susanmarie Harrington and Michael Day).

Philip Sittnick is the computer lab teacher at Laguna Middle School on the Laguna Indian Reservation. He is responsible for helping the staff integrate the use of technology into their curricula, and for assisting students who come to the lab to work on various assignments. Previously, he taught language arts for four years.

Elisa Kay Sparks is an assistant professor at Clemson University in South Carolina where she directed the Composition Program for five years while teaching English (from Freshman Comp to Science Fiction and Feminist Literary Criticism) and Women's Studies. Besides writing articles on Marge Piercy and the connections between Virginia Woolf and Georgia O'Keeffe, she is a printmaker and has been developing a web-empire of university course sites on subjects from science fiction film to contemporary women's art at her home page: http://hubcap.clemson.edu/~sparks/.

Douglas E. Wood, a former seventh-grade social studies teacher at Summit Parkway Middle School in Columbia, South Carolina, was the 1994 South Carolina Technology Educator of the Year. Currently, he is a doctoral student in administration, planning, and social policy at the Harvard Graduate School of Education, a member of the Research and Evaluation Team for the Annenberg Rural Challenge, and a course assistant at the John F. Kennedy School of Government at Harvard.